Caring for the Commonweal
Education for Religious and Public Life

Caring
for the Commonweal

Education for Religious
and Public Life

edited by
Parker J. Palmer
Barbara G. Wheeler
and
James W. Fowler

 MERCER UNIVERSITY PRESS

ISBN 0-86554-358-5

Caring for the Commonweal
Education for Religious and Public Life
Copyright ©1990
Mercer University Press, Macon, Georgia 31207
All rights reserved
Printed in the United States of America

The paper used in this publication meets the minumum requirements
of American National Standard for Information Sciences—
Permanence of Paper for Printed Library Materials, ANSI Z39.48-1984.

Library of Congress Cataloging-in-Publication Data

Caring for the commonweal :
    education for religious and public life / edited by
    Parker J. Palmer, Barbara G. Wheeler, and James W. Fowler.
    v + xxxpp. 6″ × 9″ (15 × 23cm.)
    Festschrift in honor of Robert Wood Lynn.
    ISBN 0-86554-358-5 (alk. paper)
    1. Education (Christian theology). 2. Education—United States.
3. Religion and state—United States. 4. United States—Religion.
5. Lynn, Robert W.   I. Palmer, Parker J. II. Wheeler, Barbara G.
III. Fowler, James W., 1940–   . IV. Lynn, Robert W.
BT738.17.C37   1990   89-78103
207′.73—dc20   CIP

Contents

Introduction

A Forum
on Paideia

Barbara G. Wheeler

Few historians have explored the multiple uses of expectations about America's future. For if our claims about the past often turn out to be ideological creations, so do those images of the future which have consistently moved successive generations of Americans. We have been a future-chasing nation, possessed and preoccupied by the lure of an imaginary tomorrow. These future concepts have also been employed "to control individuals, or motivate societies, or inspire classes." There has been, indeed, as much American dogma proclaimed about the future as about the past.

But when those images of the future lose their power—as appears to be the case in this country—then a double-edged challenge of peril and promise is in the making. The peril of the new situation resides in potential loss of motivating power and energy. Make no mistake about it: collective convictions about things to come can unleash incredible strength. To lose that source of energy is to risk anomic drift and inertia. The promise inherent in this loss is the necessity of thinking about the future in new and different ways.

—Robert W. Lynn[1]

---

[1]"An Historical Perspective on the Futures of American Religious Education," *Foundations for Christian Education in an Era of Change*, ed. Marvin J. Taylor (Nashville: Abingdon Press, 1976) 7-8. I am indebted to C. Ellis Nelson of Austin Presbyterian Theological Seminary, who found this and other quotations from the work of Robert Lynn that have been useful in preparing this introduction. Professor Nelson, C. Eric Lincoln of Duke University, Thomas F. Green of Syracuse University, and Robert Greenleaf, four of Robert Lynn's closest associates over the years, wrote extended reflections on his work as part of the project that produced this book. The essays helped to shape the book and these introductory comments, in which they are quoted.

This book is a tribute to the work of Robert Wood Lynn, who served as Professor of Religion and Education at Union Theological Seminary and Dean of Auburn Theological Seminary until 1976, and between then and his retirement in 1989, as Vice President of the Lilly Endowment, Inc., specializing in religion. The essays collected here treat three themes that are interwoven in his work as scholar, teacher and philanthropist: religion, education and public life.

Varied as they are in approach and topic, all the essays in this volume share two motifs with each other and with Robert Lynn's own writing. They all presuppose the accuracy of Lynn's judgment about the current state of American social and religious life: It is in disarray, indeed crisis, because older images of common purpose have lost their power, and compelling new images have not yet been formed. The essays also join in a single quest, one that has marked Lynn's whole varied career, for a *paideia*, a pattern of formation that draws from the Judaeo-Christian tradition and other rich sources the means to reform and renew our common life. Some of the essays focus on the complications and confusions in contemporary thinking about the public good, others on the crisis internal to religious communities and their own quest for binding images and appropriate educational patterns, and still others on the potential contribution of religion to the education of a public that cares for the well-being of all. But each is animated by Robert Lynn's basic commitment: to mine our national and religious histories and to search the practices of contemporary communities for elements of the *paideia* that is required to form new visions of the commonweal, those "collective convictions about the shape of things to come" that can "unleash incredible strength."

Paideia, then, is the thread that links these essays and the several themes of the book. The term has a long history in classical and Christian settings that makes it both rich in resonances and difficult to use without qualifications. As adopted for use in these essays, the concept has three prominent features. First, it is an inclusive term, as it was for the Greeks, for a kind of formation that involves not only schooling but also those patterns of social life that build character and inculcate virtue. Thus it is broader than even expansive uses of the word education. Formation is the closest English equivalent, but formation, which in current usage is associated with the molding of the individual's character or soul, does not capture a second dimension of *paideia*, its orientation to public values, to those purposes that a community or society holds in common. In this sense too the use of the term here is consonant with earlier ones. Though the substantive object of *paideia*, the values to which it is ordered, have been different in each historical period in which the term was appropriated, *paideia* has always served the larger purposes of a social group.

Paideia as invoked in these essays has a third dimension, one that is adapted to contemporary questions and complexities in a way that makes it a more dynamic concept than it has been in some periods past, especially in early Christianity. In the pluralistic setting our authors address, there is no durable agreement about the purposes and values to which patterns of teaching, learning and living should be oriented. It is, in fact, the lack of such an agreement that makes the contemporary quest for *paideia* so urgent. Thus an adequate *paideia* for our time must be more than methods of teaching and learning oriented to a commonly-held image of what is true and good. The disciplines of *paideia* must have a creative and critical component. They not only must prepare the community's members to live according to certain precepts and values; they must also become the means by which a consensus about how we should live together may be forged, continually tested and reformed.

The first group of essays focuses on the character and quality of public life and the part that religion should play in its formation. Two essays contain important warnings about the conceptual difficulties of the discussion. John Wilson explores the concept of "public," a "bedrock" term that is much used but rarely defined in recent writing on religion in America. On close examination, however, "public," as both noun and adjective, turns out to have different political meanings in the hands of different users. Almost always the use is "hegemonic": "public" serves to legitimate what the author advocates. Therefore, Wilson concludes, discussions about the relationship of religion and public life must proceed with caution and self-consciousness about *whose* idea of the public particular proposals will serve. Robert Handy urges caution in using the dyad "church/state." He provides examples from the period 1880-1920 to show that religion and government in the U.S. have so many facets, and their institutional forms have shifted so frequently, that church/state terminology always requires further definition for the specific historical context it is being used to describe.

Two other essays in the first section examine the public role of religious commitments. Robin Lovin reviews the Enlightenment ideas about society and persons that provided the conceptual context for the Constitution and its provisions for religion. He then traces how our ideas about human beings and social organization have changed, and he explores, in the light of these changes, three possible roles for religion in a liberal democracy. Lovin describes one of these roles, which he calls "articulation of religious traditions," at length, for it brings with it the possibility of public discourse among different religious and non-religious traditions. As he recounts the theories about human life that undergird this approach and the promise it offers, the outlines of a *paideia* for public life emerge. James Fowler presents a full-scale model for a *paideia* for public education. After sketching the social turbulence that creates the need for a "reconstituted" *paideia,* he calls attention to the work of several social theorists and theologians who offer antidotes to the formalism that has infected public education as well as replacements for the mistaken ideas about reason and conscience that have impoverished it. Fowler presents a model of "responsible selfhood" that weaves these materials and others from both religious and secular sources together into a pattern for character and moral formation, a *paideia* that is, he argues, appropriate for public schools.

In the second group of essays the focus shifts to religious communities and the *paideia* that is required for their reform and renewal. Three authors write specifically and critically about education in their religious traditions. Henri Nouwen, a Roman Catholic who has taught in a Protestant divinity school, describes his and his students' "ongoing struggle" against the tendency of Christian theological education to separate intellectual and spiritual formation. He argues that Christian theology is properly understood as doxology, inseparable from prayer, the building of community and proclamation, and he suggests what should be the features of a program in which "the Word" is "lived in the form of studying." From a very different vantage point, Neil Gillman expresses a similar concern, about the "religious" dimension of non-orthodox Jewish theological education. Such education retains its long-standing commitment to historical scholarship, but in recent decades, since a traditionalist view of Jewish law that defined the "religious" has broken down, it is not clear how theological education should incorporate the religious aspects of formation. Using faith development theory, Tillich's ideas about faith, and a variety of Jewish sources, Gillman makes a proposal for a form of theological reflection that he thinks can bring religious experience and formation into the core of Jewish theological schooling. This kind of theological reflection also holds rich possibilities, Gillman suggests, for education in Jewish congregations. Edward Farley brings to the problem of *paideia* for Christian congregations very different concerns about the role of religion and piety than occupy Nouwen and Gillman. In Farley's view, the situation of church education is "tragic," because a kind of idolatry is intrinsic to all religion and thus to religious education, which nonetheless aims to inculcate a faith that idolatry undercuts. Farley urges Christian education to embrace its tragic character. A "genuinely Christian *paideia*," he argues, must both interpret a tradition's past and critically challenge the elements of that past that are idolatrous.

Parker Palmer and Sara Little also take as their topic *paideia* in religious communities. Both writers ask how religious formation is related to formation for public responsibilities. Do religious education and nurture in fact lead, as is widely believed, *away* from the public sphere and toward a private, interior religious territory? Palmer and Little insist that the opposite is true, that authentic Christian *paideia* is by definition oriented to public life. Palmer maintains that the inner life and the public life co-create each other, but the deep relationship between them is obscured by "privatism," a distortion that permits the realm of family, friends and personal property to dominate everything else and to diminish the public arena. He offers congregations an alternative, rooted in a theological understanding of the "strangeness" of God: In the ways they go about education and decision-making, congregations can form their members to honor both the familiar and the strange in both the interior and the public life. Little, concerned about how social

institutions and their moral foundations are "coming apart," develops a definition of a kind of leadership that may resupply the moral commitment and sense of
collective identity that are missing. She calls such leadership "experiments with
truth" and shows how education for it has the same lineaments as education for
responsible membership in any religious or social group: It entails commitment to
truth, it is rooted in vocation, and it is oriented to both discipleship and citizenship.

The third group of essays explores the intersection of religious and public values in higher education. Glenn Miller and Dorothy Bass provide historical accounts of the Protestant stance toward education. Miller shows how the early leaders
of various branches of the Reformation all labored to create schools, most of which
were remarkable for their public and secular focus. The pattern was carried to this
country: Education continued to be Protestantism's "great cause," but its schools
soon lost their religious character, and increasingly public institutions took over
the tasks of Protestant-founded private ones. Only recently, observes Miller, has
paideia ceased to be a crusade of Protestantism, and he calls for a return to the
earlier posture: The Protestant contribution should be to develop a "theology of
the state" to undergird its support of secular education. Dorothy Bass mounts a
different argument. She uses the story of Protestant campus ministry, student religious organizations, and the growth of departments of religious studies in the
1960s as a case study of Protestant attitudes toward secular institutions. Although,
she acknowledges, the sixties were in many ways extreme, her account of this difficult period in the history of Protestant churches and higher education nonetheless reveals a persistent problem in liberal Protestantism, its tendency to sacrifice
its traditional values to contemporaneous engagement in the world. She advocates
a "truthfulness" that incorporates both secular engagement and respect for the resources of tradition, in the recognition that the strength to act on fragile Christian
values demands both.

Finally, William May asks how American higher education may have contributed to the "loss of public happiness," the increasing alienation between the
outer world and the inner self. He examines three models of higher education—
the liberal arts college, the "positivist" university, and the educational vision of
the sixties counter-culture—and shows how they seek but have often failed to cultivate "the civic self." May proposes his own scheme, which emphasizes the cultivation of critical intelligence and civic responsibility, both long strands in the
history of *paideia,* but he also asks for an unusual shift, for the reconception of
the modern professions as teaching offices. Thus like most of the authors in this
volume, he offers a *paideia* that recovers important insights and values from other
traditions and yet is newly fitted to this particular context.

* * *

This volume concludes, appropriately, with biography. Elizabeth Lynn's
narrative of her father's upbringing and education shows how ideas, institutions,

movements, teachers and mentors—indispensable ingredients of an effective *pai-deia*—molded Robert Lynn's life and profession, and brought to prominence the themes that shape this book.

The authors of the volume are Robert Lynn's students and colleagues from different phases of his many-faceted career. Like the much wider and more numerous circle of his associates whom they represent, the authors propose to resolve issues of common concern in markedly different ways. This variety has been a characteristic of Lynn's efforts to guide and sponsor of the work of others: He has often promoted projects whose conclusions differ from each other and from his own. Nonetheless, those who have worked in the diverse company that Lynn assembled have been influenced not only by his commitments to struggle with certain difficult problems but also by his approach to addressing them. Those commonalities of approach are evident in the book.

Many of the essays, for instance, use historical argument to make their point about contemporary issues. Lynn's life-long interest in history has never an antiquarian cast. Rather, writes C. Ellis Nelson, "his purpose is to look behind what happened in order to see what people in a previous era formulated as their problems, the reasons for the strategies they used to solve the problems, and an evaluation of the outcome." This "creative" use of the past is a hallmark of Lynn's own scholarship and teaching; these essays use history similarly, as a channel to clarity and honesty about the present. Thomas Green also writes of Lynn's attraction to histories, especially local ones, as ways that abstractions and generalizations are tested by "the story where actors have definite names, definite commitments, definite motives, and do definite things, in consequence of real events." Always, though, as in these essays, this focus on the past and the particular yields an enlarged sense of the character of our own times and our likely futures. Were it not for Lynn's attempts to call our attention to where we have been and where we are headed, writes Green, "we would know much less of our own surroundings and would just that much be impoverished."

These essays also reflect the scope of Lynn's interest, which spans the major religious traditions, European and American history since the Reformation, and several types of institutions, both public and voluntary. There is, however, one serious omission. Though we invited articles on the role of Black religious institutions in shaping American religion and *paideia* for the American public, the authors we approached were not free to participate. Robert Lynn has written that he learned from Lawrence N. Jones and C. Eric Lincoln, his colleagues at Union, "the significance of the Black Church as a proud, legitimate independent entity which was at the same time a vital facet of the Christian experience in America." In his work at the Lilly Endowment, Lynn consistently promoted the "Black church's study of itself," Eric Lincoln reminds us, as well as the causes of Black theological education and cooperation among the historic Black denominations.

As a result, writes Lincoln, "the Black Church will never be quite the same, and neither will religion and education in America."

Perhaps Robert Lynn's most extraordinary gift has been his capacity to teach others the significance of their own work. Each of us who contributed to this volume has benefited from that special ability of his, to help us see why what we are doing is important and what its place may be in a life-long vocation and a community of endeavor. He has made this special assistance available to many persons, in several generations. Unlike some great teachers who communicate easily only with the young, Lynn has generously encouraged his colleagues and peers and even those to whom he has looked as his mentors. One of those mentors, Robert Greenleaf, writes that "in recent years Bob has become my most dependable guide and critic, and the person who is most concerned to sustain my spirit in my declining years." All of us who write in this volume could say much the same: Robert Lynn has sustained our spirits and lovingly reminded us of the Spirit in which we all work together. We are deeply grateful for his care for us and the larger community we serve, and we offer this book in his honor and in profound thanks.

One

Paideia
for Public Life

1

The Public
as a Problem

John F. Wilson

"Public," "private," and the contrast between them have a long intellectual history. In the late twentieth century, the distinction has become, implicitly and explicitly, central to the literature concerned with the plural aspects of religion in America. But while the term *public* obviously refers back to classical times, it now bears not only the special imprint of our age but also carries an implication of hegemony that warns us to use it with care. Accordingly, it is indispensable for those who use the term to recognize its ambiguity when they consider the relationship of religion and politics. I therefore propose that we review the concept of *public*, and to some extent its companion *private,* and consider their inherent limitations while also appreciating their obvious utility.

I

One influential author who has made explicit use of the concept of the public is Martin Marty. To exhibit adequately how the term functions in his *The Public Church,* we must note the background he set out in an earlier work, *A Nation of Behavers,* published in 1976.[1] In this important monograph, Marty "mapped" seven distinctive types of religion within contemporary American society, so signaling the erosion of the tripartite Protestant-Catholic-Jewish configuration (if it ever existed) that Will Herberg posited in the post-World War II period.[2] These types were mainline religion, evangelicalism, fundamentalism, pentecostal-charismatic religion, new religions, ethnic religion, and civil religion. In his view, the older positive traditions that

---

[1]Martin E. Marty, *The Public Church* (New York: Crossroad, 1981) and *A Nation of Behavers* (Chicago: University of Chicago Press, 1976).

[2]Will Herberg, *Protestant-Catholic-Jew,* rev. ed. (Garden City NY: Doubleday, Anchor Books, 1960).

had formed the basis of Herberg's scheme were no longer monolithic; so that, to take a specific instance, Roman Catholicism had come to be prominently practiced both as a mainline religion and as a pentecostal-charismatic type. Protestantism, and to a lesser degree Judaism, have experienced the same diversification.

If *A Nation of Behavers* was Marty as citizen-cartographer, a short while later Marty as concerned churchman issued *The Public Church*. The sequel was as subjective as its predecessor had been objective. Viewed in one perspective, *The Public Church* was Marty's lament for the extent to which mainline religion had lost its influence in the culture. For the mainline had been that strand of church life that—whether Protestant, Catholic, or Jewish in name—had recognized its responsibility for the broader society. In this respect, it had kept alive the European legacy of Christendom—that vision of a universal Christian order promising the renovation of society. From another perspective, Marty's interest in the public church reflected his appreciation for the strongly Calvinist and significantly Puritan concern that Christian virtues should inform American political culture. But most of all, the public church was, in Marty's view, a grouping of religions that had some sense of responsibility for infusing transcendental perspectives into the common life. The aspirations of this group, then, were the antithesis to the essentially private objectives and goals thought to be expressed in so many of the other "regions" of the map he had drawn. Marty, seeking to explain why the claims of one special subset of religious folk (namely, the mainline) were to be viewed as more than self-serving, reached for their role in the public domain. Here they acted so as to meet the concerns of the whole as opposed to those of a part only, thus becoming the public church. Pressed for a definition, Marty explained what he meant by the "public church":

> *Public theology* is in my view an effort to interpret the life of a people in the light of a transcendent reference. The people in this case are not simply the church but the pluralism of peoples with whom the language of the church is engaged in a larger way. The *public church,* then, is a specifically Christian polity and witness. (16)

Such a point of view, in his judgment, was present in American religion from the first European settlement. Indeed, Marty does not hesitate to say that "never from the first European arrivals, has America lacked the witness of the public church," a situation that "merely extends to the new world the Constantinian ethos and framework from the old" (17). He goes on to explore fully the implications of this "communion of communions" as religious counterpart to the "political 'community of communities'" (ix). For our purposes the significance is that Marty believed that, in referring to public (as implicitly contrasted with private) experience, he was using the most far-reaching and radical (in the sense of going to the root of the matter) language available to him to plumb the current significance of religion in the United States.

Dependence on the public/private distinction is also exhibited by essays edited by Leroy S. Rouner in *Civil Religion and Political Theology*.[3] Two are particularly significant in this regard. One is a discussion by Robert Bellah, which he titles "Public Philosophy and Public Theology in America Today" (79-97). In it Bellah focuses very directly on the diversity of traditions of thought about this topic. In particular he comments on the work of two earlier twentieth-century authors, John Dewey and Walter Lippmann, concerning the individual and the community. He makes the arresting point that both were forced to embark on public theology in spite of themselves as they set out to "do public philosophy" (82). In Dewey's case, this entailed looking to natural intelligence, while for Lippmann it meant reverting to the natural law tradition. In the end Bellah finds both "abstract" in their work, and thus turns appreciatively to Reinhold Niebuhr and his book *The Children of Light and the Children of Darkness*.[4] Niebuhr's understanding that individual and community must be considered in a dialectical fashion is, for Bellah, a position both profound and relevant to the current American situation. In the work of William M. Sullivan and Richard John Neuhaus, he sees today's embodiment of much of the thrust of Niebuhr's position. He also links that position to the deeper purposes behind *Habits of the Heart,* a book he coauthored with Sullivan and others.[5] For Bellah, reference to the public and recognition of its significance finally provide the framework for dealing constructively with the need for renewal in American society.

In light of Bellah's argument, it is fascinating to turn to Richard John Neuhaus's essay, also in Rouner's book.[6] Neuhaus publishes his remarks under the title "From Civil Religion to Public Philosophy," but his subtitle, or working title, is actually "The Brief and Disappointing Life of American Civil Religion." He argues that the civil religion discussion posed the basic question that proponents of public philosophy must seek to work through. "Public philosophy, the term, is not new; but public philosophy, the task, has been long neglected" (104). Neuhaus then sketches "some of the marks of a public philosophy that might sustain the American democratic experience" (105).

What concerns us, again, is not to follow the specific course of Neuhaus's argument but to recognize that this author, too, has implicitly reached for the public/private distinction as a means of coming to terms with the problem of constructive religious action given the pluralism of our culture. Of course, he did the same

---

[3]Leroy S. Rouner, ed., *Civil Religion and Political Theology,* Boston University Studies in Philosophy and Religion vol. 8 (Notre Dame IN: University of Notre Dame Press, 1986).

[4]Reinhold Niebuhr, *The Children of Light and the Children of Darkness* (New York: Scribner's, 1946).

[5]Robert N. Bellah, Richard Madsen, William M. Sullivan, Ann Swidler, and Steven M. Tipton, *Habits of the Heart* (Berkeley and Los Angeles: University of California Press, 1985).

[6]Richard John Neuhaus, "From Civil Religion to Public Philosophy," in Rouner, ed., *Civil Religion and Political Theology,* 98-110.

in his earlier and widely acclaimed book, *The Naked Public Square*.[7] There he argued that religious pluralism has created the "naked public square" of the title, that is, a political arena without received tradition or coherent direction. The continued vitality of the American democratic experiment was threatened by this zone of moral neutrality at the heart of the common enterprise. Yet he felt that the religious-ethical claims that sought to fill it ought to legitimate themselves without recourse to privileged sources of knowledge or insights derived from revelation.

It is interesting to ask whether models of society other than Neuhaus's might enable us to foresee alternative potential futures for religiously plural cultures. There are, indeed, several kinds of religious pluralism that do not depend upon a hegemonic religion at the center. An example is the structural pluralism described by the Dutch term *verzuiling*, in which separate and largely self-sufficient cultures parallel each other and have only a minimal political connection at the level of national polity. Again, the example of Japan suggests how a functional religious pluralism can work in a modern and highly efficient social order where different religious cults or distinctive sets of traditional practices inform and minister to different aspects of human life—among them births, deaths, and national traditions. Yet another alternative is the evolving pluralism so striking in Hawaii. Here a culture is being continuously recreated in a way that acknowledges the political realities of religious groupings in a direct and responsive manner. Such an evolving pluralism does not leave the public square naked, so to speak, but encourages continuing interaction in a contracting and expanding center of the social order. These examples suggest that the problem of religious pluralism has been and is being addressed in viable social orders and in different ways—whether through preservation of distinctive subcultures or the appropriation of pluralism at the personal level. There are, indeed, distinct alternatives to a coherent religious tradition as the common cultural core thought by many to be required at the center of our modern society.

But the important immediate point for our discussion is that, in order to comprehend the interplay of deeply held American values and contemporary pluralism, Neuhaus reaches for the public/private distinction. Especially he draws on the theological proposals of David Tracy to legitimate this approach on the religious side, but his use of the term *public* reaches out beyond Tracy's work to establish it as the most powerful concept available to him in his attempt to understand American pluralism.[8]

Several further exhibits will secure our point that the public/private distinction provides an unexamined framework for most writing on this subject. One is provided by a journalist, A. James Reichley, who comes at the problem of contemporary pluralism (at least intellectually speaking) more as an outsider to religious traditions than as an insider. He has directed his considerable analytic powers

---

[7]Richard John Neuhaus, *The Naked Public Square* (Grand Rapids MI: Eerdmans, 1984).
[8]See acknowledgment in n. 6 to ch. 1, Neuhaus, *Naked Public Square*, 265.

to exploring the place of religion in America in relation to politics. Once again, the important point is not the particulars of his argument in *Religion in American Public Life*,[9] but the fact that Reichley too appropriates the concept of the public as a way to comprehend what he sees as the multifaceted nexus where religion and politics interact with the economic, aesthetic, and other dimensions of our collective existence. Here too, then, a knowledgeable observer of our current situation has reached for this term to find a generally acceptable intellectual starting point for his review of religion's power in our culture, both past and present.

Another and final exhibit of this phenomenon—and the instances given scarcely begin to tally the class—is a collaborative study, *Varieties of Religious Presence*, by David A. Roozen, William McKinney, and Jackson W. Carroll.[10] The importance of this example is that, in contrast to Reichley's, which is a longitudinal study of the place of religion in the American political culture over three centuries, it is essentially an exploration of contemporary religious institutions in one city (Hartford, Connecticut). The authors line out the respective qualities and characteristics of different types of Protestant and Roman Catholic churches as well as Jewish bodies. The net result is an investigation of, in the phrase of the subtitle, "Mission in Public Life," and it is just this sense of public—as the means of signifying that which is generally available for common inspection—that makes the book noteworthy. The public/private distinction is the axis on which turn this and the other studies named above. In virtually all of them, the term functions as a canonical reference that is not explained or explored; it is simply taken for granted.[11]

In each of these studies, my point is made by the absence of the term *public,* at least without qualification, from the index. The authors evidently think that it is a term beyond dispute, a point of reference that enables them—and us—to communicate across the cultural divisions that fracture our society. It is presumed to be one of the few universal terms available to us. Yet is *public,* and the public/private distinction it depends on, quite so self-evident and neutral as a starting point for discussion? Or does it prove to be elusive, and to shift its meaning as we use it? In taking a stand on it, are intellectual discussions really secured on bedrock or are they instead placed on foundation soil that is unstable and subject to rapid movement? At the very least we should be wary of too readily assuming that the public/private distinction permits us to move beyond contested terms to a widely acknowledged vocabulary presumed to be neutral in which discussion can take

---

[9]A. James Reichley, *Religion in American Public Life* (Washington DC: The Brookings Institution, 1985).

[10]David A. Roozen, William McKinney, and Jackson W. Carroll, *Varieties of Religious Presence* (New York: Pilgrim Press, 1984).

[11]Additional exhibits of recent literature that make use of this reference point could be multiplied almost without limit. See, e.g., Christopher F. Mooney, *Public Virtue: Law and the Social Character of Religion* (Notre Dame IN: University of Notre Dame Press, 1986); Parker J. Palmer, *The Company of Strangers* (New York: Crossroad, 1981).

place among those committed to different religions and between religious people
and secularists.

On that note, let us turn to explore some of the sources of ambiguity in this
term. In a larger perspective, what is fascinating about this contemporary consensus concerning the neutrality of the public/private distinction is its universality and
comprehensiveness. It has come to provide a framework that operates not only
across different traditions of religious discourse (Protestant, Catholic, Jewish), but
one that also involves secular authorities such as legislators and the courts. In a
highly plural and fractionated culture, *public, private,* and the contrast between
them seem to promise intelligibility and to serve as neutral reference points in terms
of which exchanges can take place. This observation suggests that the distinction
has deep cultural relevance in contemporary America. Yet hitherto the term's specific and deeper antecedent sources in the society and the special limitations and
ambiguities that attach to its use have not been sufficiently examined.

II

At root, the ambiguity associated with *public* seems to lie in the contrast between, on the one hand, adjectival and relatively static, and, on the other, nominal
and essentially dynamic constructions of the term. When used as an adjective, its
implication is that of inclusiveness. A public realm or public space is—theoretically—available to any or all who would make use of it. Thus emphasis falls upon
openness or the principle of universal access. Alternatively, when used as a noun,
the public always threatens to rule itself—taking law into its own hands—thus effectively limiting access for outsiders and perhaps constraining insiders as well.
While the European republican tradition developed specific means of limiting the
power of the mob, so to speak, the genius of American politics has been to embrace at least the possibility that the mob can be enlightened and the people benefit
from self-rule. Hence the special interest American social thinkers take in the
term—and the special tensions that arise in its use.

In the longer horizons of the West, the categories of public and private originated in Greek and Roman social and political thought. In ancient Greece, private
signaled isolation from the community, or privation from the benefits of life in the
polis. (In this respect, it is surely ironic that today privacy is valued above its antithesis, public life.) In its Roman context, the term *public,* of course, referred to
"the people" and as such was more inclusive than the notion of citizenship in the
polis that lay behind it in Greek thought. These concepts have been transmitted to
us from antiquity in the broad republican tradition of thought which J. G. A. Pocock and others have recently explored in late medieval and early modern Eu-

rope.[12] The founding of the United States gave the contemporary meaning of the term a particular content. Gordon Wood's *The Creation of the American Republic, 1776-1787*, a searching discussion of the new meaning of politics, and therefore of the public, in the aftermath of revolution, reminds us that the political achievement represented by the founding of the new American nation entailed significant innovation.[13] Commenting on the new meaning of politics he observed:

> The political struggles would in fact be among the people themselves, among all the various groups and individuals seeking to create inequality out of their equality by gaining control of a government divested of its former identity with the society. (608)

So new hopes and therefore new meaning attached to the public in the creation of the United States. But to locate the proximate source of the ambiguity we find in use of the term *public* as a noun today, we may derive most help from an explicit appropriation and elaboration of the concept by John Dewey.

A deceptively slight and unpretentious work, *The Public and Its Problems* originated as a series of lectures Dewey gave at Kenyon College.[14] It continues to bear the characteristics of those circumstances of composition and, for that matter, original mode of delivery. Dewey lays out in striking fashion how the term *public* is to be understood in the context of American self-awareness. *The Public and Its Problems* is written in the mode of systematic reflection on politics in culture, especially in the American culture.[15] Indeed, in the initial lecture of his series, Dewey offers a searching criticism of a long-standing approach to these issues. He pronounces the distinction between individual and social to be inadequate as a starting point for analyzing the nature of political life in the United States. His point is that private behavior can have social consequences (for good and ill), and that activities are not necessarily socially valuable "because carried on in the name of the public by public agents" (15). Dewey's own words make this fundamental point about the conceptual reorientation he proposes:

> Two kinds of interests and of measures of regulation of acts in view of consequences are generated. In the first, interest and control are limited

---

[12]J. G. A. Pocock, *The Machiavellian Moment* (Princeton NJ: Princeton University Press, 1975).

[13]Gordon S. Wood, *The Creation of the American Republic, 1776–1787* (New York: Norton, 1972, c1969).

[14]John Dewey, *The Public and Its Problems* (New York: Henry Holt, 1927).

[15]In passing, it is interesting to note that Robert Bellah in discussing Dewey does not make use of this particular volume but instead bases his argument on Dewey's *Individualism, Old and New* (New York: Minton, Balch, 1930), on the one hand, and, on the other, *A Common Faith* (New Haven: Yale University Press, 1934). This may be because Bellah's operative categories are philosophical and theological.

to those directly engaged; in the second, they extend to those who do not
directly share in the performance of acts. If, then, the interest constituted
by their being affected by the actions in question is to have any practical
influence, control over the actions which produce them must occur by
some indirect means.

. . . Those indirectly and seriously affected for good or for evil form a
group distinctive enough to require recognition and a name. The name selected is The Public. This public is organized and made effective by means
of representatives who as guardians of custom, as legislators, as executives,
judges, etc., care for its especial interests by methods intended to regulate
the conjoint actions of individuals and groups. Then and in so far, association adds to itself political organization, and something which may be government comes into being; the public is a political state. (35)

What Dewey here insists on is that the public is a category reflecting relationships that both occur as a result of actions and warrant further action. In this
sense, the public is not defined at one point in time; it is always coming to be. It
does not consist of a particular group or body of individuals, but rather refers to
individuals and groups insofar as they are involved in interactive relationships.
Thus Dewey insists that the public is a very dynamic concept. It is always being
formed, and perhaps taking different forms simultaneously, and struggling for influence through representation and by means of agencies. Thus the actual, or operative, public is in no sense static or formal only but is always newly emerging.
The genius of American thought is to have recognized this characteristic; the fundamental issue posed by Dewey is how the public can be made politically effective.

Pursuing this line of thought, Dewey goes on to propose how we may conceive what a state is:

The lasting, extensive, and serious consequences of associated activity bring
into existence a public. In itself it is unorganized and formless. By means
of officials and their special powers it becomes a state. A public articulated
and operating through representative officers is the state; there is no state
without a government, but also there is none without the public. (67)

He then explores the characteristics of a democratic state and laments its inade-
quacies in rising to the challenges of the modern industrial world.

But throughout his chapters, fundamental attention is directed to the problematic public as the subject of our investigation. Dewey examines the ''eclipse of
the public'': ''The Public seems to be lost; it is certainly bewildered'' (116). In
scathing terms he denounces the role of big business in performing functions more
properly exercised by government. Indeed, he abhors extralegal agencies because
they deprive the public of its true means of self-direction: ''When the public is as
uncertain and obscure as it is today, and hence as remote from government, bosses
with their political machines fill the void between government and the public''

(120). Dewey sadly comments that the shortcomings of democracy in his time had created the "prime difficulty . . . of discovering the means by which a scattered, mobile and manifold public may so recognize itself as to define and express its interests" (146). His prescription is that the community should turn to, and find itself through, "the improvement of the methods and conditions of debate, discussion, and persuasion" (208). By solving this, "*the* problem of the public," the public itself will finally be able more adequately to express its interests through a more responsive government.

At one level, Dewey's treatise on *The Public and Its Problems* stands as an exhibit of an American philosopher's frustration with the exhaustion of progressivism. But in a more fundamental sense, it is a remarkable attempt to explore the special meaning America has given to the term *public* as a category not only in relation to individual, society, and community, but also to government and state. Dewey was systematically thinking through the new reality Gordon Wood subsequently defined in his work on the creation of the American republic. Taking Dewey's study as a whole, his explorations at once suggest why the term is so appealing to contemporary authors seeking to come to terms with cultural and religious pluralism, how great the potential for serious misuse of the term, and the fundamentally political meaning that attaches to it in the United States. These are the branches of our inquiry to which our attention must now turn.

III

Dewey's conception of the public is a fascinating adaptation and application of ancient and continuing Western traditions to American life. Although it effectively establishes the sources of the term's power in contemporary usage, it is open to a line of criticism that is significant. As a dynamic construct at his hands, the public stands behind institutions, so to speak, providing for their legitimation and making possible their revitalization, an outcome he desperately sought to bring about. (Indeed, in his own time Dewey's conceptual work contributed to such new enterprises as public opinion research—an activity that takes on a somewhat different significance in light of his philosophical position [177-79].) Further, given Dewey's inclusive understanding of the term *public,* the purely private is markedly limited. His perspective requires vigorous critical questioning of any attempts to enlarge claims made on the basis of private interests.

But in this view the public can also be seen to present another face. It can appear as that subset of the whole that at any point in time is able to present itself as the whole and is able to advance its claims as bearing the interests of the whole. Dewey writes of the public as "eclipsed," and it is clear that he understands that the interests of some constituent members may be more effectively expressed than those of others less well placed to be influential.[16] In sum, the operative public (as opposed to the theoretically inclusive public) is finally a projection of influence by a subset of the collectivity in the name of the inclusive collectivity. In this sense there is no sure check upon a self-designated public's hegemony over a culture. Finally, Dewey's elegant conceptual exercise does not succeed in saving the public from being the potential instrument of cultural privilege and social control.

This kind of criticism of social concepts has become relatively commonplace. For example, reference is made to it in the Bellah essay and Neuhaus proposes by this means to identify limitations to the earlier civil religion discussion. Perhaps the most searching criticism roots in the Gramscian notion of hegemony, a recognition that to be able to set the terms of reference is to hold power over any cultural interaction. Thus while the public/private distinction initially seems promising in discussion of the role of religion in the culture, the concept of the public is finally revealed as only another means by which class and/or ethnic interests—that is to say, private interests—can express their dominant role within American society. In this light it seems clear that the term has severe shortcomings, and writers who use it should be aware of them.

In consequence of these limitations and the associated problems with the term *public*, it is interesting to turn to a relatively recent critical effort to assess "conceptions of the public and private in social life." Begun as a project at the Australian National University in 1979, it evolved into a book edited by S. I. Benn and G. F. Gaus titled *Public and Private in Social Life*.[17] A total of fifteen separate essays, most of them by faculty members at Australian institutions, explore the place of public and private in Western cultures, the liberal conception of public and private, and finally the concepts of public and private in nonliberal cultures. Taken as a whole, the essays reinforce the points that these concepts are not free of difficulties and that to make use of them requires a much more critical approach than is normal. The authors call into question precisely the uses to which public and private have been put in so much recent literature concerned with contemporary American religious pluralism and criticize their role as a cultural reference point presumed to be objective.

It would not be appropriate to report fully upon the Benn and Gaus volume here. The range of the separate essays in any case forecloses such an effort. The general introductory essay by the editors, however, does develop a more inclusive analytical framework. It analyzes "publicness" and "privateness" as "complex-structured concepts" that cover a "broad domain of activities and practices" (7). In surveying this domain, Benn and Gaus propose that there are three chief types or dimensions of publicness and privateness. One is that of control over access,

---

[16]Title of ch. 4 of Dewey, *Public and Its Problems*. See p. 137 for a useful summary.
[17]S. I. Benn and G. F. Gaus, *Public and Private in Social Life* (London, Canberra: Croom Helm; New York: St. Martin's Press, 1983).

itself a complex issue for it entails not only physical access but access as well to "activities and interests," to "information," and to "resources" (7-9). Another dimension relates to "the status of agents," whether acting publicly or privately (9-10). A final dimension is that of interests—who purportedly benefits from the operation of institutions (10-11).

Beyond identifying this complexity of the terms, Benn and Gaus call attention to a significant ambiguity concerning the relationship between public and private. Under some circumstances, these terms are conceived to form a bipolar continuum (a construction that has a special affinity with liberalism), while under others they tend toward multipolarity (13-18). At this level of analysis the authors clearly recognize that these terms as they actually operate relate directly to religious conceptions that claim an authority rooted outside the culture (19-23). In this sense, the contemporary appropriation of the public/private distinction we have remarked upon is not so much the solution to the question of religious pluralism in America (that is to say in more traditional terms the church-state issue in the culture) as it is itself a particular version of the problem.

The significance of the Benn-Gaus book is that it forces careful readers to analyze precisely the ambiguous and hegemonic qualities of this ostensibly bedrock term, *public*. Through the rigor of their analysis and the range of their alternative cultural strategies, the authors force us to recognize how these seemingly neutral terms—apparently situated beyond partisanship and privilege—are themselves laden with particular meanings and roles, especially in the context of late liberal Western cultures. This should not in the end surprise us, but if the insight is taken seriously there are some important implications to be drawn.

For one, as problematic terms *public* and its implied companion *private* should be used critically. This means asking what we mean by them, especially when they are to bear the burden of constructive and prescriptive work. To give a concrete example, when we are dealing with systematic exclusion from position and privilege, whether caused by racism or sexism, it will not do to suppose that the public as a reference point transcends the social structures that are alleged to embody the problem. People never have a single voice, so the question becomes, who speaks for others? The great political issue of modernity is the absence of instrumentalities that would permit the chorus of actual voices to be heard. The insights offered in the Benn and Gaus study ought to lead us to recognize that public and private as reference points may, and possibly do, systematically reflect, embody, and reinforce just the social biases and interests at the center of an issue. Publicness as a culture-dependent quality is not a neutral description—however much it may seem to masquerade as such in normal usage. What from one vantage point may seem to be a progressive political program (here recall Dewey's exploration of the concept), from another may appear as repressive.

As another implication, we must be careful in using the terms adjectivally to specify other discrete activities—as in such examples as public theology, public philosophy, and for that matter, public life and public square, where used metaphorically. It would be much better to recognize that *public* (and its companion *private*) are political and relational terms in our culture, that is to say, concerned with power. If it is the quality of publicness we are concerned with, then to modify such terms as philosophy or theology with it compounds already complex activities—for in so using them we effectively politicize them. Adjectival usage is invariably affected by the nominal usage that America has given to the term. If we have carefully thought through such strategies, there is no reason not to adopt these uses. But that entails a burden of explicating exactly what we might mean by such compound terms. To use them is the beginning of a project, not its conclusion. Nor is it even the adoption of a framework that can be taken for granted. An adjectival reference should not turn out to be a substitute for or an evasion of analysis.

Finally, and most important, this kind of exercise ought to make us wary of substantive uses of the term *public*. What can we mean by "the public" in light of the Benn-Gaus critique? As a concept it has a particular history and set of meanings. But the preceding review, sketchy as it is, suggests significant evolution in uses of the term. And the deeper point of the Benn-Gaus inquiry may be to signal that widespread consciousness of interaction among cultures is remaking our most basic terms of reference. It may even be that "the public"—or in an American version "We the people," freighted with the substance of our political traditions—is a normative concept we can give to other cultures as our most basic political and cultural legacy. But if that is our understanding and intent, our definition is far from self-evident and certainly is more political and moral than philosophical and analytical. And paradoxically it may also turn out to embody direct tension with the classical republican heritage with which the term is linked.

The problem with the public is that, as with so many other terms and concepts, we must not take for granted that the meanings we assign it are self-evident and universally true. In this particular case the term is irreducibly political and hegemonic. The problem with the public is that it is so politically charged as a concept that it cannot without qualification and refinement play the constructive critical role intended by many of those who use it. To appropriate the language of Gordon Wood, to claim to speak for the public is irreducibly a political act, a "seeking to create inequality out of . . . equality."[18] In the final analysis, with the help of Dewey we see that to make this claim is to seek to gain control of a government under the pretense that the interests of some (including ourselves) are coincident with the interests of all. We may in fact wish to do this and cannot be prohibited from so making use of the term *public*. But to use the term unaware of its hegemonic role, believing it has delivered us from the political perils of religious pluralism, is a form of self-deception. Whenever we see the term, we ought to ask whose public and in the service of whose purposes?

---

[18]Wood, *Creation of the American Republic*, 608.

2

Changing Contexts
of Church-State Relations
in America, 1880–1920

Robert T. Handy

As many have observed, the familiar terminology of "church and state," rooted in European historical experience, is really not adequate for the religious situation of the United States.[1] Here for a century and a half there have been no established churches but rather a widening spectrum of many types of churches, synagogues, temples, meeting houses, associations, and other institutions of religion in bewildering variety. What we so glibly call "the state" has long operated through an array of various governmental units at local, county, state, and national levels, while in the twentieth century the proliferation of a range of official administrative agencies of many types has further increased its complexity and growing omnipresence. The old church-state terminology, however, has become so standard as to be virtually unshakable as an overall rubric. Only by being aware of the broad, continually changing contexts in which the issues have emerged we can seek to use the hackneyed terms more accurately.

This essay is an effort to trace some of the connections between what have been familiarly known as church-state problems and other issues for the period 1880–1920. On the surface, those years do not seem to mark a time in American history in which there were great public controversies on matters that come under the conventional rubrics of church and state. Other periods seem to have been far more fertile fields for scholarly digging and controversial debate. One thinks, for example of the time of the shaping and adoption of the Constitution with its Ar-

---

[1]E.g., see John F. Wilson and Donald L. Drakeman, eds., *Church and State in American History: The Burden of Religious Pluralism*, 2nd ed. (Boston: Beacon Press, 1987) ix-xx; and Wilson, ed., *Church and State in America: A Bibliographical Guide*, 2 vols. (New York: Greenwood Press, 1986–1987).

ticle Six ("no religious Test shall ever be required as a qualification to any Office or public Trust under the United States") and the religion clauses of the First Amendment ("Congress shall make no law respecting an establishment of religion, or prohibiting the free exercise thereof"); of the early decades of the nineteenth century when the patterns of Protestant cultural hegemony were shaped under the conditions of voluntaryism in religion; or of the years since 1940 with their escalation of hard-fought, split-decision, "landmark" church-state cases, when the free exercise and establishment clauses were specifically applied to the states by the incorporation of the First Amendment into the Fourteenth. In comparison, the four decades considered here seem to have been a relatively quiet period; the basic patterns that had been worked out in the relations of church and state were generally accepted, and the Supreme Court was not often called on to deal with controversies in this area. The massive changes in American life and thought that were going on, however, were undermining the familiar patterns and alignments in this relationship as in others, and to understand later controversies and present predicaments, an examination of this period may prove to be fruitful indeed.

I

In the heart of the 1880-1920 period philosopher George Santayana perceptively pointed to what was going on: "The civilisation characteristic of Christendom has not disappeared, yet another civilisation has begun to take its place. We still understand the value of religious faith; . . . . On the other hand the shell of Christendom is broken."[2] The pattern that had marked nineteenth-century Christendom in America was certainly not the same as those that marked the medieval, Reformation, or even American colonial periods, with their continuing legal establishments of state religion. It was a modified, voluntaryistic version of Christendom, which promised religious freedom for all, yet within which the leading Protestant denominations confidently expected to maintain their prominence. At heart it was pluralistic, yet the pluralism was distinctly Protestant in cast; both Roman Catholicism (though already the largest single religious body in the United States by 1850) and certain distinctive sects and indigenous groups (like the Mormons) were tolerated but not perceived by either side as part of the dominant "Protestantdom" of the time. Believing itself to be fully committed to a religious freedom consistent with the First Amendment, evangelical Protestantism still expected not only to hold the allegiance of the dominant elites of American life but also to march on to make the country even more fully a "Christian" (as evangelicals defined it) nation by means of continuous revivals and the network of vol-

---

[2]George Santayana, *Winds of Doctrine: Studies in Contemporary Opinion* (New York: Charles Scribner's Sons, 1913) 1.

untary societies they spawned. Despite growing tensions and difficulties, these patterns were carried confidently by the evangelical leaders from the late-nineteenth into the twentieth century.[3]

The four decades we focus on here have been selected primarily with reference to the decisive change in patterns and scope of immigration at the beginning of the ninth decade of the nineteenth century and the close of the decade of World War I. Various descriptive phrases have been used to characterize all or parts of these years, which, for example, fall largely within Richard Hofstadter's "age of reform" and Howard Mumford Jones's "age of energy." From the perspective of this church historian, however, the term "age of crusades" seems to point to certain characteristics important for understanding the changing church-state situation at the time. When Gaius Glenn Atkins, a prominent theological educator, looked back at the opening years of the twentieth century, he declared:

> The first fifteen years of the twentieth century may sometimes be remembered in America as the Age of Crusades. There were a superabundance of zeal, a sufficiency of good causes, unusual moral idealism, excessive confidence in mass movements and leaders with rare popular appeal. . . . The air was full of banners, and the trumpets called from every camp.[4]

To be sure Atkins refers to just those fifteen years, but in view of the preceding intense revivalistic campaigns under Dwight L. Moody and Samuel P. Jones and the remarkable resurgence of interest in both foreign and home missions, it seems appropriate to extend the terminology of the crusade backward into the late nineteenth century, and to remember that World War I was often known as the "Great Crusade" while it was being waged. Though the image of the crusade is especially useful for the leading Protestant denominations, many aspects of Roman Catholic history in those decades also show the crusading pattern, as in such vigorous movements as the planting of new parishes to serve the millions of Catholic immigrants, the molding of the vast parochial school system to educate children under church auspices, and the drawing on the resources of faith to meet the needs

---

[3]On the "Christian America" theme, cf., e.g., Sidney E. Mead, *The Lively Experiment: The Shaping of Christianity in America* (New York: Harper & Row, 1963); Martin E. Marty, *Righteous Empire: The Protestant Experiment in America* (New York: Dial Press, 1970); Robert T. Handy, *A Christian America: Protestant Hopes and Historical Realities* (New York: Oxford University Press, 1971, 1984); Mark A. Noll, Nathan O. Hatch, and George M. Marsden, *The Search for Christian America* (Westchester IL: Crossway Books, 1983).

[4]Gaius Glenn Atkins, *Religion in Our Times* (New York: Round Table Press, 1932) 156. For the Hofstadter and Jones references, see the former's *The Age of Reform: From Bryan to F. D. R.* (New York: Vintage Books, 1955), and the latter's *The Age of Energy: Varieties of American Experience, 1865–1915* (New York: Viking Press, 1970, 1971).

of working people. There were significant crusading aspects also in the life of the black Protestant denominations at the time, although their energies often had to be directed against the growing hostility of the movement for white supremacy.[5] From the perspective of the confident leaders of white evangelical Protestantism and their hosts of followers, however, a crusade to win not only America but also the world seemed destined to bear rich fruit, for it was a crusade for the kingdom of God.

The leaders of the crusade were not unaware of the massive changes that were going on in American life and the problems that were mounting as industrialization transformed the economy, as unprecedented waves of immigrants poured in, and as vast urban areas with their mounting social problems spread steadily. There were many watchers on walls calling attention to what was going on. Henry George dramatized what was to become a stubborn paradox of the period in his *Progress and Poverty* in 1879; six years later Josiah Strong, then moving from home mission work to head the Evangelical Alliance, highlighted the major perils that lay in the path of the crusaders in his widely read book of 1885, *Our Country: Its Possible Future and Its Present Crisis.* The prolific Congregational pastor in Columbus, Ohio, Washington Gladden, later labeled "the father of the social gospel," called attention to the dangers of deepening conflict between capital and labor; while from her base at Hull House in Chicago, Jane Addams vividly portrayed the realities of life among immigrants caught in the warrens of the deteriorating slums. Protestant leaders were aware of the widening spectrum of denominations and especially of the growth of Catholicism, for as children of the Reformation they had an instinctive fear of Rome, intensified by persisting memories of Britain's encounters with that church in the sixteenth and seventeenth centuries. Yet they were confident that they were still in the ascendancy, that the programs of Americanization would work, and that the familiar patterns of voluntaryistic Christendom in which they had been reared were firm and well founded, yet flexible enough to meet the challenges. They were convinced that the way of freedom in religion had abundantly proved itself as it allowed individuals to go their own way in matters of faith and yet opened doors of opportunity for religious bodies to make their witness as they chose and to gather in whomever they could reach.

An eloquent, informed, somewhat cautious spokesman for this point of view was the eminent church historian Philip Schaff, a prolific scholar born and educated in Europe whose career as educator and author unfolded in America. Toward the climax of his nearly half-century of service on this side of the Atlantic, on the occasion of the centennial celebration of the American Constitution, he praised the American tradition of religious freedom that "protects us against the despotism of a state church," for "the relationship of church and state in the United

---

[5]E.g., see James Melvin Washington, *Frustrated Fellowship: The Black Baptist Quest for Social Power* (Macon GA: Mercer University Press, 1986).

States secures the full liberty of religious thought, speech and action, within the limits of public peace and order.'' Though he was a firm believer in religious freedom, Schaff remained under the spell of the ideal of Christendom that had long guided much Protestant thought and action. He was convinced that "the American nation is as religious and as Christian as any nation on earth, and in some respects even more so, for the very reason that the profession and support of religion are left entirely free.'' He interpreted the First Amendment as providing the opportunity for the churches to secure the allegiance of the vast body of Americans to their persuasion, and cited cases to show that in a limited way Christianity was part of the law of the land, "as far as the principles and precepts of Christianity have been incorporated in our laws, and as far as is consistent with religious and denominational equality.''[6] He was one of many who showed awareness of the magnitude of change around them but who believed that Protestant patterns of faith and life were more than adequate for whatever lay ahead.

Certainly the massive changes going on in American life were among the factors at work to crack the weakening shell of Christendom, important among them the increasing pluriformity of religious life, but Santayana's comment had been set in an essay on the intellectual temper of the age. It was the revolutions in thought evidenced by such things as the growing prestige of natural science, the impact of evolutionary hypotheses, the ripening of historical consciousness, and the strengthening of empirical trends in philosophy and naturalistic strains in literature that were also preparing the way for a post-Christendom era. It was a strange time of commingled faith and doubt. Faith in God, faith in progress, faith in humanity, faith in democracy, faith in freedom were given eloquent expression by both laity and clergy. But the authorities invoked for many such statements of faith were often not those that had the ring of Christendom, classic or voluntary, even when they were uttered by certain prominent ministers. For though there were expressions of faith aplenty, somehow it was no longer an age of faith. Critical study of the Bible suggested to many that while it was still an authority in matters of the spirit, it was not in matters of geography and science. Historical examination of creeds made clear to growing numbers that they were products of a particular time and place and that popular understandings of them were questionable. Once such questions were raised, they would not easily be put down, and many traditional beliefs fell under scrutiny. As Washington Gladden put it in his autobiography, "the sound of inquiry was abroad,'' while Henry Van Dyke, in a book

---

[6]Philip Schaff, *Church and State in the United States* (New York: G. P. Putnam's Sons, 1888; reprint, 1972) 5, 12, 55, 58. On Schaff, see John F. Wilson, "Civil Authority and Religious Freedom in America: Philip Schaff on the United States as a Christian Nation," in Henry W. Bowden, ed., *A Century of Church History: The Legacy of Philip Schaff* (Carbondale: Southern Illinois University Press, 1988) 148-67; and George H. Shriver, *Philip Schaff: Christian Scholar and Ecumenical Prophet* (Macon GA: Mercer University Press, 1987).

he significantly entitled *The Gospel for an Age of Doubt,* reported that ''the questing spirit is abroad, moving on the face of the waters, seeking rest and finding
none.''[7] From the point of view of many of the traditionally minded who identified faith with Christendom, it was indeed an age of doubt, the spirit of which they
opposed. They saw those who were trying to mediate between Christian faith and
a changing culture as too easily finding their authority in that culture and not in
the faith.

The very idea of Christendom is predicated on consensus, enforced or voluntary. The hope evangelical Protestants had of maintaining and extending their
hold on the culture was weakened as tension increased between those who adhered
to the familiar authorities of Bible, creed, and church and those who found illu-
mination not only in their understanding of those authorities but also in the world
about them as they drew on the expanding sciences and humanities and their new
methods. The differences were often not sharp, as many parties were aligned across
a wide and changing spectrum of opinion. Within particular denominations battles
between varying groups could become very intense and give the appearance of a
house utterly divided. It has been all too easy to project the vehement bitterness of
the fundamentalist-modernist controversy of the 1920s back into previous decades.[8]
But the major evangelical denominations, especially those with their strength focused
toward the north and east, held together despite the continuing tensions. Between
groups that tended toward one side or the other of the liberal/conservative cleavage
were mediating groups that sought to maintain denominational loyalties by focusing
on its practical work, soft-pedaling the theological differences.

One of the most enduring studies of that process in a denomination in our period was that of Lefferts A. Loetscher many years ago. He summarized his analysis in these words:

> As the Presbyterian Church dealt with these theological issues, the
> forces that were really decisive in the discussion were not theological,
> but ecclesiastical; not ideological, but sociological and physical. This was

---

[7]Washington Gladden, *Recollections* (Boston: Houghton Mifflin Co., 1909) 262; Henry
van Dyke, *The Gospel for an Age of Doubt,* The Lyman Beecher Lectures on Preaching,
1896 (New York: Macmillan Co., 1896) 7.

[8]A vast literature has gathered around these topics; for reliable guides, cf., e.g., Ken-
neth Cauthen, *The Impact of American Religious Liberalism,* 2nd ed. (Washington DC:
University Press of America, 1983 [1962]); William R. Hutchison, *The Modernist Impulse
in American Protestantism* (Cambridge: Harvard University Press, 1976); George M.
Marsden, *Fundamentalism and American Culture: The Shaping of Twentieth-Century
Evangelicalism, 1870–1925* (New York: Oxford University Press, 1980); James R. Moore,
The Post-Darwinian Controversies (Cambridge: Cambridge University Press, 1979); C.
Allyn Russell, *Voices of American Fundamentalism: Seven Biographical Studies* (Phila-
delphia: Westminster Press, 1976); Ferenc M. Szasz, *The Divided Mind of Protestant
America* (University AL: University of Alabama Press, 1982).

the case . . . especially after the turn of the twentieth century. Amazing activity in Christian service at home and abroad has been the chief glory of American Christianity and to this activity the Presbyterian Church has contributed its full share.[9]

In his recent study of Protestant foreign missions, William R. Hutchison is very much aware of how the conservative (especially the premillennial) outlook in these years was becoming steadily more antagonistic to liberal and social gospel emphases, yet he finds that in the common crusade abroad those of differing viewpoints found ways to work together. He writes, "with the help of conciliatory attitudes among missionary statesmen, and with just a little obfuscation (on both sides) of theological issues, premillennialists for some fifty years seemed able to march in step with liberals and moderates in the exultant campaign for speedy world evangelization."[10] Thus a consensus of a sort was maintained throughout these crusading decades, and the illusion that Christendom was still intact persisted, yet the underlying tension was increasing. The commitment to activity can be seen as a rather external way of holding to a semblance of a consensus that had been undermined, of maintaining the form of Christendom after its time had really passed.

In a book that ran through a number of editions in the late nineteenth century, a perceptive Episcopal priest, William Reed Huntington, called attention to the deeper changes in emphatic terms. He was aware that "there still linger among the usages of our governmental system some traces of the old concordat between Church and State." But to the arguments, so frequently made, that such usages as piously worded Thanksgiving proclamations, Bible reading in the schools, the appointment of military chaplains, and the stamping of religious mottoes on coins meant that a certain Christian complexion still clung to the government, he responded:

These vestiges of Christianity, as we may call them, are printed on the sand. The tide has only to crawl up a few inches further to wash them clean away. There is nothing in the theory of the Republic that makes such usages an essential part of the national life. They rest for the most part upon the precarious tradition of colonial days: or if on statute law, what is statute law but the creation of temporary majorities? The moment popular opinion sets against them, all these relics of an established religion must go by the board. They are not the natural fruit of our system; they are but reminders of an old order of things that has passed away; fossils embedded in the rock on which the existing structure now stands. One by one they will probably be chipped out and set aside as curiosities.[11]

---

[9]Lefferts A. Loetscher, *The Broadening Church: A Study of Theological Issues in the Presbyterian Church since 1869* (Philadelphia: University of Pennsylvania Press, 1954) 92.

[10]William R. Hutchison, *Errand to the World: American Protestant Thought and Foreign Missions* (Chicago: The University of Chicago Press, 1987) 112.

[11]William R. Huntington, *The Church-Idea: An Essay Toward Unity*, 4th ed. (New York: Charles Scribner's Sons, 1899) 101-102.

The waves of enthusiasm of an age of crusades extended the life of voluntary Christendom, and not until near the middle of our century did the chipping-out process Huntington foresaw become highly visible in Supreme Court decisions. But in the turmoil of the exciting decades of the crusading period, forces were at work that played significant roles in later efforts to reconceive the relationship between what has conventionally been called church and state, and that lay behind later moves to set aside the old church-state concordat. A look at two of these developments, which were seemingly moving in quite opposite directions, may deepen our understanding of what happened later, and suggest how efforts to deal with the way religious institutions and governmental agencies might relate became so narrowly and negatively focused.

II

The pervasive influence of Protestantism in American culture was illustrated on the eve of the crusading period by government efforts to eliminate the practice of polygamy among Mormons by passing laws forbidding it. Tested in the courts, the Supreme Court found that American law, in harmony with Christian morality, regarded monogamous marriage as the basis of society and polygamy as offensive to society. The opinion drew on the writings of Madison and Jefferson, and quoted from the latter's famous letter of 1802 to the Danbury (Connecticut) Baptists:

> Believing with you that religion is a matter which lies solely between man and his God; that he owes account to none other for his faith or his worship; that the legislative powers of the Government reach actions only, and not opinions,—I contemplate with sovereign reverence that act of the whole American people which declared that their Legislature should "make no law respecting an establishment of religion or prohibiting the free exercise thereof," thus building a wall of separation between church and State.

The judgment meant that an individual or group could claim the freedom to hold any religious principles but that they were not protected if such principles broke out into overt acts against peace and good order. The Mormons had to repudiate the practice, clearing the way for Utah to become a state. Of great significance for later court actions was that for the first time the Supreme Court had put the words "wall of separation of church and State" into the legal record, to be echoed many times since. At that point the opinion/action dichotomy meant that the protection of the wall was not available for an unpopular religious minority. This was even more apparent in another case a few years later when the Supreme Court upheld congressional acts that voided the charter of the Mormon Church and declared its property forfeited, observing that the practice of polygamy was a return to barbarism and was "contrary to the spirit of Christianity and of the civilization which

Christianity had produced in the Western world.''[12] But before the crusading decades were over, Protestant definitions of what the spirit of Christianity was and how the civilization to which it was related should be construed had come under increasingly sharp challenge. The value of the wall of separation then began to seem more important than it had at the outset of the period, for now it could be invoked to protect the evangelical faithful against hostile attack either from other groups or from a state that might become less benevolent in its attitudes toward religion.

Another trend toward emphasizing the wall of separation came in reaction to the terrible and tragic story of the treatment of the native Americans, which was slowly becoming better known in the 1880s as such works as Helen Hunt Jackson's *A Century of Dishonor: A Sketch of the United States Government's Dealings with Some of the Indian Tribes* (1881) were published. One period in that history that was hopefully to be better than previous ones was initiated by Grant's "peace policy" (1869-1882). This policy allowed the churches to control Indian agents and greatly expanded and intensified the program of federal aid to Indian missions and education. Of the seventy-three agencies allotted to the religious forces, Protestants held the large majority, for only seven went to the Catholics, even though they were the largest single denomination and had long been at work in Indian missions. From the perspective of historian Robert H. Keller, Jr., the policy "provided federal support for sectarian missions and worship, violated the constitutional ban against religious tests for public office and, perhaps most serious of its legal transgressions, denied religious liberty [especially to the Indians] as guaranteed by the First Amendment." In his concluding section, Keller observed that "as for the relationship between Church and State, the Peace Policy can be viewed equally as the culmination of the idea of a Christian Commonwealth and as a flagrant violation of the First Amendment, but the second possibility simply did not occur to many people in the 1870s.''[13] By the early twentieth century, however, increasing numbers of people were to be much more watchful about such violations, not so much with concern for the Indians as with anxiety that one denomination might gain an advantage over others.

A main reason for the new awareness was the continued numerical growth of the Roman Catholic Church. The census figures show that the population more than doubled in size, from just over 50 million in 1880 to well over 105 million in 1920. The significant fact for church-state study is not so much the sheer in-

---

[12]The critical passages of the first case, *Reynolds* v. *United States*, 98 U.S. 145 (1878, 1879) are printed in Anson Phelps Stokes, *Church and State in the United States*, 3 vols. (New York: Harper & Bros., 1950) 2:276-78; on the subsequent decision in *Church of Jesus Christ of Latter-day Saints* v. *United States*, 136 U.S. 1 (1890), see ibid., 2:278-79.

[13]Robert H. Keller, Jr., *American Protestantism and United States Indian Policy, 1859–1882* (Lincoln: University of Nebraska Press, 1983) 176, 213.

crease as it is the sources from which the immigrants came, for in the ninth decade
the flow from predominantly Catholic central, southern, and eastern Europe
markedly increased, though in the 1880s Irish immigration continued, and that decade actually marked the high point of German arrivals, of whom about 30 percent
were probably Catholics. Among the greatly augmented arrivals from Italy in the
1880s, the vast majority were Catholics. The same can be said of the new wave
of Poles, Czechs, and Slovaks, while many Catholics were present among the
Lithuanians and the Ruthenians (Ukrainians). Two other major groups of immigrants also contributed vast numbers to the rapidly growing Catholic Church:
French Canadians and Mexicans. Thus, as Jay P. Dolan sums up a complex situation, "These ten groups of immigrants made up the bulk of Catholics living in
the united States in the early-twentieth century," the total number of whom was
estimated as close to sixteen million by 1916.[14]

As these new waves of immigrants poured in, there was a resurgence of the
anti-Catholic spirit that had long marred American claims concerning freedom.
Political and nativist often intertwined with religious factors. There was no repetition of the outright violence that had taken place earlier in the century, when an
Ursuline convent was burned by a mob in Charlestown, Massachusetts, in 1834,
several churches and other Catholic institutions torched in Philadelphia ten years
later, and a riot in Louisville left more than a score dead.[15] Yet the resurgence of
anti-Catholicism in this period was marked by ugly and bitter overtones and was
spurred on by the formation of the American Protective Association (APA) in 1887,
which interpreted religious liberty as guaranteed for the individual and not for "any
un-American ecclesiastical power."[16]

As the Roman Catholic Church struggled to meet the religious needs of its
diverse immigrant masses and to help them and their children find their way in a
strange land, it sincerely upheld the traditions of religious freedom and the separation of church and state on the American scene. The titular leader of the Catholics in the United States from 1877 to 1921, the archbishop of Baltimore, James
Gibbons, who received the red hat of a cardinal in 1886, and many of his fellow
bishops made their stand in favor of liberty and separation very clear, though it
was hard for many outside the church to hear and believe them. Gibbons was a
staunch patriot who wanted to make the Catholic immigrants at once firm in their
faith and at home in America.

---

[14]Jay P. Dolan, *The American Catholic Experience: A History from Colonial Times to
the Present* (Garden City NY: Doubleday & Co., 1985) 135.

[15]The story is compactly reviewed in James Hennesey, *American Catholics: A History
of the Roman Catholic Community in the United States* (New York: Oxford University Press,
1981) 116-27.

[16]Donald L. Kinzer, *An Episode in Anti-Catholicism: The American Protective Association* (Seattle: University of Washington Press, 1964) 45.

The public school system was also committed to making good Americans of children born to both immigrants and natives. But the public schools were saturated with the religious spirit of a generalized Protestantism in its crusade for a Christian America. A typical statement of this phenomenon came from the educational leaders of Oregon in 1884 when they declared that:

> there *must* be a *religious* basis to our educational system; an acknowledgment of our religious obligations, and the natural and common presentation of incentives to piety, must have their place in the common schools, or it utterly fails of its mission, and will soon go the way of all effete institutions. . . . This *does not* involve either cant or sectarianism.[17]

It was not sectarian from the Protestant point of view, perhaps, but clearly so from the Catholic. For though Protestants remained denominationally divided, they had long since committed the basic educational task to the common schools, confident that those public institutions would communicate the substance of their goals for a Christian America. "The cultural hegemony of Protestantism and an ensuing sense of dominance in school affairs—these are some of the factors that have propelled Protestants toward a complete embrace of the cause of public education," wrote Robert W. Lynn a quarter-century ago. "What had been, in the beginning, a matter of social necessity and a way of keeping the civil peace was transformed in later years into a matter of belief, an article of faith in the unofficial but operative credo of American Protestantism." By the turn of the century the school had become "symbolic of both our national unity and God's handiwork in history. As such it was a sacred cause, worthy of religious devotion."[18]

It was not, however, a cause congenial to Catholic leaders, to many of whom such a pattern seemed to be thinly disguised secularism. At the Third Plenary Council at Baltimore in 1884 the bishops came down firmly for the building up of the parochial school system, requiring that Catholic schools be built near each church where one did not exist, that the parishes support them, and Catholic parents send their children to them. Though such an ambitious plan could not be fully carried out, it did indeed lead to a remarkable expansion of parochial education. As the expanding system provided general education along with religious, Catholics mounted a vigorous campaign for some support from public funds, which, except in a few experimental settings, were not forthcoming. The Catholic step was a bold challenge to the Protestant commitment to public education, and was one of the factors leading to the founding of the APA in 1887.

---

[17]As quoted by David Tyack, "The Kingdom of God and the Common School," *Harvard Educational Review* 36 (1966): 465.

[18]Robert W. Lynn, *Protestant Strategies in Education* (New York: Association Press, 1964) 22, 30.

One of the side effects of the bitter controversy was to heighten the Protestant emphasis on the wall of separation between church and state. A clear illustration of this trend was what happened to denominationally sponsored schools for Indians that drew on federal funds. Though Grant's peace policy had come to an end in 1882, what were called "contract schools," in which the federal government contributed to church-run institutions, were continued. But the Protestant bodies involved realized that their protest against public funds for sectarian schools was weakened by their acceptance of such funds for the special Indian schools, and so by 1892 they had quietly withdrawn from the contract arrangements, preferring, as Francis Paul Prucha has observed, "to lose their own meager benefits than to see the Catholics profit." Funds for the contract schools were soon reduced and disappeared altogether by 1900 as "the close ties between the churches and government in Indian matters were finally cut by the sharp knife of intolerance."[19] The wall separating church and state was raised higher, and some of the breaches in it were closed. As Keller rather ironically comments, "not until American Catholicism began to grow in size did 'strict separation' become a Protestant constitutional doctrine."[20]

When David S. Schaff, Philip's son, wrote an article on "The Movement and Mission of American Christianity" in 1912, he went beyond his father's position of a quarter century earlier in declaring boldly that the primary mission of American Christianity "seems plainly to be to demonstrate that the complete separation of church and state, as we have practiced it, is the principle most favorable for the development of the Christian religion."[21] The forcefulness of the word "complete" reflected a shift in emphasis among many Protestants as the religious situation changed, to a considerable extent because of the increasing pluralism in the institutional forms of religion in America.

III

Even as the separation of church and state was being accentuated in much of religious America, other voices were calling for a closer relationship between the two. Philosophies of individualism had come largely to dominate social and political thinking, among Protestants especially, during the nineteenth century. Individualistic attitudes reinforced concepts of minimal government, and such phrases as Jefferson's "he governs best who governs least" and Emerson's "the less government we have the better" were often quoted. But as the economic effects of

---

[19]Francis Paul Prucha, *American Indian Policy in Crisis: Christian Reformers and the Indian, 1865–1900* (Norman: University of Oklahoma Press, 1976) 318, 56.

[20]Keller, *American Protestantism and the United States Indian Policy,* 214.

[21]David S. Schaff, "The Movement and Mission of American Christianity," *American Journal of Theology* 16 (1912): 63.

the philosophy of individualism were magnified in the rapidly expanding nation, allowing a few to amass much wealth while great masses lived at or near the poverty level, reformers and their organizations began to call for a stronger, more centralized state to deal effectively with mounting social problems. The term social gospel soon came into general use for those Protestants among the spectrum of reformers who based their views primarily on religious attitudes and teachings. The scholars of the movement have shown how controversial and diverse it was, for it included many varieties of theological and social opinion. The most conspicuous proponents of the social gospel tended to be informed by liberalism in theology and by progressivism in political leanings as that movement developed. A number of them advocated a more positive role for the state, and a closer relationship between it and the churches. Though they were challenging the individualism that was so deeply rooted in Protestant thought at the time, they were in harmony with the crusade for a Christian America, believing that social reform was necessary to that end.

The most prominent early advocate of the social gospel was the energetic Washington Gladden. In sermons, addresses, and books he tirelessly emphasized what he called one of the "ruling ideas of the present age," the coming kingdom of God, a theme at the very center of the social gospel vision. "When we are bidden to seek first the kingdom of God, we are bidden to set our hearts on this great consummation; to keep this always before us as the object of our endeavors," he proclaimed. "The complete Christianization of all life is what we pray and work for, when we work and pray for the coming of the kingdom of heaven.[22] That meant that every department of human life, specifically including politics, was to be governed by Christian law and controlled by Christian influence. Though he was a romantic idealist and an optimist, he knew the reality was far different, and called for basic changes in attitude and practice. His views on these and related topics were touched on in many of his writings; Richard D. Knudten has systematized them in a useful volume. Gladden, recognizing that there was a serious lack of political ethics and morality, traced it to the principle of separation of church and state, believing that the American nation had traveled "much further in separation than the nation's forefathers imagined or intended." The "divorce" of church and state, he argued, was influenced by the rise of sectarianism and the acceptance of the artificial distinction between secular and sacred. He called attention to the need for increasing cooperation and unity among the churches so that a united church could "work closely with the State to reintegrate society." The democratic state opens the way for humans to work together to reformulate the laws and Christianize the state, at which point, Gladden envisioned, both church and state will appear to be "equally sacred, while equally secular," and "there will be no dis-

---

[22]Washington Gladden, *The Church and the Kingdom* (New York: Fleming H. Revell, 1894) 8.

tinction between them because they will be united in the work of social construction and reconstruction."[23] He was moving in a different direction from many
Protestants who stressed separation to resist Catholicism. He forcefully protested
the anti-Catholic feelings expressed by the APA and was later honored by receiving an honorary degree from the University of Notre Dame.

While Gladden's career in social Christianity was a long one, George D. Herron's in the 1890s lasted less than a decade before his move to the theological and
social left, combined with divorce and remarriage, led to his rejection by the
churches and to his defrocking as a Congregational minister and teacher. But during that period he made a strong, attention-getting, and controversial plea for a
very positive if rather vaguely stated role for the state in human affairs. In a series
of lectures, later published, given in a number of cities in that decade when the
social question was a major topic of general discussion, Herron denounced existing political and religious institutions and declared that the state is "the only organ
through which the people can act as one man in the pursuit of righteousness; the
only organ through which the people can act together in the organization and perfection of their common life in justice. . . . Only through industrial democracy
can the state obtain and insure political freedom, and Christianity cannot accomplish its world mission, save it effect the political organization of human life."[24]
He seemingly had no plan as to how this was to be accomplished except through
the proclamation of his vision and had trouble understanding those like Gladden
who found his message impractical, naive, and much too anti-institutional.[25] At
the height of his fame, however, this magnetic speaker riveted the attention of vast
audiences from coast to coast.

Far different was the impact made by a lay Episcopal economist, Richard T.
Ely. His active leadership in the social gospel movement was also limited to the
last few years of the nineteenth century, but he never repudiated his social Christian writings of that period, and they long continued to be widely read and influential. After earning his doctorate in Germany, where he was steeped in the
historical school critical of classical economics, he taught at Johns Hopkins and
the University of Wisconsin. In an early book, he exclaimed that "it may ration-
ally be maintained that, if there is anything divine on this earth, it is the state, the
product of the same God-given instincts which led to the establishment of the church

[23]Richard D. Knudten, *The Systematic Thought of Washington Gladden* (New York:
Humanities Press, 1968) 146, 103, 147. The definitive biography is by Jacob H. Dorn,
Washington Gladden: Prophet of the Social Gospel (Columbus: Ohio State University Press,
1966, 1967).

[24]George D. Herron, *The Christian State: A Political Vision of Christ* (New York:
Thomas Y. Crowell & Co., 1895) 53-54, 108.

[25]Washington Gladden, "Shall We Abolish Institutions?" *The Congregationalist* 79
(January–June 1894): 791.

and the family."[26] In a book published in 1889, *The Social Aspects of Christianity*, he took his place as a central figure in the social gospel movement. The next year he delivered the Carew lectures on "The Church and the World, the Church and the State" at Hartford Theological Seminary, repeating them later in the year at the well-known conference grounds at Lake Chautauqua. After analysis of the function of a state church, as in England, he referred to some of the problems in American disestablishment, which "has led to the separation of our life into two parts, the one sacred and the other secular and to many these are mutually exclusive in the sense that where one begins the other stops." He admitted that the forms of the former established churches were too narrow and were wanting the true idea of a state church, which he described in these words, mingling elements from both classic and voluntary Christendom:

> A state church in modern times cannot be a mere sect. It cannot be an organization for the propagation of any narrow and exclusive creed. It must within itself contain room for a great multiplicity of dogmas and its emphasis as a church must be laid on righteous life. It must not through the coercive power of the state nor yet through its own churchly punishments like excommunication attempt to fasten the minds of men to certain speculative views in regard to the nature, purposes and methods of the Almighty. It must recognize the inner spiritual life as the domain of sovereign individuality and adopt in its attempt to influence rightly this inner individual life the methods of persuasion and not coercion. . . . A state church must be regarded as occupying essentially the large and generous ground of the public schools. . . . It must represent one side of the life of the people and must supplement the activities of the state. It must serve the state, regarding the establishment of just and loving relations among men as its peculiar mission and as a holy work.

He recognized that because of the multitude of denominations, "it is manifestly impossible to reestablish a state church among us," and suggested the solution lay "in the conception of the state as the true church of the future."[27]

The impact of these unpublished Carew lectures was limited, but their essential thesis was stated in Ely's other writings, especially in his chapter on "The State" in *The Social Law of Service*. Noting that family, church, and state are frequently mentioned together as the three preeminently divine institutions known to

---

[26]Richard T. Ely, *The Labor Movement in America* (New York: Thomas Y. Crowell & Co., 1886) 325-26.

[27]Richard T. Ely, "The Church and the World, the Church and the State" (Carew Lectures, Hartford Theological Seminary, 1890, typescript) 137-39, 159, a copy of which was made available to me through the courtesy of Eugene Y. Lowe, Jr., author of an informative thesis, "Richard T. Ely, Herald of a Positive State" (Ph.D. diss., Union Theological Seminary, New York, 1987).

humanity, he concluded "that God works through the State in carrying out His purposes more universally than through any other institution; that it takes the first place among His instrumentalities."[28] Though to the end of his long life in 1943 he did not change the point of view of his social gospel period and remained active in parish life, he withdrew from social gospel work and turned his full professional attention to economics, perhaps seeing it more directly relevant to the most universal of the three divine institutions.

Walter Rauschenbusch is remembered today as the most prominent prophet of the social gospel. Several of his major works have been reprinted, and various selections from both his ephemeral and well-known writings have been published.[29] He became an advocate of social Christianity soon after he took the pulpit of a German Baptist congregation in New York in 1886 and participated actively that year in the campaign of Henry George for mayor. As an involved member of a denominational tradition that had long taken a strong stand on church-state issues, he was more guarded in his statements on the matter. Yet in an address before the Baptist Congress in 1889 he was wary of rigidities in the matter, saying,

> Brethren, I feel sometimes that in our strong statements of the separation
> of Church and State, we have come to gather up our skirts and to act as
> if the State had no more claim on us; that somehow our life as christians
> and as citizens can be cut asunder; that on one side we can be christians
> and on the other side we can be citizens. It is not true. We must be the
> two things at the same time, and we can be that in just one way—by being
> animated by the life of Jesus Christ, and by carrying that life into the State
> in every direction.[30]

The positive connection that the church must have with the state is to declare that truth which is not recognized, to perform that duty which has not yet been performed.

It was eighteen years after that, when he had been teaching at Rochester Theological Seminary for a decade, that Rauschenbusch became internationally known through the publication of a remarkable work, *Christianity and the Social Crisis.* He was still cautious in stating his views: "Historical experience has compelled us to separate Church and State because each can accomplish its special task best without the interference of the other." But they can cooperate with each other, for "the output of each must mingle with the other to make social life increasingly wholesome and normal." They are both but partial organizations of humanity for special ends; their common aim "is to transform humanity into the

---

[28]Richard T. Ely, *The Social Law of Service* (New York: Eaton & Mains, 1896) 162-63.
[29]E.g., Winthrop S. Hudson, ed., *Walter Rauschenbusch: Selected Writings* (New York: Paulist Press, 1984).
[30]*Proceedings of the Baptist Congress, 1889,* 140.

kingdom of God.''[31] But five years later in his most programmatic book, *Christianizing the Social Order,* he came somewhat closer to the position of Ely, a man he much admired. In that book he made the often-criticized claim that four great sections of the social order (family, church, education, and the political organizations of our nation) ''have passed through constitutional changes which have made them to some degree part of the organism through which the spirit of Christ can do its work in humanity.'' For when special privilege was thrust out of the constitution and theory of our government and it was based on the principle of personal liberty, he contended, ''the fundamental redemption of the State took place.'' It was therefore part of the state's role to move into the fifth and unregenerate section of the social order, business. He thus interpreted certain events in the progressive era, then at its height, as evidence that the democratic state ''had to step in with its superior Christian ethics and put certain limits to the immoralities of Capitalism.''[32] The tendency of the social gospel to magnify the positive role of the state in the struggle against social evil was clearly illustrated in this aspect of Rauschenbusch's work.

One of the dimensions of social gospel thought was thus an emphasis on a rethinking of nineteenth-century patterns about the relationship of church and state. Such reconsiderations were reflected in the writings of such persons as Gladden, Herron, Ely, and Rauschenbusch. In the flood of social Christian writings in the crusading years, there were many other writings along the same lines, some briefly popular, but few attaining the impact of the ones mentioned. To select one by way of illustration, a 1909 book by Samuel Zane Batten, a close friend of Rauschenbusch and like him prominent in Baptist affairs, bore the same primary title as one of Herron's, *The Christian State.* The themes were typical of the progressive religious reformism of the prewar period: ''The State we find is the one organ great enough and varied enough to express and correlate the varied powers and talents of mankind, the one medium through which all men can cooperate in their search after social perfection. . . . The Church and the State are both institutions of the kingdom, and as such each has a work to do, and both sustain a vital relation to one another.'' He was keenly aware of the tensions between Catholic and Protestant and sought to name strengths and weaknesses in their church-state positions as he understood them:

> The Romanist is eternally right when he claims that the State must be subordinate to Christ, and must seek his kingdom in the world; but he is eternally wrong when he claims that Christ has delegated his authority to another, be that a man or an institution. The Protestant is eternally right

---

[31]Walter Rauschenbusch, *Christianity and the Social Crisis* (New York: Macmillan Co., 1907) 380.

[32]Walter Rauschenbusch, *Christianizing the Social Order* (New York: Macmillan Co., 1912) 154, 148, 239.

when he demands the separation of Church and State in the interests of
both, but he is as eternally wrong when he construes this separation to
mean the divorce of religion from civil affairs and the abandonment of
the State as a secular institution.[33]

Once again, that rootage of social gospel thought in both liberal kingdom-of-God
interpretations of Christianity and also in progressive reformism is evident, along
with the tendency to find new ways of relating church and state for the demands
of an industrial era, yet within the boundaries of the familiar quest for a Christian
America.

Nor did the positive views of the state as advocated by the social gospel remain only in the realm of theory. The formation of the Federal Council of Churches
of Christ in America in 1908 served as an official agency of some thirty denominations in which missionary, cooperative, and social concerns were conspicuous.
In its adoption of what came to be called "the social creed of the churches," a
platform for social action was laid. The Federal Council then played a leading role
in the important cooperation between churches and the state during World War I.
John F. Piper, Jr., has told that story in *The American Churches in World War I,*
referring, for example, both to the thought of Walter Rauschenbusch and the activity of Samuel Zane Batten in showing how closely both Protestant and Catholic
churches cooperated with the state during "the Great Crusade."[34]

IV

Looking back on that first global war from the perspective that time provides,
interpreters have documented how great its impact on twentieth-century history
has been, and how different the period since has been from the one before. In Barbara Tuchman's words, "The Great War of 1914-18 lies like a band of scorched
earth dividing that time from ours. In wiping out so many lives which would have
been operative in the years that followed, in destroying beliefs, changing ideas,
and leaving incurable wounds of disillusion, it created a physical as well as psychological gulf between two epochs."[35] In a probing review article, Michiko
Kakutani wrote:

> That earlier conflict, as Paul Fussell argued in his brilliant study,
> "The Great War and Modern Memory," destroyed an entire set of val-
> ues and beliefs and in so doing also remade language and generated a new

[33]Samuel Zane Batten, *The Christian State: The State, Democracy and Christianity*
(Philadelphia: Griffith & Rowland Press, 1909) 31, 288, 291.
    [34]John L. Piper, Jr., *The American Churches in World War I* (Athens: Ohio University
Press, 1985).
    [35]Barbara Tuchman, *The Proud Tower* (New York: Macmillan Co., 1966) xiii.

way of interpreting the world. In that respect, it served as the crucible in which modernism was formed; the sense of irony, of dislocation, of fragmentation that we now accept as commonplace would have been unimaginable in the innocent days before the war.[36]

In his book, Fussell even says "that there seems to be one dominating form of modern understanding; that it is essentially ironic; and that it originates largely in the application of mind and memory to the events of the Great War."[37]

There were, however, certain important continuities. Though the pluralistic pattern of religion in America had been evident from the early days of European settlement, it dramatically increased in the years from 1880 to 1920. One of the reasons for that was the startling rise of the number of immigrants in those decades. That has been mentioned above primarily in connection with the growth of Catholicism, but among the new arrivals were those who introduced previously unrepresented denominations of Lutheran and of Eastern Orthodox traditions, for example. Millions of Jews were part of the immigrant tide of these decades, and the full organization of Reform, Conservative, and Orthodox bodies followed. But it was not only the influx of immigrants from Europe, Asia, and Africa that increased the religious pluriformity of the nation: The new, indigenous denominational families of the Holiness and the Pentecostal people were largely products of this period, and the number of churches arising out of the Christian or Disciples movement increased. Though the major black denominations had been shaped earlier in the nineteenth century, some others arose at this time, a number of them related to the Holiness and Pentecostal movements, others clustered around colorful leaders. It was also in these decades that a number of the bodies arising out of the Spiritualist, New Thought, and Divine Science movements were formed. These trends toward religious multiplicity have continued to be evident throughout the twentieth century as now well over a thousand bodies have been recorded. But in 1920 the prevailing view that this was a nation in which the historic Protestant churches were religiously predominant meant that most of the recently arrived and newly emergent denominations were identified as "fringe groups." The deeper significance of the growing pluriformity became apparent only later.

Another point of continuity has been the persistence and continuation of social concern in religion. Though the controversial social gospel, in the theologically liberal form in which it developed in the early years of the century, survived for many decades, it changed with the times as other theological movements came to the fore and as societal needs changed. Though vigorously rejected in various quarters, the social concern and spirit it had cultivated persisted and spread, man-

---

[36]Michiko Kakutani, "Novelists and Vietnam: The War Goes On," *New York Times Book Review* (15 April 1984): 39.

[37]Paul Fussell, *The Great War and Modern Memory* (New York: Oxford University Press, 1975) 35.

ifesting itself in many forms, in Catholicism and Judaism as well as in Protestantism.[38] A number of the major Protestant denominations continued their social service/social action bureaus, many also supporting the social emphasis through various cooperative agencies. The earlier emphasis on the positive role of the state in industrial society was part of the reason why many religious leaders favored the governmental welfare programs launched by the New Deal in the depression years. In 1932 the Federal Council of Churches sponsored a statement concerning the social ideals for which the churches should stand. As John C. Bennett has observed, it was "surely a product of the social gospel," for ten of its seventeen goals "called for specific economic changes such as social insurance, the right of labor to organize, a minimum wage, and the abolition of child labor."[39]

At least at these two points, especially relevant for understanding "church-state" issues, there were important continuities with major developments in the prewar period. There was also, however, a major discontinuity. The informal hegemony that Protestantism had long held over American cultural life by its numerical pluralities and the power of its organizational networks was seriously weakened. Though the reasons for this shift are complex, many of them related to the secularizing trends in twentieth-century Western culture, one that cannot be dismissed was the growing strength of other religious traditions in what I have elsewhere analyzed as "the second disestablishment." The first disestablishment had cleared away most of the remnants of the old legal establishments of religion; the second slowly eroded the dominance of nineteenth-century patterns of voluntary Christendom in American life.[40] Protestantism continued to grow and maintained an active inner institutional life, but increasingly the fastest growing bodies tended to be newer movements outside the circle of older denominations that had dominated the nineteenth century. All this caused some internal discomfort and sense of crisis within these bodies. The disillusionment that plagued American life in the early 1920s was hard on the churches. The postwar Interchurch World Movement was cast in the familiar patterns of crusading enthusiasm that had worked so well for more than a century, but it failed in 1920. The historian of the movement concluded that "the long-developing pattern of a rising urban, secularized, religiously and culturally and racially pluralistic, American population, which had caused increasing alarm to Protestant leaders since the Civil War, had begun to come of age after World War I."[41] The bitter fundamentalist-modernist controversy, which was at its peak in 1925, revealed inner turmoil in

---

[38]See esp. Ronald C. White, Jr., and C. Howard Hopkins, *The Social Gospel: Religion and Reform in Changing America* (Philadelphia: Temple University Press, 1976).

[39]Ibid., 285-95, in a concluding essay by John C. Bennett, "The Social Gospel Today," 289.

[40]Handy, *A Christian America*, ch. 7, "The Second Disestablishment."

[41]Eldon G. Ernst, *Moment of Truth for Protestant America: Interchurch Campaigns Following World War I* (Missoula MT: Scholars Press, 1972).

the Protestant world; the hammer blows of the economic depression fell on a house already shaken. As historian Theodore H. White sharply summarized the situation later, ''This American Protestant culture dominated politics until 1932—when all of it broke down in the market-place, where hunger and unemployment mocked the Emersonian philosophy of self-reliance and independence.''[42]

A perceptive participant in the religious life of the stormy 1930s—the general secretary of the Federal Council of Churches—realized what was happening and perceived its meaning for the relationships between religious bodies and governmental agencies: ''We can no longer discuss the relation of Church and State, even in America, on the basis of the old assumptions which have held the field down to our own day.''[43] The effects of crucial changes in the years from 1880 to 1920, compounded by what happened since, was showing that the long-term drift was away from a benevolent interpretation of the government's neutrality toward the institutions of religion to one of strict neutrality. A flood of Supreme Court decisions from 1940 onward set that trend into the law of the land.

---

[42]Theodore H. White, *In Search of History: A Personal Adventure* (New York: Warner Books, 1981, c1978) 626.

[43]Samuel McCrea Cavert, ''Points of Tension between Church and State in America Today,'' in Henry P. Van Dusen et al., *Church and State in the Modern World* (New York: Harper & Bros., 1937) 191.

3

Beyond the Pursuit of Happiness: Religion and Public Discourse in Liberalism's Fourth Century

Robin W. Lovin

Problems of faith and politics have suddenly become major issues in America in the 1980s. As courts, politicians, school boards, and legislatures attempt to sort our questions about public prayer, evolutionary biology, and family values, more and more people realize that these are not just separate issues that can be adjudicated one by one. They raise a more comprehensive question about the public role of religious commitments that must be resolved, if it can be settled at all, in more comprehensive terms.

Many writers today seek those terms in an understanding of the separation of church and state in the United States' Constitution. According to one's interpretation, this either mandates a rigorous exclusion of religious symbols and values from any normative role in public life,[1] or forbids preferential treatment of any one religion while encouraging substantial public recognition of religious norms and institutions generally.[2] In this essay, however, I want to suggest that we must consider not just the constitutional provisions for religious freedom but the Enlightenment ideas about individualism and freedom that gave shape to the constitutional system. What is at issue is not just the legal foundation for certain institutional relationships, important as these may be, but the whole way in which

---

[1]Leonard W. Levy, *The Establishment Clause: Religion and the First Amendment* (New York: Macmillan, 1986).

[2]A. James Reichley, *Religion in American Public Life* (Washington DC: Brookings Institution, 1985). See especially Reichley's arguments on the interpretation of the establishment clause.

we understand the society in which such questions arise. Before we can decide what the Constitution says about the manger scene on the lawn at City Hall, we have to reexamine how we think about the public world in liberal democracies and why we have been reluctant to let religion into it. For that purpose we must attend to a world somewhat wider than the American constitutional context, one that includes the main points of Enlightenment politics generally. We must also pursue the issues farther back into history, reaching about a century beyond the American constitutional revolution to the Glorious Revolution of 1688 in Britain, and to the ideas about religion, politics, and society in which John Locke summed up that Revolution's achievements and bequeathed them to subsequent political thinkers.[3] The third century of the U.S. Constitution will also be the fourth century of Anglo-American political liberalism, and it is in that context that I want to think about the issue of religion in public discourse.

The essay proceeds, then, by first attending to Enlightenment politics and its ideas about the public role of religion (Section I). We will then be able to see more clearly how our ideas have changed, not so much about religion but about the persons who live their lives and pursue their goals in a political context. While our preference for the institutions of liberal democracy may still be intact, it is nonetheless clear that many of the explanations of them that appealed to our constitutional founders are no longer credible to us (Section II). This leads to the third and longest section of the essay, in which I explore three ways that American religious thinkers and communities might respond to the problems of liberal politics and suggest that it may be possible to reconstruct public discourse by articulating religious values within it, rather than excluding them from it.

I

We might begin our inquiry with Immanuel Kant, who summed up the pursuit of political Enlightenment by saying that human freedom means that "'no man can compel me to be happy after his fashion, according to his conception of the wellbeing of someone else. Instead, everybody may pursue his happiness in the manner that seems best to him, provided he does not infringe on other people's freedom to pursue similar ends.'"[4] The individualism of modern politics grows directly out of this Enlightenment precept, for the implication of Kant's statement

---

[3]John Locke, *Two Treatises of Government*, ed. Peter Laslett (New York: New American Library, 1965); also *A Letter Concerning Toleration*, ed. James H. Tully (Indianapolis: Hackett Publishing Company, 1983). Although Locke's *Treatises* could not have been published in the political climate prior to 1688, Laslett offers convincing evidence that they were written several years before. The *Letter* was published in 1689.

[4]Immanuel Kant, *On the Old Saw: That May Be Right in Theory, But It Will Never Work in Practice*, trans. E. B. Ashton (Philadelphia: University of Pennsylvania Press, 1974) 58.

is that each of us must make his or her own assessment of the political system, must take it or remake it as our own way to pursue happiness, since no one else's idea of happiness can serve the purpose for us.

Traditional religions, whether Catholic or Protestant Christianity, or Judaism, posed a problem for the individualism that followed from political Enlightenment. These religions appeared to be the leading contenders among the ways of forcing people to be happy according to the plans of others. They sought to convince or even to coerce people to take up a way of life by claiming that, left to their own devices, people could not even know what would make them happy. They backed up their own claims with appeals to supernatural truths, miracles that did not fit at all well with the Enlightenment's skeptical assessment of claims to knowledge that transcends ordinary experience.[5] At the same time, however, the new forms of theistic or deistic rationalism suggested also that traditional religion might not be entirely false, and no one could deny that these beliefs were part of many of those plans by which persons seek to be happy.

The practical resolution to this difficulty was to assign religion to a sphere of private judgment within which persons devised their plans for happiness without the interference of public powers and authorities. A little reflection on the problem suggested that quite apart from the strife and violence that might easily result from religious coercion, the nature of beliefs is such that no other policy is workable. As John Locke put it:

> The care of Souls cannot belong to the Civil Magistrate, because his Power consists only in outward force; but true and saving Religion consists in the inward perswasion of the Mind, without which nothing can be acceptable to God. And such is the nature of the Understanding, that it cannot be compell'd to the belief of any thing by outward force. Confiscation of Estate, Imprisonment, Torments, nothing of that nature can have any such Efficacy as to make Men change the inward Judgment they have framed of things.[6]

The beliefs of one sect might appear bizarre or even blasphemous to members of another, and all of them might strain the credulity of a true rationalist, but the person who accepted those beliefs sincerely was entitled to enjoy them unmolested.

The solution, in short, was mutual toleration. For obvious reasons, this toleration was restricted to those who accepted the imperative to tolerate others, and it was denied in any event to those whose beliefs and practices threatened disrup-

---

[5]Kant himself, of course, was something of an exception to this skepticism since he sought to ground his ethics in necessary truths known a priori, apart from experience. Like others, however, he tried to redraw the lines between what could and could not be known in ways that excluded appeals to special, unique experiences of revelation or to truths that could not be critically evaluated by human reason.

[6]Locke, *Letter*, 27.

tion of civil peace and order. Those eminently logical parameters, however, also reveal some limits to the solution since the perceived requirements of peace and order will in fact vary with the dominant religious beliefs. Locke argued that the principle of toleration extends to both Christians and pagans,[7] and he explicitly suggested that it might reach so far as to protect the rites of a sect that practiced animal sacrifice,[8] but he stated the subject of his famous *Letter* as "the mutual Toleration of Christians in their different Professions of Religion,"[9] and he clearly argued that even Roman Catholics could not be tolerated if they held certain doctrines about the relationship between civil and ecclesiastical powers.[10] Other authorities who endorsed tolerance in principle declined to extend it to atheists since these persons presumably would have no fear of the consequences of swearing falsely,[11] or to polygamists since that practice "has always been odious among the Northern and Western Nations of Europe."[12]

The pursuit of happiness according to one's own plan was thus subject to limitations that did not all follow from "other people's freedom to pursue similar ends." What is most important for our purposes, however, is to understand how religious choices and values are conceived under this regime of toleration. Liberalism does not protect the individual pursuit of happiness from religious intrusions by restricting the activities of religious institutions. Indeed, churches in the United States have achieved a special status in constitutional law[13] that goes far beyond the resolute refusal even to recognize their existence that ought, according to some theorists, to mark the religious neutrality of a truly secular state.[14] Religious institutions have flourished in the liberal democracies, especially in the unregulated marketplace of ideas the founders sought to create as the foundation for religious and civil liberty.[15] So long as competent adult human beings are presumed to come to the marketplace of ideas with their own well-formed notions of happiness, there is no problem in allowing religions to purvey their beliefs on terms that fit that currency.

---

[7]Ibid., 31.

[8]Ibid., 42. By contrast, British authorities recently attempted to prosecute a Muslim resident of a fashionable London neighborhood for cruelty to animals after he celebrated the end of Ramadan with the ritual slaughter of a sheep in a public street.

[9]Ibid., 23.

[10]Ibid., 49-51.

[11]See J. B. Schneewind, *Sidgwick's Ethics and Victorian Moral Philosophy* (Oxford: Oxford University Press, 1977) 20.

[12]The United States Supreme Court in *Reynolds* v. *U.S.*, 98 U.S. 145 (1878).

[13]Lawrence Tribe, "Church and State in the Constitution," in Dean M. Kelly, ed., *Government Intervention in Religious Affairs* (New York: Pilgrim Press, 1982) 33.

[14]See, for example, John M. Swomley, *Religious Liberty and the Secular State* (Buffalo NY: Prometheus Books, 1987) 43-73.

[15]See William Lee Miller, *The First Liberty* (New York: Knopf, 1986) 112-17.

A church, as John Locke understood the term, is simply "a voluntary Society of Men, joining themselves together of their own accord, in order to the publick worshipping of God, in such a manner as they judge acceptable to him, and effectual to the Salvation of their Souls."[16] So long as people are seeking religion as a means to happiness conceived according to their own plans, their pursuits make sense according to the instrumental rationality of liberal individualism, however unverifiable the particular creeds they take up may be. If they gather to sing hymns and share sacraments, or to organize soup kitchens and shelters for the homeless, or to send their money to help evangelists purchase air time, those activities are perfectly intelligible to anyone, even a complete skeptic, who considers them as free individuals trying to be happy according to their own plans. It is when we begin to ask how they know what will make them happy that the puzzles begin.

II

Three hundred years after Locke wrote his ideas about religion and politics, we read them with a mixture of appreciation and wariness. We value the democratic institutions that were developed from the idea of a government based on consent, and we are so used to the pursuit of happiness according to our own plan that we can hardly conceive social and political life on any other terms. We admire the intellectual and political courage of those who first dreamed that societies might be ordered without an enforced religious unity, but we are also immediately aware that something is wrong with the Enlightenment picture of rational persons examining the evidence and voluntarily affiliating with the religious community that seems most likely to be "acceptable" to God and "effectual to the Salvation of their Souls."

Today, we understand that the criteria of acceptability and efficacy are formed in the context of the very social practices that Locke intends for them to judge. Given some experience with the results of our own choices and a modest amount of reflection on the kinds of persons we are and want to become, it is fairly easy to decide whether season tickets to the opera or a woodshop in the basement will make us really happy. It is even possible, with some practice, to arrive at principled judgments about how to balance the demands and pleasures of friends, family, and students against the solitary time required to write books. But when we are asked which of several apparently satisfactory ways of life is really the *best* life for human beings, the criteria of choice and the objects of choice become confused. If we are asked, more to the point, how we know that our own way of life, with its particular pleasures, vocational choices, and religious commitments really is the right one for us, we are apt to respond that we know it just by living it, or

---

[16]Locke, *Letter*, 28.

—in a more analytical mood—to point out to the questioner that there really is no way to put such a question except in terms provided by some possible answer: How do we know that this way of life enables us to cultivate detachment from the illusions of material reality? How do we know that it adds something to the sum of objective value in the world? How do we know that it is "effectual to the Salvation of our Souls?"

We are too well aware of the social influences that affect both our lives and our questions to think that the affinities that develop are merely voluntary associations of persons who have independently come to the same reasonable conclusions. H. Richard Niebuhr, whose understanding of the Christian tradition gave him acute and critical insights across a broad range of modern culture, nonetheless remarked that a "historical qualification" of one's relationship to God is inescapable.[17] In addition to the social influences that bias explicit reasonings, we are also aware of economic interests and psychological dynamics that may influence us more profoundly than the explicit arguments we give. Marx and Freud have penetrated the consciousness at least of educated moderns, to the extent that we often trust our opinions least when they concern those matters that are most important to us.[18]

All of which is to say that we can no longer separate reason from superstition as neatly as Locke and his contemporaries did, or even as neatly as Marx and Freud could distinguish them. If Horatio Alger's moralizing tales of virtue, opportunity, and initiative now appear as a religious ideology in support of capitalist economics, the criticism of ideology itself now appears less as a scientific endeavor than as the expression of a different ideology. At each step, what appears to be a new method of obtaining knowledge independent of the observer's biases proves itself to be the product of a community of inquiry with its own presuppositions, while the domain of "objective" truth shrinks to the vanishing point.

This change in the way that modern, educated people think about knowledge and truth has taken place gradually, almost imperceptibly, so that most of us still use a language of objectivity to describe claims that are made with a measure of methodological rigor or a certain detachment from the immediate situation under review. A scientist can be objective about the results of a particular experiment.

---

[17]H. Richard Niebuhr, *The Responsible Self* (New York: Harper & Row, 1963) 45.

[18]It is possible that this "hermeneutic of suspicion" so refined by Marx and Freud is implicit already in the critical habits of the Enlightenment mind. Kant, at least, was no stranger to it when he wrote in the *Groundwork*, "It is indeed at times the case that after the keenest self-examination we find nothing that without the moral motive of duty could have been strong enough to move us to this or that good action and to so great a sacrifice; but we cannot infer from this with certainty that it is not some secret impulse of self-love which has actually, under the mere show of the idea of duty, been the cause genuinely determining the will." See Immanuel Kant, *Groundwork of the Metaphysics of Morals*, trans. H. J. Paton (New York: Harper Torchbooks, 1964) 74-75.

A judge can be objective about a minor criminal case involving people she has never met. But if the scientist begins to prescribe objective, "scientific" solutions for basic social problems, or the judge claims that the law works by objective principles, independent of the beliefs of particular lawyers and judges, our suspicions are immediately aroused.

The problem these developments pose for liberal politics is that liberalism has always assumed that there is just such an objective position from which to assess the basic social arrangements under which we live. Persons may have dramatically different views of happiness, especially when that idea of happiness encompasses the eternal fate of their souls, but liberalism expects them to stand aside from those particular goals and values to make an objective decision about the arrangements that will allow them to live together while each "pursues his happiness in the manner that seems best to him."

Thus liberal utilitarianism typically presupposes a commensurability between different views of happiness and a willingness on the part of individuals to have their different pursuits cashed into this common currency so that the social sum of it can be maximized. "Pleasure" occupies an important place in these calculations,[19] and there is a corresponding tendency to deprecate pursuits that do not frame their goals in its terms.

"Deontological liberalism,"[20] by contrast, stresses objectivity in setting up the rules of justice that govern society as a whole. The terms of this social contract are usually the results of an imaginative reconstruction in which persons achieve objectivity by simulating the ways that they might think if they set aside their particular pursuits. Locke achieves this by imagining a state of nature in which the absence of law and government creates "inconveniencies" that impinge on everyone more or less equally since they threaten the success of all pursuits.[21] Rawls creates elaborate conditions for an "original position" in which persons with a general knowledge of human nature and conditions set up rules for a society without knowing which roles they will occupy in it.[22]

An understanding of the social context of knowledge suggests that this construct is incoherent because the self on which it relies cannot exist, even in imagination. The oddity of Locke's notion that a church is a voluntary association of

---

[19]I use the term "calculation" advisedly since utilitarianism has often attempted to formulate its objective in mathematical terms. Both Bentham's crude "hedonic calculus" and the sophisticated mathematics of welfare economics illustrate this.

[20]Michael Sandel coins this term for those forms of liberalism that stress the independence of the right pursued by justice from any particular conception of the human good. See Sandel, *Liberalism and the Limits of Justice* (Cambridge: Cambridge University Press, 1982) 1.

[21]Locke, *Two Treatises of Government,* 395-97.

[22]John Rawls, *A Theory of Justice* (Cambridge MA: Harvard University Press, 1971) 118-92.

persons who have apparently formed their beliefs about God in some other context exemplifies a larger problem: the incredibility of the self that is able to choose rules for the pursuit of the good with no particular notion of what that good might be. As Michael Sandel puts it:

> [Deontological liberalism] insists that we view ourselves as independent selves, independent in the sense that our identity is never tied to our aims and attachments. . . . To imagine a person incapable of constitutive attachments such as these is not to conceive an ideally free and rational agent, but to imagine a person wholly without character, without moral depth. For to have character is to know that I move in a history I neither summon nor command, which carries consequences nonetheless for my choices and conduct. It draws me closer to some and more distant from others; it makes some aims more appropriate, others less so. As a self-interpreting being, I am able to reflect on my history and in this sense to distance myself from it, but the distance is always precarious and provisional, the point of reflection never finally secured outside the history itself.[23]

What is wrong with liberal politics from this perspective is that it requires us to formulate a basis for moral life in community that ignores the real bonds that make life in community morally compelling. The self that could make such choices is not available to us except by a sleight-of-hand that incorporates some particular community of reference into its idea of objectivity. Locke's assumption that the scope of toleration that reason requires extends for practical purposes to British Protestant sects[24] serves as a reminder that liberalism's reasoned claims to universality often prove in time to be quite particularistic. The result of that illusive universality will either be a repressive liberalism that mistakes a limited, historical conception of the good for a human universal or a minimalist liberalism that employs a concept of the good so limited that in the end it cannot adequately define the rules of justice that were the reason for its construction.[25]

III

At the end of the twentieth century, the problems of religion and politics are curiously reversed from their positions in the Age of Enlightenment. From a skepticism about religious claims that draw us away from empirical realities available

---

[23]Sandel, *Liberalism,* 179.

[24]Catholics (and Muslims) were conveniently excluded because their faith supposedly made them subject to foreign authorities. See n. 10 above.

[25]For a more extensive treatment of the integral relationship between justice and ideas of the good, see William R. Galston, *Justice and the Human Good* (Chicago: University of Chicago Press, 1980).

to everyone's experience, we have come to a recognition that all discourse is rather like religious discourse in that it is sustained by a community that shares a set of assumptions that allow them to get on with the conversation. But we have also come from a confidence that the public, objective language of rational men is equal to the demands of managing their shared civic interests to a nagging doubt that there is any adequate basis for political community except power. Not Locke's rational contractors who join forces to remedy the inconveniences of a state of nature but Hobbes's desperate victims who flee the insecurity of nature for the predictable constraints of sovereignty become the paradigms of citizenship in modern states.[26]

The theoretical problems of public discourse have produced a certain confusion in the statements of religious denominations who clearly want to speak to the issues of public life but are no longer sure how to do it. Recent statements by the American Roman Catholic bishops, for example, attempt to speak both to the church and to the wider society, but they largely abandon the language of natural law, which Catholics took for many years to provide a universal standard of moral objectivity. Instead, the bishops frame their arguments in terms of Scriptures that have uncertain authority for the wider society to which they want to speak.[27] "Mainstream" Protestant denominations, who assumed for many years that they spoke for the value consensus in American society, now tend to stress the differences between their Christian values and the aspirations of the culture. The United Methodist bishops, in their statement on the threat of nuclear war, simply gave up the effort to speak to society as a whole and addressed their pastoral letter strictly to "all those people called United Methodist in every land."[28] While this may be a realistic recognition of who is most likely to pay attention to their letter, it seems also to avoid the problems of public theology at the price of a sharp restriction of the scope of their message.

In this brief essay, it is impossible to analyze these recent church statements in detail or to give their important policy recommendations the full consideration they deserve. I call these pastoral letters to mind because they are particularly important examples of the more general problem of speaking as a church to a society

---

[26]Cf. Thomas Coleman, *Hobbes and America* (Toronto: University of Toronto Press, 1977).

[27]National Conference of Catholic Bishops, *The Challenge of Peace: God's Promise and Our Response* (Washington DC: United States Catholic Conference, 1983); National Conference of Catholic Bishops, *Economic Justice for All: Pastoral Letter on Catholic Social Teaching and the U.S. Economy* (Washington DC: National Conference of Catholic Bishops, 1986). On the changing forms of argument in American Catholic social teaching, see James M. Gustafson, "The Bishops' Pastoral Letter: A Theological Ethical Analysis," *Criterion* 23 (Spring 1984): 5-10.

[28]United Methodist Council of Bishops, *In Defense of Creation: The Nuclear Crisis and a Just Peace* (Nashville: Graded Press, 1986) 91.

that can no longer trust the objectivity of its political discourse the way it once did. To explore this problem, I want to turn to other theological works to identify some main currents of response to these historic changes I have outlined. Readers will no doubt be able to supplement my limited footnotes with other examples of the positions I describe, though there will also be statements and authors that do not fit neatly into these categories.

A. Witness. First, there are those who greet the collapse of liberal ideas of objectivity as a confirmation of what one strand of the Christian tradition has known all along. If there is no neutral, objective form of public discourse in which we might try to frame the truths of Christian faith, then perhaps the best guidance comes from the Anabaptist traditions of the Radical Reformation. These Christians refused to put their faith in terms that fit the world's language, even when people thought that was possible. They have seen themselves from the beginning as "encumbered" selves. Meaningful human life goes on in a particular community of faith, and it is to that life, rather than the politics of large, diverse communities that we want to speak.

It comes as no surprise to them to hear that the order of the wider society is dependent in the end on force rather than on moral bonds. In any event, that order simply is not a task for which Christians have any special responsibility. "Let those who aspire to nothing higher perform the task of the magistracy, the police, and the military. There will always be more than enough people ready to fill these positions, but candidates for the higher place, which the nonresistant Christian alone can fill, are altogether too few."[29]

Christians are not necessarily indifferent to needs and suffering that happen to fall outside the circle of their community. They may be quite active in alleviating these needs, but they do not make the mistake of supposing that secular society could be reformed in ways that would make it truly Christian rather than merely less brutal and destructive. Historically, these communities have often withdrawn from the politics and institutions of the wider society, leaving behind not only its police and its army but also its elections, news media, schools, and social insurance schemes. John Howard Yoder, a contemporary Mennonite voice, assures us however that this withdrawal is not normative.[30] What is required is not nonparticipation but an appropriately limited set of expectations about the kind of transformations one will be able to achieve without resort to the same kinds of force and power that create the problems.

It is just at that point that the vision of the Radical Reformation connects with the dilemmas of contemporary politics, for it provides a model of action that does

---

[29]Guy F. Hershberger, *War, Peace, and Nonresistance* (Scottdale PA: Herald Press, 1944) 301.

[30]John Howard Yoder, *The Politics of Jesus* (Grand Rapids MI: Eerdmans, 1972) 157-59.

not measure effectiveness by a set of moral premises that everyone is assumed to share. The point of action in the wider society is neither persuasion nor social transformation but *witness*. One does not register as a conscientious objector in expectation that the draft board will be convinced of the moral necessity for non-resistance, nor does one feed the hungry in hope that others will be inspired to give of their resources so generously that hunger will be eliminated. One acts, rather, in response to the community's story of God's action and in witness to an alternative way of ordering life together. The nonresistant Christian can hardly expect that those outside the community will understand these actions, that the story of God's peaceable kingdom will give them reasons to act in the same way. If they understood that, they would themselves be part of the community! But the Christian can act in ways that demonstrate in the action itself that there are other ways to order life than the reliance on force and power that dominates most human relationships.

In the absence of a shared public moral discourse, this "sectarian" Christianity begins to appear to some "mainstream" Protestants as in fact the most realistic way to think and act as a Christian in modern society. One need not set narrow limits on the social changes that can be achieved by electoral campaigns and effective local organization, and one need not, as a Christian, draw back from participation in these democratic processes. But one must avoid any notion that a victory at the ballot box or a successful reform movement in the legislature is also a victory for Christian faith. Such changes do not mark a general acceptance of the Christian understanding of life because in the terms in which those political choices must be made, that Christian understanding cannot even be expressed.[31]

B. Foundations. When there seem to be no shared social assumptions on which to depend, theology and action based on witness look to traditions that have long accepted a distinction between their faith and the assumptions of society as a guide for Christian life. Another viewpoint, however, suggests that if society lacks foundations on which to build its moral life, then the task of Christians is to provide them. Where the traditions of the Radical Reformation limit moral community to the community of faith, this position insists that society itself must be a moral community if it is to survive and prosper. The aim of Christians in society must be nothing less than to provide the basis on which such a community can be built.

Despite the apparent differences in their aims, those who speak of Christian witness to a society without moral foundations and those who provide Christian foundations for society as a moral community do share several important assumptions. For one thing, they agree that people can achieve a moral ordering of their own lives and their communities only in the context of shared values and

----

[31]Stanley Hauerwas, *A Community of Character* (Notre Dame IN: University of Notre Dame Press, 1981).

symbols. They also agree that these symbols and values cannot simply be created by imaginative leadership or by common consent. They have to grow out of a long history of shared experience, and they derive their authority from a wisdom that transcends the patterns of history and nation, even as it is deeply embedded in them. In short, the concern for witness and the concern for moral foundations both reject the liberal idea of a self that is free of history and tradition. They affirm the "encumbered" self as the only kind of self there is. They differ only on whether the smaller community of faith or the larger society is the appropriate place to seek and sustain these encumbrances.

Religious concern for a moral society is often linked to cultural pessimism that sees a loss of common values and a preoccupation with individual gratification as the underlying cause of many more obvious social evils. One form of this pessimism appears in Alasdair MacIntyre's *After Virtue,* with its evocation of a new Dark Age that is already upon us, and in Allan Bloom's immensely popular *The Closing of the American Mind,*[32] but the profound humanism of MacIntyre and Bloom is also echoed, oddly, in fundamentalist Christian attacks on "secular humanism." In both cases, what is lamented is the loss of shared moral convictions and the substitution of individualistic goals that lack the power to keep society from flying apart in all directions.

Perhaps the most thoughtful theological response to this pessimism comes from Richard John Neuhaus, who stresses that the loss of public values and symbols is not just the result of long-term cultural trends. There has also been a conscious effort, supported by philosophical liberalism, to create a neutral environment for government and public action, a space devoid of encumbrances that might remind the free, rational, and equal individuals of the different communities from which they are sprung.[33] So long as most Americans in fact understood their lives and their society in terms drawn from Christianity and from the Hebrew prophets, the illusion of neutrality worked fairly well. It is only when we really begin to replace those commitments with a utilitarian calculation of costs and benefits or a bland and undemanding civil religion that we discover in practice the unworkability of the liberal model.

To preserve society over the long run, we must restore a tradition capable of making real moral demands. Since this will have to be some particular tradition, the solution clearly requires a reassertion of the values, symbols, and standards of

---

[32]See Alasdair MacIntyre, *After Virtue,* 2nd ed. (Notre Dame IN: University of Notre Dame Press, 1984), and Allan Bloom, *The Closing of the American Mind* (New York: Simon & Schuster, 1986). Cultural pessimism does not determine a single theological response. MacIntyre's work is also read appreciatively by Stanley Hauerwas, who suggests a return to limited, self-conscious communities of witness as the most effective response to the crisis MacIntyre describes.

[33]Richard J. Neuhaus, *The Naked Public Square* (Grand Rapids MI: Eerdmans, 1984).

a "Judeo-Christian consensus."[34] Neuhaus is clearly aware of the anxiety this may provoke, not least in the Jewish parties to the consensus, but he suggests that a freedom grounded in the values of liberal individualism is over the long run less secure and more susceptible to majority intolerance than the respect for the stranger that is deeply engrained in the biblical ethic.[35]

Neuhaus's doubts about modern society thus do not run as deep as those of MacIntyre and the pessimists who see a long-term decline in Western culture nor as those of the sectarian theologians who see no possibility of a meaningful expression of Christian values in public life. Neuhaus is, in fact, quite confident that Judeo-Christian foundations can renew society as a moral community and do so in a way that respects the personal differences and makes the allowances for individual weakness that any large, modern society must make. We need not create the Holy Commonwealth envisioned by our Puritan forebears, but we must build a moral society with enough discipline and commitment to the future to sustain itself.

Perhaps because the advocates of a Judeo-Christian consensus have larger expectations for social transformation than their counterparts who stress the role of Christian witness, they say rather less about present suffering and human problems. Christian witness, precisely because it expects only very limited changes in society, often takes the form of care and concern for the homeless, hungry, or abused persons who are society's victims. Concern for moral foundations need not imply indifference to personal sufferings, but those who seek to renew social morality will often trace these problems back to individual failures of morality or morale that result from the loss of a firm set of social expectations. For this reason, religious groups that aim at the creation of a moral society often find themselves aligned today with the agenda of neoconservative politics, despite the fact that neoconservatism rests on an almost unlimited respect for individual freedom that cannot easily be reconciled with the encumbrances of moral and religious traditions.

C. Articulation. We have seen, then, that both the sectarian concern for witness and the renewal of the foundations of social morality accept the failure of the search for a universal, rational public ethic that would be free of ties to traditional religious beliefs. Neither of the positions we have examined doubts that the liberal version of this search has collapsed, and both stress the "encumbered self" as the starting point for moral identity, as a religious community or as a whole society.

A third approach, which we may call the "articulation" of religious traditions, also accepts the reality of the "encumbered self," with its links to history, communities, and symbols. It also insists, however, that in modern society, these encumbrances are inevitably multiple. They arise out of religious traditions, shared ethnic identities, tastes and experiences shaped by mass communications; local,

---

[34]Ibid., 146.
[35]Ibid., 144-47.

regional, and economic interests; and the identity-forming pressures of the work-place—to name but a few. A realistic approach to public discourse locates it nei-ther in some single system of values identified as superior to all the rest nor in a set of minimal, rational requirements that could sustain an argument apart from any of these systems. Public discourse develops as persons with a variety of pri-mary moral commitments learn to articulate these commitments in the midst of a variety of encumbering identities, both within themselves as individuals and be-tween themselves and others in society.

Those who are concerned with moral foundations for society tend to see the "Judeo-Christian" consensus as a source of definitive moral guidance. A public discourse based on the articulation of traditional values, by contrast, stresses the indeterminacy of the tradition, its power to exercise a normative influence over a variety of social contexts, though only as it is understood in quite specific rela-tionships to them. Reinhold Niebuhr's "Christian Realism" represents one such effort.

> Human society represents an infinite variety of structures and systems in which men seek to organize their common life in terms of some kind of justice. The possibilities of realizing a higher justice are indeterminate. There is no point in historical social achievement where one may rest with an easy conscience. All structures of justice do indeed presuppose the sinfulness of man, and are all partly systems of restraint which prevent the conflict of wills and interests from resulting in a consistent anarchy. But they are also mechanisms by which men fulfill their obligations to their fellow men, beyond the possibilities offered in direct and personal relationships. The Kingdom of God and the demands of perfect love are therefore relevant to every political system and impinge upon every so-cial situation in which the self seeks to come to terms with the claims of other life.[36]

Articulation of the Christian tradition brings Christian symbols and values to bear on public choices by relating them to arguments and analyses that are already going on in other frameworks of discussion. Contemporary Roman Catholic bish-ops transform conventional notions of justice by reference to the biblical claim that "the justice of a community is measured by its treatment of the powerless in society, most often described as the widow, the orphan, the poor, and the stranger (non-Israelite) in the land."[37] Walter Rauschenbusch, theologian of the Social Gospel, saw how the movement of democracy was transforming modern theology.[38]

---

[36]Reinhold Niebuhr, *The Nature and Destiny of Man,* 2 vols. (1941, 1943; reprint [2 vols. in 1], New York: Scribner's, 1964) 2:192.

[37]*Economic Justice for All,* 21.

[38]Walter Rauschenbusch, *A Theology for the Social Gospel* (Nashville: Abingdon Press, 1945) 178.

Reinhold Niebuhr, tracing the influences in the opposite direction, offered a reconstruction of democracy based on an understanding of human nature that owed more
to Christian ideas of sin and finitude than to Enlightenment rationalism.[39]

In recent years, some critics have dismissed these formulations as "Constantinian," suggesting that they borrow their legitimacy from the presumption of a
social consensus on Christian values that simply does not exist. An examination
of the sources suggests, by contrast, that even as early as Rauschenbusch, these
theologians were aware that they were speaking to a society that was largely secular, in which biblical ideals and norms had lost whatever presumptive hold they
once had had, and needed now to be expounded and defended against well-formed
and widely accepted alternatives.[40] What articulation presumes is not that Christian values and symbols are culturally legitimated, but the more modest hope—
which, admittedly, some sectarians would deny—that the Christian tradition can
be made intelligible to people who are largely shaped by quite different values.
The idea of articulation, in fact, turns on people being able to see a difference between what Christian and other values imply for public choices. Articulation locates public discourse just at the point where those differences can be identified
and where choices must be made between them.

Theologians of the "Social Gospel" or of "Christian Realism" have seldom
presented a fully developed theory of this intelligibility between competing understandings of human life. Confidence that it is possible rests largely on the experience of conflict and choice between alternative goods in one's own life and
on a critical awareness of the way that our perceptions of the world can be distorted by social pressures, interests, and anxieties. Honest self-examination does
not reveal a mind so completely formed by a single set of values and beliefs that
the alternatives can be understood only in those terms. Rather, we find ourselves
shifting from one frame of reference to another, understanding each in terms of
the others, and all the while becoming aware of the larger, less conscious influences that shape our choice of these frames and help to determine where we will
locate the good for our lives in any given choice. The "encumbered self" is a more
accurate understanding of human life than the liberal idea of an objective observer
choosing values and affiliations without prior commitments, but in the modern
world, these encumbrances are complex, and often conflicting. We no sooner set
out to pursue happiness according to our own plan than we realize that we have

---

[39]Reinhold Niebuhr, *The Children of Light and the Children of Darkness* (New York:
Scribner's, 1944).

[40]Reinhold Niebuhr wrote in 1937 that "For the past two hundred years the Christian
Church has been proclaiming its gospel in a world which no longer accepted the essentials
of the Christian Faith." See Reinhold Niebuhr, "The Christian Church in a Secular Age,"
in *Christianity and Power Politics* (New York: Scribner's, 1940) 203.

been loaded with a great variety of plans, that we understand each of them imperfectly, and that they are often inconsistent one with the other.

The multiple encumbrances that complicate the experience of individuals yield an even wider range of possibilities for society. It is little wonder that theologians of witness insist that persons must sort out this confusion by identifying a "canonical story,"[41] or that advocates of moral foundations seek a "Judeo-Christian consensus" that would reduce the number of contending visions entitled to serious consideration in public choices about the human good. A realistic theology, by contrast, insists that facing this multiplicity candidly discloses that it is a fact about the world and about ourselves, the given with which we must work.

The encumbered self does not look out on the world through the lens of a single tradition or narrative. Rather, we are acutely conscious of the contingent, historically relative social matrix that gives us a tentative grasp on the human good, revealing to us a range of possibilities but concealing others from us. When we explore the Christian tradition through history, spirituality, or theology, we are able to expand that range of socially given possibilities, challenging the limitations of our cultural conditioning. But we also distort Christianity by assimilating it to our own history. Reflecting on the Hebrew prophets and the covenant community in which persons are responsible to God for the well-being of others, one may come up with an idea of justice that challenges the rigorous rewards and punishments of the marketplace. That is the possibility envisioned by the Roman Catholic bishops in their pastoral letter on the U.S. economy. But one may also come up with an understanding of Christianity that assimilates it to the Darwinian competition of the market, transforming it into a tool for survival. "Pray to win," trumpets the cover of one evangelical self-help text, "God wants you to succeed."[42]

The Christian tradition itself may challenge some of the grosser distortions of its import. No interpretation that makes it the tool of a particular social class or national community can fully grasp the idea of human good that has challenged and sustained persons across so many cultural and historical boundaries. In other cases, however, the boundaries between ideal possibility and assimilative distortion are less clear and must remain the subject of continued discussion. In the long controversy over the relationship between Christianity and democracy, we have surely moved beyond the starting point that found popular government incom-

---

[41]Stanley Hauerwas, *Truthfulness and Tragedy* (Notre Dame IN: University of Notre Dame Press, 1977) 38-39.

[42]Pat Boone, *Pray to Win: God Wants You to Succeed* (New York: Revell, 1980). One might also note as an earlier example of this Bruce Barton's 1925 best-seller, *The Man Nobody Knows,* in which, as Robert Handy puts it, Jesus appears as "a young executive who put together the best management team in history." See Robert T. Handy, *A Christian America: Protestant Hopes and Historical Realities,* 2nd ed., (New York: Oxford University Press, 1984) 173. Also consider again those stories of youth, wit, and initiative (and, often, marriage into money) spun by the Rev. Horatio Alger (see above).

patible with divine sovereignty, but we must also resist a view that reduces Christianity to a legitimation of Enlightenment republicanism. Rauschenbusch was no doubt right, too, that as Christian assessments of democracy have changed, the experience of the democratic search for justice has also given new insights into the Christian idea of God. Similar complexities attend efforts to state a Christian understanding of the relationship of technology, military power, or labor to the human good.

Thus the implications of Christian faith are discovered gradually, in concrete cases, as the Christian understanding of human good challenges our other encumbrances and reveals the limitations with which we have distorted it and other human possibilities. Christian faith is neither a good that can be chosen on rational grounds from some objective standpoint outside itself nor a way of life that we can take up so completely that we need no other insights to tell us what it means.

From this perspective, the problems that attend religion's public role in liberal thought largely disappear, for religion is no longer something that individuals pursuing happiness must freely choose according to their own individual plans. Religion is rather a way of understanding what happiness, what the human good is and how its place in public discourse is not so different from the place it has in the private reflections of complexly encumbered selves. Religion provides a necessary challenge to the limited and distorted possibilities with which we inevitably begin, but those limitations and distortions also provide the context in which we learn, concretely, what the possibilities for human life presently are. Religion has a place in the conflicting visions and values that make up public discourse in the modern world, not only because people of faith can make clear to others what faith means for public choices, but also because it is only in that discourse that people of faith find its meaning for themselves.

4

Reconstituting Paideia *in Public Education*

James W. Fowler

This chapter investigates three fresh angles of approach to the challenge of reconstituting a *paideia* in American public education. Then it presents and elaborates a model designed to provide guidance for an interdisciplinary approach to ethics education in American public schools. The inquiry proceeds as follows: First, it examines the critique of "formalism" in American education marshalled by E. D. Hirsch, Jr., in his recent book *Cultural Literacy: What Every American Needs to Know*.[1] Second, it explores a critique of this society's privatization of dialogue regarding normative perspectives on what are worthy ends for human lives. Here the study draws on work by Robin Lovin and David Tracy. Third, it directs attention to Thomas E. Green's critique of approaches to moral education based on conceptions of the domain of the ethical that are too narrow.[2]

Taken separately, each of these critiques suggests that our present crisis in education will not be helpfully addressed until we relinquish certain assumptions that have gained the status of dogma. In turn, each proposes an alternative to the dogma that it intends to dismantle. Each of these approaches, I will contend, contributes an essential dimension toward the reconstitution of an American *paideia*. Taken together they provide a rich framework within which to present and examine a model for ethics education in the public schools.

The model for ethics education to be presented is being developed and tested by the Center for Faith Development of Emory University. Using a title familiar to every student of the ethical thought of H. Richard Niebuhr, the model is called "Responsible Selfhood." It will be presented and discussed with an eye to seeing

---

[1]E. D. Hirsch, Jr., *Cultural Literacy: What Every American Needs to Know* (Boston: Houghton Mifflin Company, 1987).

[2]Thomas F. Green, *The Formation of Conscience in an Age of Technology,* The John Dewey Lecture, 1984 (Syracuse NY: Syracuse University, 1984).

how it can inform the shaping of the ethos of schools, as well as the style and substance of teaching and the curriculum.

Paideia and the Challenge of Public Education in the U.S.

Before proceeding, let us bring into focus the central concept with which we are working. *Paideia* is a Greek word often translated into English as "education." Education comes from the Latin *educare*, which means "to lead or draw out," implying that education has a double meaning or movement. On the one hand to educate is to lead or lure persons out of ignorance toward new vistas of knowledge and insight. On the other, it involves drawing out toward explicit recognition and possession truths or insights latent within persons. While the term education captures some of the dimensions of *paideia*, it misses others. The German concept *Bildung* (formation) comes closer to the more comprehensive range of the meanings of *paideia*. It involves all the intentional efforts of a community of shared meanings and practices to form and nurture the attitudes, dispositions, habits, and virtues—and in addition, the knowledge and skills—necessary to enable growing persons to become competent and reflective adult members of the community.[3]

In the Greek city-state where the term had its origins, *paideia* was informed by a reasonably coherent worldview and shared consensus about the virtues and passions needed for citizenship. This consensus was shaped by the language, the myths, and the heroic stories of the polis. Each city-state had its heroic figures by whose actions the city was founded, given its distinctive character, or saved from internal or external danger at crucial points. Through schooling, through athletic competition and military training, through attendance at public enactments of drama, music, and ritual, and through the crucial theater of the political process itself, the young, at least those destined for citizenship, were formed in the *paideia* necessary for adulthood and full citizens' participation.

In contrast to the coherence, homogeneity, and the relatively small populations of the Greek polis, today's United States has a population of more than one-quarter billion. It is made up of people from the most diverse range of racial, national, cultural, ethnic, and religious backgrounds found in any nation of comparable size in the world. From the beginning of our national period public education has been assigned a principal role in the task of forming and maintain-

---

[3]The classic study of the concept and practice of *paideia* among the Greeks is the monumental three-volume work by Werner Jaeger, *Paideia: The Ideals of Greek Culture*, trans. Gilbert Highet (London and Oxford: Oxford University Press, 1939, 1943, 1944).

ing moral coherence in the nation.[4] Across these years the population has grown rapidly in numbers and diversity. The nation has filled the continent and has come to include states in the far Northwest and the Mid-Pacific. It has been split and bloodied by a great Civil War.

In the century since that Civil War the nation has struggled toward the incorporation into full and untrammeled citizenship of former slaves and their descendants. In addition, great waves of immigrants have flooded in, first in the nineteenth century as the nation underwent a technological transformation into the full realization of industrial revolution, and second, in the twentieth as it presently reorders its economy and technology in accordance with the unprecedented changes brought by the high-tech and electronic communications era. In between, the nation undertook the total mobilization of the population in two world wars, which, interspersed by a great depression, brought about a vast centralization and increase in national government, with its initiatives, power, and control.

In the post-World War II era the nation experienced unprecedented economic growth, which made possible a wider range of consumer and life-style options than in any previous era of history. The high water mark of religious affiliation and participation in the fifties was followed by a rapid secularization during the sixties and seventies. During that same period the quasi-religious fervor of the cold war's anticommunist crusade gave way to the more muted and continuous tensions of superpower nuclear buildup and standoff. During those two decades civil rights and liberation movements forever changed the identity and participation of the nation's racial, sexual, and ethnic groups. Psychologies of growth and the dynamics of intensive groups fostered preoccupation with self-actualization and experimental intimacy. Revolutions in sexual mores and sex roles accelerated coupling and uncoupling, loosened the bonds of marriage, destabilized patterns of family life, and brought hundreds of thousands of gay men and lesbians to a public owning of their sexual identities. Meanwhile, the political and social impacts of the indecisive or losing outcomes of this nation's involvement in two Asian land wars showed up in legacies of deep division and bitter disillusionment. We were left struggling over the meaning of our recent history. At present we find ourselves in the unaccustomed and ironic position of being the world's greatest debtor nation. And we are saddled with an economy overdependent on defense-related industries and tied to the international sale of arms.

---

[4]See Lawrence A. Cremin, *American Education*: vol. 1. *The Colonial Experience*; vol. 2. *The National Experience*; vol. 3. *The Metropolitan Experience* (New York: Harper Torchbooks, 1970, 1980, 1990). For a condensation of these studies see Lawrence A. Cremin, *Traditions of American Education* (New York: Basic Books/Harper Torchbooks, 1977). See also Robert Michaelson, *Piety in the Public School* (New York: Macmillan Company, 1970); and James W. Fowler, "Pluralism, Particularity and *Paideia*" in *Journal of Law and Religion* 2/2 (1984).

Against the backdrop of the turbulence of the past three decades, expectations have not diminished that the nation's schools should continue to meet the challenges of providing continuity and moral coherence for our national society. However, the ecology of socializing institutions, that once augmented the efforts of schools and churches—YMCAs, YWCAs, Scouting, community youth clubs and centers—has deteriorated. The corps of volunteer workers with children and youth has thinned dramatically as single parent and two-parent working families have become the norm. For growing thousands of residents of our inner cities the daily violence and the humanity-obliterating impact of the drug culture seem to seal their consignment to a permanent underclass. Myriad programs and specialists have emerged to try to deal, in often uncoordinated ways, with the overwhelming symptoms of societal transition and breakdown we are experiencing. It is against this background that we must consider the possibilities and challenges of reconstituting a national *paideia*.

In light of this overview, it is tempting to give way either to abstract and grandiose visions of cultural and social renewal or to overwhelming despair. What is refreshing about the perspectives we will now consider, however, is that they can be focused upon the schools, their ethos and curricula. While in the long run the reconstitution of *paideia* will no doubt play a role in societal transformation and renewal, in the short run the task is to try to rethink and reground the institutional contexts that are devoted most directly and publicly to the conduct of *paideia*—the schools.

Cultural Literacy, Formalism and the Fragmentation of Curriculum

E. D. Hirsch, Jr., and the sources on which he has drawn in *Cultural Literacy*, point to a period at the turn of the present century as the time in which a transformation of fundamental importance in thinking about the conduct of public education occurred. One might say that the public signal of the coming ascendancy of progressivism in public education was given in the 1918 document entitled, *Cardinal Principles of Secondary Education*.[5] This report was the work of a commission on the reorganization of secondary education appointed by the National Education Association. It consciously aimed to replace and supersede the influential 1893 *Report of the Committee of Ten*, the product of a prestigious panel

---

[5]C. D. Kingsley, ed., *Cardinal Principles of Secondary Education: A Report of the Commission on the Reorganization of Secondary Education, Appointed by the National Education Association*, bulletin, 1918, no. 35 (Washington DC: Department of the Interior, Bureau of Education, Government Printing Office, 1918), cited in Hirsch, *Cultural Literacy*, 235.

chaired by President Charles W. Eliot of Harvard University.[6] This earlier committee had undertaken its task in the 1890s in the midst of new pressures to diversify secondary education, opening it to wider populations and making it responsive to the needs for vocational training to meet the more complex demands of an urbanizing industrial society. In summarizing the position of the Eliot committee Hirsch writes:

> The earlier report assumed that all students would take the same humanistic subjects and recommended giving a new emphasis to natural sciences. It took for granted that secondary school offerings would continue to consist of just the traditional areas that its subcommittees had been formed to consider—Latin, Greek, English, other modern languages, mathematics, physics, chemistry and astronomy, natural history, botany, zoology, physiology, history, civil government, economy and geography.[7]

In important ways the Eliot committee resisted the turn to formalism in education. (Formalism is the subordination of particular subject matter disciplines and their "canons" of required information to the task—using whatever subject matter is at hand—of evoking and strengthening the formally describable capacities of intellectual inquiry.[8]) The committee explicitly rejected the teaching of English composition as a skill to be pursued in isolation from other subject matter. It held out for requiring of all secondary students an encounter with the substantive contents of the subjects included in the curriculum, even as it insisted on the importance of integrating the contents of the various subject areas. Only a hint of formalism appeared in its justification for including the study of ancient languages and of geography in the curriculum. "It subscribed to the claim that studying Latin and Greek 'trains the mind' and that studying geography enhances '(1) the power of observation, (2) the powers of scientific imagination, and (3) the powers of reasoning.'"[9]

The 1918 *Cardinal Principles of Secondary Education* went directly contrary to the emphases on subject matter and content of the 1893 report. "Instead," says Hirsch, "it stressed the seven fundamental aims of education in a democracy:

---

[6]National Education Association, *Report of the Committee of Ten on Secondary School Studies* (Washington DC: Government Printing Office, 1893), cited in Hirsch, *Cultural Literacy,* 235.

[7]Hirsch, *Cultural Literacy,* 117.

[8]By "formalism" I mean the position that identifies certain operations of knowing and understanding as requisite for full adult participation in society and its enterprises of science, business, government, family life, and the like. As the subject matter of the particular disciplines began to grow geometrically in the early twentieth century, educators began to see the futility of hoping that everyone could master the requisite *contents* of the several fields of inquiry. Moreover, that content rapidly became obsolete. The important thing became "learning to learn" and developing the requisite intellectual capacities to enable one to operate effectively in a complex society.

[9]Hirsch, *Cultural Literacy,* 117.

'1. Health. 2. Command of fundamental processes. 3. Worthy home membership. 4. Vocation. 5. Citizenship. 6. Worthy use of leisure. 7. Ethical character.' '' He continues,

> The shift from subject matter to social adjustment was a deliberate chal-
> lenge to the 1893 report and to conservative school practices generally.
> American education should take a new direction. Henceforth it should
> stress utility and the direct application of knowledge, with the goal of
> producing good, productive, and happy citizens.[10]

In contrast to the 1893 report, the *Cardinal Principles* called for a commitment to provide for a high school education for the entire eligible population, despite the new situation created by immigration and the doubling of the school
population every ten years. In order to achieve this aim, however, it envisioned
differentiated curricula in which students with different aptitudes and career objectives would follow significantly diverging paths. Hirsch and his sources con-
vincingly attribute this commitment to differentiated curricula to the impact of the
work of John Dewey and, through him, of Jean Jacques Rousseau. He writes:

> From the perspective of intellectual history, the conception of natural hu-
> man growth has been the most decisive influence on American educa-
> tional theory over the past six decades. Although schools of education
> have clothed this romantic idea in the language of developmental psy-
> chology, their basic assumptions owe more to Rousseau than to Piaget.
> As the originator of these ideas, John Dewey is usually given too much
> credit (or blame), and Jean Rousseau too little . . . . Even today, Rous-
> seau's principles reappear in the doctrine, straight from *Emile,* that a
> child's positive self-concept is the true key to learning. Dewey and his
> followers agreed further with Rousseau and Wordsworth in scorning sec-
> ondhand, bookish education. Dewey attacked the abstract, rote-learned
> material of literate culture, which he considered to be, as Wordsworth
> put it, ''a weight/ Heavy as frost and deep almost as life.''[11]

Hirsch's book recounts the dramatic victories that progressive ideas and
methods, relying more and more extensively on formalistic methods, won over
the older ideals of a substantive, coherent, and uniform curriculum. Hirsch recognizes strong reasons for the emergence of formalism and for the de-emphasis
of substantive consensus. And he acknowledges that it is difficult to determine
which of the two reports—the Eliot committee's of 1893 or the *Cardinal Principles* of 1918—is more democratic in basic thrust. His own deep preferences come
to expression in two quotable statements: ''Certainly the 1893 idea that everyone
can and should start out from the same educational foundation was an admirable

---

[10]Ibid., 118.
[11]Ibid., 119.

democratic ideal that needs to be renewed.''[12] And, commenting on the excesses of the romantic effort to center the curriculum in the experiences and unique needs of the child, ''Indeed, if traditional facts were to be presented unimaginatively or taught ignorantly or regarded as ends in themselves, we would have much to deplore in a return to traditional education. But dry incompetence is not the necessary alternative to lively ignorance.''[13]

If we look at the history of efforts at moral education from the 1920s to the present we, indeed, see striking developments in the direction of formalism. It is interesting to note the parallelism of the decline in emphasis on character education from the twenties and thirties with the de-emphasis on common standards and established fields of required subject matter in school curricula. In a history of character education in America, B. Edward McClellen discusses the Character Education Movement, which had a fragmentary time of ascendancy in the Midwest and West from about 1880 to 1935. This movement, McClellan suggests, was always more programmatic than theoretical. It was ''built not so much on a thorough and coherent analysis of social change as on a vague sense that modern specialization threatened the wholeness of both the society and its individuals.''[14] During the first decade of this century this movement proposed specific courses in ethics or morals and sought a place in the curriculum for issues that seemed to be neglected elsewhere in the school program. By the middle of the second decade, however—when the *Cardinal Principles* report was written—the character development proponents

> . . . had lost their faith in the adequacy of specific courses and began instead to try to suffuse the whole program of the school with the goals of character education. Now their hope was to encourage all teachers to emphasize the ethical dimensions of their subjects, to exploit the educational value of student codes of conduct, and to suffuse extracurricular activities with moral purpose.[15]

(Just as Hirsch's program of restoring cultural literacy returns to the Eliot report of the nineties for some of its vision, alert readers will note that the ''Responsible Selfhood'' proposal to be offered later in this paper shares, in a similar way, some of the aspirations of the Character Education Movement.)

Such coherence as the Character Education Movement's proposals had came from the use of ''morality codes,'' which amounted to lists of desirable traits of character and behavior. Such lists are what Lawrence Kohlberg, forty years later,

---

[12]Ibid., 121.

[13]Ibid., 125.

[14]B. Edward McClellan, ''A History of Character Education in America'' (unpublished paper, Conference on Moral Education and Character, Washington DC: U.S. Office of Education, September 1987) 9.

[15]Ibid., 10.

would refer to scornfully as "bags of virtues." The list proposed by William Hutchins in 1917 is representative. It outlined "ten laws of right living": self-control, good health, kindness, sportsmanship, self-reliance, duty, reliability, truth, good workmanship, and teamwork.[16] Although such lists exerted considerable influence and came to provide the basis for district and statewide emphases in character education, they remained vague and were subject to a wide variety of interpretations.

Progressivism's growing insistence on professionalization and specialization in teacher education led to a de-emphasis on the nineteenth century commitment of teachers to use every means available to them to ingrain good moral habits in their students. The publication from 1928 to 1930 of the now famous studies by Hugh Hartshorne and Mark A. May raised serious scientific questions about the effectiveness of teachers' use of heavily didactic approaches to moral education. Such perspectives, McClellen observes, "gave the critics powerful ammunition and put the character education movement in a defensive posture that it was never able to abandon."[17]

Though the emphasis upon character education continued on well into the 1950s, it was the principles of progressivism that shaped the most influential thinking about moral education between the 1930s and the 1980s. The same formalistic tendencies that Hirsch and others have criticized in progressivism generally can be clearly seen in its approaches to moral education. Impressed by "modernism," progressivism expressed an impatience with tradition and convention. Over against ideals of consistency and dependability in character, it called for recognition of the need for flexibility in moral judgment and action. Impressed by the differentiation of spheres of action in modern society, it taught the relativity of contexts and norms. Progressivism gave rise to the concept of "values"—portable attitudes centering in commitments to excellence and to the worth and uniqueness of each individual that could be "applied" insightfully in many different and unprecedented situations.[18] McClellan writes:

> Rejecting the notion that the school should teach specific moral precepts or encourage particular traits, progressive educators hoped to cultivate in students both a quality of openmindedness and a general ability

---

[16]Ibid.

[17]Ibid., 13.

[18]Thomas F. Green writes, "It would not be too much to say that until about the third decade of this century nobody had values. They had beliefs, virtues, expectations, hopes, sometimes good fortune, luck, and even a bit of happiness. What they *did* was to *value* (verb) certain things, some more than others, because they believed those *things* were of greater or less *value* (predicate) or had greater or less *worth*." "Teaching and the Formation of Character" (unpublished paper, Conference on Moral Education and Character, Washington DC: U.S. Office of Education, September 1987).

to make moral judgments. Their model for ethical behavior was the disinterested expert, the professional who brought both a spirit of inquiry and a high level of competence to the solution of problems. What worked in the world of science and technology, they believed, would work as well in the solution of other human problems, if only students could be taught moral imagination, "the ability to picture vividly the good or evil consequences to self and to others of any type of behavior."[19]

Progressive approaches to moral education placed heavy burdens on teachers. They expected, without being very clear or specific about how to do these things, that teachers would use the full range of curricular resources as contexts for consistently raising and addressing moral issues. With its emphasis on rational analysis of moral problems, and on the need for technical knowledge, it is not surprising that progressivism shifted its attention on moral education from the elementary years to the high schools. Influenced by positivism in science and by an optimistic confidence in the scientific method, progressivists bought the distinction between facts and values. Many of them were not able to see the ideological biases that informed their own precommitments regarding moral education. McClellan helpfully points to some of these:

> Their values were the values of elite professionals, and their approach to moral education encouraged a strong deference to expertise and a relatively uncritical acceptance of scientific method. Their politics tended toward collectivism of various shades, but their cosmopolitanism sometimes kept them from appreciating the potential value of such primary associations as the family, the parish, the community, and the ethnic neighborhood.[20]

Marked by vagueness, unable to identify specific virtues that it wanted to teach, disenchanted with traditions and conventions, progressivist moral education depended on good will, certain abstract ideals, and, unconsciously, on the diminishing capital of traditions of character education and religious teachings for its substance. In trying to assess its pre-World War II impact McClellan writes, "In the end, progressive theorists may have done more to destroy conventional approaches to moral education than to provide a compelling modern alternative."[21]

Between 1945 and the early 1960s little direct attention was given to moral education in the public schools. In 1951 a blue-ribbon panel of public figures and educators, sponsored by the National Education Association, published a report that warned that schools seemed to be neglecting their time-honored central roles as the nation's moral educators. The heart of the report can be found in a list of

---

[19]McClellan, "A History of Character Education," 16.
[20]Ibid., 18.
[21]Ibid., 19.

values the writers prepared on which, they believed, "all American people are agreed." The list of values, which reflects the influence of formalism in moral education, includes the following: (1) human responsibility—the basic value, (2) moral responsibility, (3) institutions as the servants of men, (4) common consent, (5) devotion to truth, (6) respect for excellence, (7) moral equality, (8) brotherhood, (9) the pursuit of happiness, and (10) spiritual enrichment.[22]

McClellan cites three reasons for the shift away from character education in the postwar era: (1) The heavy emphasis on developing technical and scientific skills, associated with the revolutions in electronics, physics, and medicine coming out of the war. (2) The obsession with countering the threat of communism as an ideological alternative to Western democracy, which turned the teaching of civics and moral education in the direction of arming American youth for international competition in an ideologically divided world. (3) The growing tendency of Americans to draw sharp distinctions between the private and public realms in their lives and to establish different behavioral norms in each sphere.[23]

When efforts were made to return to an explicit agenda of moral education in the public schools in the sixties and seventies, the two dominant models that emerged seemed to signal the complete victory of formalistic approaches over character education or the teaching of virtue. "Values Clarification" canonized values relativism as the fundamental truth about the moral domain. It also served to confirm that morality and values were domains where emotions and subjectivity prevail, thus furthering the privatization of ethical considerations. The second approach that emerged in the seventies was the cognitive developmental approach to moral reasoning of Lawrence Kohlberg. At first blush Kohlberg's work seemed to partake of the same formalism that had begotten concern with "values" and "values clarification." Orienting to "justice" as a unitary virtue, Kohlberg's Kantian and Rawlsian project seemed to stay in the realm of the formal, with its deontological and procedural characterization of justice. Nonetheless, it aimed strong blows at the emotivism and the relativism upon which the values clarification approach rested, affirming in robust ways that moral deciding and acting have strong rational foundations and that public forms of reasoning can and must be used in moral adjudication and persuasion. We will return later to a discussion of what needs to be conserved from Kohlberg's important project.

From Covenant to Social Contract:
The Privatization of Moral Reasoning

In an astute article published in 1986[24] Robin W. Lovin suggested that the tendency for Americans to separate the public and private domains of their lives, and to restrict moral concerns to the latter, has a long history. He points to fun-

---

[22]Quoted in Robert Michaelson, *Piety in the Public School,* 242.
[23]McClellan, "A History of Character Education," 22-24.

damental changes occurring in English political and economic thought between the 1630s and the 1780s as a primary source of the relegation of the discussion of the substantive ends and standards for human living to the realm of the private and the religious.

As a benchmark for his argument, Lovin offers us a fresh characterization of the meaning and power of the idea of a covenant society—the primary informing political and social vision for the New England colonies:

> A covenant idea of society emerges when people are not content to see their relations to one another simply in terms of natural ties such as kinship, marriage relations, or the accidents of being born in the same village, or speaking the same language, or living under the same ruler. A covenant society is one in which the members are bound together by choice, by mutual commitment, more than by chance. A covenant society is one in which the members see their moral obligations as growing out of this commitment, so that they not only hold their neighbors to a higher standard of conduct than they might if they were just thrown together at random; they expect more of themselves and they acknowledge that others who share in the covenant have a right to examine and criticize their behavior. Above all, the covenant creates this sense of mutual accountability not only to one another, but before God. It is not the moral health of each individual which is under scrutiny, but the righteousness or waywardness of the whole society. This sense that there is a common good, a well-being of the whole society that cannot be measured just by summing up the achievements and faults of all the individuals in it, is crucial to the covenant idea.[25]

Within this framework of covenant, the need for public discourse about matters affecting the common good was understood and expected. Because of accountability to each other and to God, it was reasonable to debate and try to persuade one another regarding the meaning of Scripture or tradition as guides for the community's responding to specific situations of challenge or policy choice. Moreover, it was reasonable to argue out the possible implications of legislation or policy for the collective and personal virtues of the population. Law was understood to be an organ of moral education as well as social order. For a variety of reasons, however, seventeenth-and eighteenth-century political philosophy, in the hands of Thomas Hobbes, John Locke, Adam Smith, and others, began to formulate rationales for government that increasingly undermined the basis for public dialogue about virtue, the question of worthy ends for human living, and substantive conceptions of the common good. Instead, their approaches brought forward an

---

[24]"Social Contract or a Public Covenant?" in Robin W. Lovin, ed., *Religion and American Public Life* (New York: Paulist Press, 1986) 132-45.

[25]Ibid., 135.

awareness of the multiplicity of human desires and ends and stressed the individ-
uality and irrationality of each person's subjective notions of the good. In an irony
not lost on Lovin, these philosophers of an "age of reason" presided over the de-
thronement of reason as a central participant in establishing and confirming substantively normative visions of the purposes of human life and community. Lovin
writes:

> Reason, said the empiricist philosophers of the eighteenth century,
> is the servant of the passions. Reason helps us to choose the best means
> to get what we want. Reason may keep us from pursuing our desires in
> ways that are apt to do us harm, but reason does not choose the goals that
> we pursue. If we want to discuss matters rationally, the Age of Reason
> suggested, we would do well to keep the talk within fairly narrow bounds.
> Reason can help us to choose the best means to reach an end that we al-
> ready want, but it cannot choose the ends for us. Above all, the philos-
> ophers added, there is no way that your reason can penetrate my desire
> and no basis for you to say that I should not want what I want.[26]

By the Constitutional Convention of 1789 the idea of the covenant community had become somewhat strange and distant. The conception of a community
where people acknowledged accountability to each other for their personal and
corporate ideals did not fit well with the assumption that each person's goals were
established by factors of subjective impulse or desire and were not susceptible to
alteration through rational persuasion. Reason itself, on the way to becoming restricted to the establishment and investigation of matters of fact, no longer seemed
available for forming or reforming agreements regarding the ends of human life.
Increasingly the role of reason, as envisioned in the new political theory, was instrumental: It functioned personally and corporately to protect and/or further the
individual interests and ends of persons. This view led to a conceiving of the role
of government in terms of the rational relinquishment of a measure of personal
autonomy for the sake of establishing a central authority. This central authority—
of which Hobbes's *Leviathan* is one symbol—would insist on that degree of fairness and respect for the rights of each member of society compatible with the equal
respect for all others to pursue their personal conceptions of the good. These are
the essential foundations on which the idea of covenant was replaced with the concept, in its several forms, of the social contract. In Lovin's words,

> The contract that Hobbes and Locke had in mind was a commitment
> made for quite definite purposes. One accepts the constraints of life in
> society, not because that commitment makes one a better person or im-
> proves the quality of one's goals and aims. One accepts the constraints
> because a certain amount of mutual restraint, reason suggests, is the only

---

[26]Ibid., 137.

way that we will be able to live together at all. In a world where we are all continuously engaged in the pursuit of essentially irrational desires, our rational capacity to make agreements with one another does not necessarily bring unanimity to our choices, but it does give some order and predictability to public life. That in turn will allow us as individuals to lay plans to pursue our goals more effectively.[27]

Harking back to our previous discussion of formalism in education in general, and in moral education in particular, we are reminded by Lovin's analysis that these twentieth century emergences have strong antecedents spanning the decades back to the late eighteenth century. It is ironic that contemporary interpreters of democracy who call themselves ''conservative'' should be such articulate advocates of eighteenth-century liberalism, with its stress on individual rights and the sovereign subjectivity of individual notions of the good.[28] Lovin's summary of the implications of that tradition for our concern with *paideia* is important:

> Public life is no longer thought of as a place to learn and practice virtue. Virtues, if we are to have them at all, must be inculcated in the home, or the church, or perhaps in the understandings that provide a code of decent professional conduct for lawyers, scholars, bankers, and so forth. Public life does not so much require virtue as it requires the restraint of vice.[29]

Both Lovin and his colleague David Tracy[30] make a strong case for retrieving and reconstituting an understanding of reason that recognizes its power to illumine questions of the worthy and just ends of persons and societies. In a formulation that anticipates some of our own conclusions, Tracy both clarifies the dangers of a reductionist understanding of reason and points toward a more robust conception and practice of reason in public discourse:

> If strictly positivist and instrumentalist notions of reason and publicness are alone allowed, then the possibility of the concrete experience of the truths of art and religion as truth-as-disclosure and transformation is, of course, disallowed. Then, as the public realm itself becomes more and more scientized and technicized, art becomes marginalized and religion becomes privatized. But if—to employ classic Aristotelian terms— poetics and rhetoric are also allowed to make claims to truth (poetics through persuasive argument, not fanciful ornamentation), then the role

---

[27]Ibid., 138.

[28]The best example is Michael Novak, *The Spirit of Democratic Capitalism* (New York: Simon and Schuster, Touchstone, 1982).

[29]Lovin, ed., *Religion and American Public Life,* 139.

[30]See David Tracy, ''Particular Classics, Public Religion, and the American Tradition'' in Lovin, ed., *Religion and American Public Life,* 115-31.

of reason itself is properly expanded—and properly focused in its *de facto* effects, not its speculative "origins."[31]

As a step toward such retrieval of reason, especially in the moral domain, let us turn now to a proposal in moral education that has as one of its animating concerns that moral education should be, from the outset, *civic* education.

The Formation of Conscience for Participation in Public Life

Thomas F. Green's John Dewey Lecture for 1984 is entitled "The Formation of Conscience in an Age of Technology."[32] Green has read widely in contemporary literature on moral development and education. It is evident, however, that his deepest love and favored resources are the classics—Plato, Aristotle, and, interestingly enough, the Bible. Green's goal at the outset is to reclaim a more comprehensive understanding of the *moral* in moral development than either the cognitive developmentalists or the Durkheimian sociologists have employed. In choosing *conscience* as his unifying and inclusive term for that aspect of human knowing and being that needs to be formed in moral education, he knows that he is taking a unique tack in the present discussion. He also knows something of the richness of this term, historically, though he does not, in this lecture, take time to trace its variety of meanings. His principal thesis is that moral education has to do with the forming of attitudes and virtues, which, in the light of the liberal political and ethical theories discussed above, would be regarded as "nonmoral" virtues or qualities. Green wants to show the ways in which conscience both permeates and draws from such qualities as our manners of doing our work and conducting the business of everyday life, our loyalty and fidelity as members of groups and associations, our sense of identity and rootedness in a place and with people, and our capacity for imagining and keeping solidarity with generations yet unborn. Conscience involves all these dimensions, Green says, as well as that more usual understanding of the term that refers to the imperativeness of doing what is one's duty, even when it requires the sacrifice of one's pleasure or going against the sense of one's own best interest. Let us overhear Green's own formulation:

> It is a simple fact that each of us has the capacity to judge our own conduct and even to stand in judgment on what we discern to be the composition of our own affections. The point I want to stress about this experience is not that it involves judgment of moral approval or disapproval, but simply that it is judgment that *each of us makes in our own case.* In short, it is reflexive judgment. Furthermore, it is judgment al-

---

[31]Ibid., 120.
[32]Published as a small monograph, *The Formation of Conscience in an Age of Technology.*

ways accompanied by certain emotions which, if not exactly the same, are nevertheless like moral emotions. I can feel guilt, shame or embarrassment at a job poorly done and these are the same feelings I have when viewing some moral failure of mine. This capacity of ours to be judge, each in our own case, is all that I mean by conscience. Conscience, as St. Thomas put it, is simply reason commenting upon conduct. And this capacity, please note, extends far beyond the capacity to comment merely upon matters of morality narrowly conceived. It can extend to self-judgment even in such matters as washing the car, planting the garden, getting dressed, or crafting a good sentence. These are all activities that can be done well or badly in our own eyes. They are all activities subject to the commentary of conscience.[33]

While Green understands conscience in this unitary and comprehensive way, he points out that it speaks to us in different voices. He identifies and discusses five such voices. They include (1) the conscience of *craft,* (2) the conscience of *sacrifice,* (3) the conscience of *membership,* (4) the conscience of *memory,* and (5) the conscience of *imagination.* Let me try to characterize each of the voices briefly. As we consider them it is helpful to keep in mind Green's statement regarding their relations to each other:

We may speak of these different voices as existing not in sequence but simply side by side. That is to say, none come first, none come later, and none should be lost in the formation of conscience. In short, I do not suppose that there is any invariable and definable sequence in the emergence of these voices of conscience through several stages. There is development, of course, but it may be that all these voices are present from the beginning. Certainly, all must be present at the end. Development is simply their elaboration and composition, the way that each finds a place in the four or five or eight part chorus of the mature conscience.[34]

The Conscience of Craft. At the most obvious level, Green is proposing that conscience involves making habitual an attitude of doing the things one undertakes thoroughly and well. This means acquiring a sense of the standards for excellence in the domains of one's activity. It also means conscientious work at the acquisition and practice of the requisite *skills* involved. "Developing a sense of craft is not all there is to the formation of conscience," says Green. "Still it is an important part. . . . We make a serious mistake if we fail to recognize the conscience of craft and to acknowledge that *it may be in the acquisition of a 'sense of craft' that the formation of conscience takes place most clearly.*"[35] Following the Greeks, Green invites us to see that forming the conscience of craft is part of the

---

[33]Green, "Formation of Conscience," 2-3 (italics in original).
[34]Ibid., 3.
[35]Ibid., 12.

larger task of learning to live well. The principal sin for the Greeks, Green says, was not, as is commonly thought, *hubris,* the inflation or pride that "goeth before a fall." Rather, he suggests, the cardinal sin is properly *hamartia*—missing the mark or the target, as in archery. In *hamartia* one fails to live well, in some comprehensive sense, through repeated carelessness, inattentiveness, or through a stubborn refusal or inability to learn.[36]

The Conscience of Membership. Green observes that most discussions and approaches to moral education focus upon conscience and the development of judgment as primarily individual matters. Only after attending to the qualities needed in the management of one's individual life do we ask about one's fitness for public life or service. He proposes an arresting counterpoint: " . . . [A] conscience formed for conduct in the skills of public life is more likely to be a conscience suited to private life than a conscience formed merely for private life is likely to be suited for public life."[37]

This thesis represents a strong claim that the community is prior to the individual. We should note, in passing, that this thesis runs directly counter to the assumptions underlying social contract theory. The person is indelibly social and the formation of the person occurs in the context of the relations, meanings, rules, laws, and culture of the community. Moral development as the formation of conscience means forming a set of bonds—of attachment—to the community. It means forming the moral emotions that are appropriate norms giving permanence, legitimacy, and stability to the community's *praxis*—its way of living and being. If we take this priority of community over the individual seriously, Green says, it significantly alters our approach to moral education:

> By such a thesis, civic education can no longer be viewed as a mere addendum, a mere footnote, to moral education, something that comes after the main business has been accomplished. On the contrary, education for a public life would have to be viewed as the central problem which, being understood, then allows us to understand the formation of private conscience.[38]

Green points to two essential sets of skills required for effective exercise of the conscience of membership. Each involves an attitude of commitment to the common good; each involves certain skills of empathy and imagination. The first skill he points to involves learning that whenever one is asked whether a given policy or proposal is a good thing for *us,* the group, to do, it is never sufficient merely to answer "No." "It is necessary," Green says, "to go on and add some proposal for improvement." After trying to exercise this skill one may decide that

---

[36]Ibid., 6.
[37]Ibid., 7.
[38]Ibid.

though the present proposal is less than ideal, it is the best possible now. Or one may decide that one must develop more skill in order to be able to propose an improvement. In either case one has entered more deeply into the proposal, the situation, the minds of one's fellows, and into one's own responsibilities and possibilities for growth.

The second set of skills required for the conscience of membership involves a disciplined use of empathy. "Whenever it is asked whether X is a good way for us to do Y, then if you answer 'no' and offer a better way, or if you answer 'yes,' you are obliged to confront three more questions. (1) Whose interests are you expressing? (2) Whose interests are you *not* expressing? and (3) How does your proposal balance the goods being sought (from these *several* perspectives)?'' Green goes on to say,

> . . . [I]n this lesson in the curriculum of civic skill I do not speak merely of a utilitarian, arithmetic, or intellectual calculation. It is not enough to simply *think* about or merely entertain the interests of others. We are called upon to actually enter into those interests or, better yet, permit them to enter into us. Indeed, the very act of *stating* the interests of others, *as others see them,* and stating them out loud and, if possible in the actual presence of those others—that is often in itself a powerful exercise in empathy, an exercise by which the interests of others are allowed to actually enter into our own. . . . Such a lesson requires the actual *employment* of empathy and at the same time promotes its *acquisition.*[39]

In his critique and rejection of the work of Lawrence Kohlberg, Green seems to be unable to recognize just how central to Kohlberg's developmental theory and his practice of the ''Just Community School'' this kind of disciplined empathy— social perspective taking, Kohlberg calls it—really is. Nor does Green seem to see or acknowledge that Kohlberg's explicit goal in moral education is to provide for the practical acquisition of the skills, understanding, and commitment to the common good that Green himself calls for. Green's impatience with Kohlberg stems, in part, from his concern with other aspects of the conscience of membership, which have to do with entering into and taking upon one's own identity the stories and myths, the morals and the meanings of the community. These factors Kohlberg does neglect. We will give more attention to them when we speak of the conscience of *memory.*

The Conscience of Sacrifice. In his brief section on this voice of conscience Green seeks to drive home two important points. On the one hand he affirms the moral responsibility of self-love and (after Bishop Butler) of attending to one's own happiness. But if such self-regard is at least part of what we mean by *pru-*

---

[39]Ibid., 13-14.

dence,[40] then the conscience of sacrifice (or of duty) calls, in Green's view, for a radical contradiction of, or a going beyond, self-interest.

> To the *merely* prudential man or woman this voice of conscience speaks harshly. It says, in effect, "You must have other desires than you have. You must have the desire to serve the good of others even at the cost of what you desire now as your own good." And it will not do to say merely that I *desire* to have other desires than I have. . . . Nothing will satisfy that voice, nothing will quiet it, except to actually *have* those other desires.[41]

In a manner that reminds us of W. D. Ross's justly famous discussion of *prima facie* duties,[42] Green wants to impress upon his readers that

> there are certain moral practices of almost daily experience within which the voice of conscience as duty speaks clearly. I have in mind the keeping of promises, as well as the keeping of contracts and confidences, which are like promises. When I say, "I promise," the future becomes firmly fixed. By pronouncing those words I declare that whatever may be my prudential interests at some future time, I shall lay them aside. Instead, I shall perform the promised act.[43]

Conscience of Memory. The final two voices of conscience that Green identifies can be understood as closely related to the voice of the conscience of membership. By reference to the conscience of memory, Green affirms the importance of narrative—especially the myths and stories that link us to the past and meanings of our peoples and place—in the formation of our characters and our sense of "rootedness." By rootedness he means the deep sense of identification with and assent to the distinctive sources of strength (mixed always with some weaknesses or limits) that form the soils that have nurtured us toward personhood, language, meanings, myth, and aspiration.

> What I am here attempting to point to as rootedness is often called for in the modern world as commitment. . . . But the word "commitment" is inadequate and misleading. It rings with overtones of will, as though I

---

[40]I think that Green, usually so adroit an interpreter of the classical sources, may have misrepresented the classical understanding of *prudence* or *phronesis* in this passage by reducing it to "enlightened self-interest." Though it undoubtedly includes that dimension, it also pertains to good judgment, informed discernment, and an ability to see "reality" in depth. See Joseph Pieper, *Four Cardinal Virtues* (Notre Dame IN: University of Notre Dame Press, 1964); and Gilbert C. Meilaender, *The Theory and Practice of Virtue* (Notre Dame IN: University of Notre Dame Press, 1984)

[41]Ibid., 19.

[42]W. D. Ross, *The Right and the Good* (London: The Oxford University Press, 1930) esp. ch. 2.

[43]Green, *The Formation of Conscience,* 19-20.

am free to choose what I am not free to choose. . . . We are not free to choose it, but we can reach a point where we possess as our own what already we have been given. And . . . [w]e might attain that point where we learn to work not only within but *upon* our inheritance. That is rootedness, and it is hard to suppose that there can be any education complete without it or any *moral* education at all without it.[44]

The conscience of memory means keeping faith with those persons and traditions who have formed us. It means claiming as our own the legacy of value and worth they sacrificed for; it means endeavoring with all we are to be as faithful and generative in our time with the inheritance as they were in theirs.

The Conscience of Imagination. It is the lure and pull and corrective power of the conscience of imagination that, while faithful to the past, allows us to engage it critically and transformatively. This is the imaginative faithfulness by which persons claim solidarity with and ethical responsibility for generations yet unborn. For Green, this is that aspect of conscience formed by prophets, poets, and visionaries. Green quotes Walter Brueggemann to help make his point:

> Prophetic speech is characteristically poetic speech. The importance of this cannot be overstated. . . . They are speakers (not writers) who commit linguistic acts that assault the presumed world of the king, who expose the pretensions of the royal system, and who invite listening Israel to entertain new dimensions of social possibility which they had never before considered. . . . [T]hey have the . . . fundamental task of nurturing poetic imagination. . . . They seek to form an alternative context for humanness by creating a different presumptive world which is buoyed by different promises, served by different resources, sobered by different threats, and which permits different decisions.[45]

The critical and visionary imagination of the prophetic conscience is rooted in the conscience of membership and memory. It seeks always to radically enlarge the inclusiveness of membership, however, and it looks for those sources and promises in the memory that guide the community toward its most humane calling. It also attends to the "dangerous memories"—the repressed, denied, and shameful past—that are the source of distortions in the present and a resource for identification with those who are afflicted and oppressed by our ways of being.[46]

---

[44]Ibid., 21-22.

[45]See Walter Brueggemann, *The Creative Word: Canon as a Model for Biblical Education* (Philadelphia: Fortress, 1982) 52. See also Brueggemann, *The Prophetic Imagination* (Philadelphia: Fortress, 1978).

[46]See Johannes Metz, *Faith in History and Society* (New York: Crossroad/Seabury, 1980) esp. ch. 5 and following.

Responsible Selfhood:
A Model of Character Development and Education

This model did not grow out of a reading of the sources we have considered to this point. Work on the model has been pursued over the past two years in the context of the Project on Ethics and Public Education at the Center for Faith Development of Emory University. It arises out of our practical involvement with preparing and pilot-testing a manual for teacher education in collaboration with the Orange County Public Schools in Florida.[47] Center Research Associate John Shippee has contributed a great deal to the construction of this model, and he will continue to work on and with it in his own future writings and research. The perspectives of Hirsch, Lovin, Tracy, and Green, however, do provide a rich context within which to explicate and elaborate on the approach to ethics education we are taking.

Let us examine the chart entitled "Character and Character Education: Responsible Selfhood."

CHARACTER AND CHARACTER EDUCATION: RESPONSIBLE SELFHOOD

STORIES

—Belonging and Inclusion
> *Family*   *Religion*
> *Nation*   *Global*
> *Collegial*   *Friendship*

—Suffering and Heroism
—Virtue and Vice
—The Meaning of Community(s)
—The Nature and Being of God(s)

DEVELOPMENTAL ABILITIES

—Social Perspective Taking

—Moral Reasoning and Understanding
> *Future*: Cost-Benefit Analysis
> *Present*: Character Consistency
> *Past*:   (from Future): Justice,
>   Principled Reasoning

MORAL ATTITUDES

—Voices of *Conscience:*

—Of Craft
—Of Sacrifice
—Of Membership
—Of Memory
—Of Imagination

INFORMATION AND KNOWLEDGE

STRENGTHS OF CHARACTER: VIRTUES

—Prudence: Good Judgment, Dialogue and Discernment, Seeing Things Whole

---

[47]John Shippee and Linda Johnson, eds., *Responsible Selfhood: Teacher Training Unit* (Orlando FL: Orange County Public Schools, 1988) prepublication pilot draft.

—Justice: Fairness, Equity, Network of Care, Inclusion
—Courage: Resoluteness, Resourcefulness, Loyalty, Determination,
 Sacrificial Commitment
—Temperance: Self-Management, Discipline, Balance and Proportion

[THEOLOGICAL VIRTUES]
—Faith   —Hope   —-Love

The chart shows the interrelated components of character formation as we have identified them. It seeks to convey that the components, while separably identifiable, work in interaction with each other and in a more or less comprehensive and coherent unity in persons and in communities. There is no suggestion that one or another of the components precedes the other in development, or that there is a necessary sequence in which they emerge. Rather, development of certain sorts of components is built into the model. There is, however, a kind of cumulative richness intended in the spatial representation of these components that results in or constitutes character and the virtues. Crudely, it might be put this way: The provision of rich normative *Stories*, plus the forming of *Moral Attitudes*, plus the stimulation and support of *Developmental Abilities*, plus the systematic provision of *Information and Knowledge*, taken all together in environments where students are known, and experience care and accountability, maximize the possibility of the formation and nurture of *Virtues and Strengths of Character*. The value of such a model is that it clarifies how each subject matter area in the curriculum, each curricular or extracurricular activity, as well as the leadership approaches of teachers and administrators and the ethos of the school as a community can contribute to one or more of the aspects of character education. Theoretically and practically the cumulative flow of the model also helps us begin to appreciate, in contemporary terms, the remarkable multidimensional range of meanings that the classical concept of the virtues comprehends. Now let us look at each component of the model in a bit more depth.

Stories. Our discussion of Green's work on the conscience of membership and the conscience of memory sets the stage for our consideration of the fundamental importance of *narrative* in the development of character. Of course there is, in our time, a growing body of literature in the so-called "ethics of character" that compellingly delineates the ways in which certain kinds of stories provide us with indispensable moral orientation, motivation, and identifications.[48] As the chart

---

[48]See Steven Crites, "The Narrative Quality of Experience," *Journal of the American Academy of Religion* 39/3 (September 1971): 291-311; James Wm. McClendon, *Biography as Theology* (Nashville: Abingdon, 1974); Stanley Hauerwas, *Vision and Virtue* (Notre Dame IN: Fides, 1974), *Truthfulness and Tragedy* (Notre Dame IN: University of Notre Dame Press, 1977), *A Community of Character* (Notre Dame IN: University of Notre Dame Press, 1981); and Craig R. Dykstra, *Vision and Character* (New York: Paulist Press, 1981). For important background sources for these perspectives see H. Richard Niebuhr, *The Meaning of Revelation* (New York: Macmillan, 1941), and James G. Gustafson, *Christian Ethics and the Community* (Philadelphia: Pilgrim Press, 1971).

suggests, normative stories of belonging and inclusion (Green's conscience of membership and memory) come to us from our families, our nation, our religious traditions, our colleagues and friends. Increasingly in our time we are receiving stories that invite us to membership in the global community (Green's conscience of imagination). Such narratives help to establish our sense of rootedness. They provide important sources of identity and identifications. They establish the moral horizons in which we construe present situations requiring moral initiatives or responses, as well as giving us a repertoire of the previous initiatives and responses of others. Narratives portray vivid examples of the virtues and of vice. They conserve and convey the sacred history and meanings of our communities. And some narratives—our religious "classics"—bring to expression our community's memories of the disclosure-transformation events that reveal the character and being of the transcendent.[49]

For purposes of character education in the public schools the stories of the school itself, its mission and character are important, as are the "myths" that teams or classes within the school create as they live and work together. Helping children and youth reclaim some of their family, racial, or ethnic stories can provide important dimensions of identification and membership, as the tremendous influence and energy generated by Alex Haley's book and television series *Roots* so powerfully demonstrated. Moreover, the history of the nation and of states or regions must be taught in ways that provide opportunities to glean from the narratives and biographies identifications with instances of suffering and heroism, fidelity and compassion, oppression and liberation.[50] Most of all, the story of this nation must be compellingly told in ways that make vivid and accessible a vision of covenant solidarity and accountability, as well as dedication to equality, freedom, and the inalienable rights of each person to life, liberty, and the pursuit of happiness. It must be told as an inclusive "Story of our stories" and must include accounts of the "dangerous memories" that require that we continue to widen the bounds of membership and stay responsive to prophetic criticisms and visions.[51]

---

[49]For the idea of the "classic" see David Tracy, *The Analogical Imagination* (New York: Crossroad, 1981) esp. chs. 3-5.

[50]For an important discussion of the teaching of history in such ways that it contributes to character development see Charles Strickland, "Curricular Approaches to Character Education: History and Biography" (unpublished paper, Conference on Moral Education and Character, Washington DC: U.S. Office of Education, September 1987).

[51]This chapter begs one very central, very important question: There must be a "cultural canon" of normative stories and information pertinent to formation in civic education. Such stories must indeed be part of a rich, inclusive "Story of our stories." In the project on ethics and public education, we are addressing this question but are not yet prepared to offer such a canon or criteria for establishing it. Unlike biblical canon, the civic canon should not be closed, though there certainly will be certain nonnegotiable "classics" that must be included in any listing. For efforts at establishing such a canon see Horace M. Kallen, *Cultural Pluralism and the American Idea: An Essay in Social Philosophy* (Philadelphia: University of Pennsylvania Press, 1956); and Hirsch, *Cultural Literacy,* ch. 4.

Developmental Abilities. There is an important place in character and civic education for the contributions of cognitive developmental theories and approaches to moral education. As our discussion of civic education in Green's perspective suggested, the cognitive ability and willingness to grow in the disciplined empathy of social perspective taking contributes to a crucial set of skills that are integral to character development. As the work of Lawrence Kohlberg and his associates has shown, social perspective taking is constitutive for moral and ethical reasoning. They have demonstrated a developmental sequence of stages in the acquisition and exercise of these cognitive functions. While Kohlberg's theory and research is less helpful in accounting for the role of moral emotions in disciplined empathy, to include the Kohlberg perspective in a more comprehensive account of character helps us to make that connection.

In working out the Responsible Selfhood model, we will want to make explicit what is at best implicit in the Kohlberg stage theory, namely that there is a plurality of modes of moral reasoning that need to be constructed and developed in the course of cognitive moral development. My colleague Jon Gunnemann has written a ground breaking essay in which he suggests that the different modes of moral reasoning traditionally recognized in philosophical ethics are not mutually exclusive, but rather, in use, are correlated with different time frames. Utilitarian ethical reasoning, concerned with cost-benefit analyses, he suggests, primarily serves us in trying to assess the impact of certain actions or policies on affected parties in an unknown future. Deontological ethics, oriented to principles or rules that define duty or obligation, he suggests, curiously locate us in an imagined future time looking back at presently contemplated decisions or actions. Deontological perspectives enable us to look at an action presently being considered as if it were in the past. Then, as if we were a judge or tribunal evaluating our own contemplated actions, we can determine if they are right or wrong, just or unjust. The ethics of character, Gunnemann suggests, help us within the present by asking, Is this contemplated action or response *consistent* with my identity or character? Does it *fit* with the story or stories that guide my life and my images of what it means to be a good man or a good woman?[52]

To flesh out the plurality of modes of moral reasoning begins to suggest links between developmental abilities and both the components of story and moral attitudes. Developmental capacities also affect students' appropriations of the component of *information and knowledge,* which Hirsch's concern with the necessary contents for cultural literacy highlights. Such developmental abilities can be nurtured in engagement with each and every subject-matter area of the curriculum. The skills of perspective taking can, of course, be cultivated in classroom activities and interactions and in extracurricular community involvements. But they can

---

[52]Jon P. Gunnemann, "Theses on Language, Moral Difficulty, and Religion" (unpublished paper, Emory University, 1986).

also be augmented through the study of literature, through the engagement with conflicts in science or social studies, and through historical and biographical studies. The different forms of moral reasoning can be taught, not as abstract theories, but as frameworks of analysis for understanding and evaluating critical moments in the nation's past (Lincoln's decision to write the Emancipation Proclamation) or in a particular figure's biography (Daniel Ellsworth's decision to release the *Pentagon Papers*). When actual issues arise in the life of the school or community, the preparation made by utilizing and understanding these different modes of ethical reasoning and the skills of disciplined empathy can be crucial resources in civic education.

Moral Attitudes. After having read and digested Green's lecture on the voices of conscience, I found his imagery and account of the moral emotions to be the most adequate characterization I have found for the attitudes we seek to inculcate in the Responsible Selfhood approach. The voices of conscience he has identified hold together the cognitive operations accounted for in our Developmental Abilities component and the normative perspectives deriving from our Stories component. While highlighting the moral emotions, Green's discussion suggests their interpenetration with the other aspects of character and civic interaction.

Schools, as communities, can nurture these voices of conscience and the moral attitudes they bring into focus. While we must acknowledge at the outset that family and home, and perhaps religious contexts, provide the first and perhaps most influential early influences on the formation of the voices of conscience, as day care and nursery school childcare programs expand, there is both increased possibility and responsibility for influencing the development of these moral attitudes in school settings. Clearly the conscience of craft represents an area in which schools can make great contributions. The provision of materials and contexts, the teaching of techniques and modes of approach, the offering of support, and the teaching of standards can occur at every level of education in ways that nurture conscientiousness, confidence, and competence. As regards the conscience of membership, schools can provide vitally important and formative experiences of belonging, and they can foster the skills and attitudes of effective and loyal membership. Through the stories they make accessible to their students, and through the way community and order are administered, students can form deep respect for duty and for the importance of truth-telling and promise-keeping, for honesty and respect for property, and for loyalty in friendship and fidelity in confidences. They can come to understand the point of rules and laws, and develop their capacities to discern what fairness and justice require. In all these ways schools can help to form the conscience of sacrifice. Previous discussions in this paper illustrate how the school's potential for nurturing the voices of memory and imagination can be spelled out.

Information and Knowledge. Hirsch's work on cultural literacy jars us out of an unreflective repetition of the notion that what is "basic" in education is learn-

ing "Readin', 'Ritin', and 'Rithmatic." He and his sources show how real literacy involves having information enough at our disposal, and practice enough at
ordering it into cognitive maps, that we can process, evaluate, select, understand,
digest, and utilize the overwhelming amounts of information that are accessible
to us in print. What one of his sources calls "world knowledge," Hirsch calls
"cultural literacy," by which he means,

> . . . the network of information that all competent readers possess. It is
> the background information, stored in their minds, that enables them to
> take up a newspaper and read it with an adequate level of comprehen-
> sion, getting the point, grasping the implications, relating what they read
> to the unstated context which alone gives meaning to what they read. In
> describing the contents of this neglected domain of background infor-
> mation, I try to direct attention to a new opening that can help our schools
> make the significant improvement in education that has so far eluded us.
> The achievement of high universal literacy is the key to all other funda-
> mental improvements in American education.[53]

Without laboring the obvious, it becomes clear how interrelated the acquisition of
information and knowledge is with each of the other components of the Responsible Selfhood approach to character education.

Strengths of Character: Virtues. In the introduction to the Responsible Selfhood model, I indicated that cumulatively the components of character that it depicts flow together to form and fund the strengths of personhood that have
traditionally been called "virtues." Reading an account of the classic Greek virtues like that of Joseph Pieper[54] makes one aware of just how rich a range of interrelated and interdependent qualities those concepts integrated. One of the
revelations for me connected with our work on the Responsible Selfhood approach has been the recognition that virtues are dynamic qualities of person constituted by the convergence of *at least* as many aspects of moral personality as this
model seeks to depict. In this concluding section neither space nor my expertise
will allow anything like a full-orbed consideration of the virtues toward which we
aim in an American *paideia* based on this model. For the time being, therefore, I
take this traditional listing and offer brief explications of a contemporary reinterpretation of the virtues, based on what has gone before in this chapter. To make
these meanings truly contemporary, however, care must be taken not to let these
old names bring with them the legacy of gender, ethnic, or racial exclusivism, and
class privilege that citizenship connoted in the Greek polis.

Prudence. In this redrawing of the virtues, prudence becomes the composite
term for "good judgment." Good judgment involves, of course, having sufficient

---

[53]Hirsch, *Cultural Literacy*, 2.
[54]Pieper, *Four Cardinal Virtues*.

knowledge of the relevant circumstances in any situation requiring response or initiative. But, following Hirsch, it also means having the cognitive ordering or mapping of that knowledge so as to illumine in relevant ways the complexities and subtleties of the situation. Moreover, prudence involves skills of consultation, dialogue, and discernment with others. Informed by moral attitudes and conscience, and by stories that offer both motivation and models of effective concern for the common good, prudence, as good judgment, reaches decisions—or contributes to group decision-making—on the basis of a deliberate effort at seeing things whole.

Justice. Traditionally justice meant "giving to each his/her due." We cannot here rehearse Aristotle's rich account of the different modes of justice. In this contemporary reconstitution of the virtues, justice includes such capacities as the commitment and competence to establish fairness. It includes equity and evenhandedness, both in interpersonal relations and in social policy and the treatment of groups. It means consideration and care for the networks of care and interdependence that make being and well-being possible. And it embraces the imperative to keep open and expanding the membership of those entitled to regard and treatment with full humanity and humaneness.

Courage. For the Greeks courage was the quality of emotional and intellectual fortitude sufficient to carry out what prudence and justice determined to be the proper course of action in any situation. It is hard to improve upon that conception. However, informed by the conscience of imagination, courage in the service of the common good in a covenantally based society must have a forward looking component—the nerve and resoluteness to hold in view the future dangers and threats to the common good and to insist upon engaging them. Courage also exhibits resourcefulness, a determined readiness to find means to do what justice and prudence require. Finally, courage involves the strengths of loyalty and fidelity to those causes, persons, and institutions for which one has covenant responsibility.

Temperance. In contemporary terms the traditional concept of temperance becomes "self-management" or "discipline." It is related to the conscience of membership and memory and grows out of self-knowledge and clarity about what constitutes worthy manhood or womanhood. Temperance is also grounded in the conscience of craft in the sense of learning to live well and being a kind of artist with one's life. Involving balance and proportion, temperance is proficiency in the ability consistently to discern and "hit the mark."

On the chart that depicts the Responsible Selfhood approach I have also listed the traditional "theological virtues" of faith, hope, and love. This is not the place to try to demonstrate that these virtues do not depend, for their validity and imperativeness, upon their biblical roots.

Suffice it to say that without love, commitment to the other virtues tends to deteriorate and fall too much into the self-regarding use of virtues to establish one's own worth. Similarly, without hope—hope in the responsiveness and fidelity of others, hope for a future in which to be virtuous and committed to the common good, the virtues tend to lose their point. Finally, the whole setting of the virtues, as conceived here, is one of covenant commitment to a common-weal, a common good. And without faith—a trust in and loyalty to that covenant community, and the body of story and myth that gives it its determinate character and corporate vocation—concern with the virtues can deteriorate to a kind of individualistic manicuring of one's own soul. Faith, hope, and love are not dispensable in the Responsible Selfhood approach, though in order to be constitutional, their inclusion cannot depend upon or be justified solely upon the basis of their formulation in the New Testament.

Two

Paideia
for Religious Education

5

Theology as Doxology: Reflections on Theological Education

Henri Nouwen

During my years of teaching theology, I have often asked myself: "How will a critical study of the Word of God help the students to live the Word more fully?" Theological students who explore with their minds the mysteries of God's presence among God's people without letting that Word mold their own hearts will eventually find themselves bored and dispirited.

General Introduction

To keep intellectual formation and spiritual formation from becoming separated has been an ongoing struggle for me. I have always tried to stay close to the words of the Evangelist John: "Something which has existed from the beginning, which we have heard, which we have seen with our own eyes, which we have watched and touched with our own hands, the Word of life—this is our theme" (1 John 1:1-2). If, indeed, the word we study is the word of life, we cannot study it from a distance. Just as we cannot judge the quality of bread without eating it, so we cannot speak with authority about God's word without letting that word touch our heart, that is, the core of our being.

But, having said this, it is far from easy to let this conviction take shape in the classroom. I have failed in many ways. Sometimes I felt I was giving sermons to students instead of good theological education. Sometimes I felt that I was giving in to current controversies that stimulate more the curious mind than the listening heart. Sometimes I found myself so eager to be relevant that I did not pay enough attention to the hard-to-grasp fundamental issues. Sometimes I wanted to prove myself to my students and colleagues instead of helping them to discover

God's ways in their lives. Sometimes I was far too personal and sometimes far too distant. But I did try, and sometimes I did sense that something happened that was good theological education.

Since I have left the academic world to live and work with mentally handicapped people, I have felt a need to express my vision for theological education as it has emerged over the years.

The focus of these reflections is not pragmatic. I am not trying to suggest concrete theology programs or teaching techniques. My primary concern here is to articulate a "spirituality" for teachers and students in theology.

In the first part of these reflections I want to present a theological approach to the study of theology and in the second part I want to show the implications of this approach for the different modes in which theology is studied.

I. Theology as Doxology

Introduction. In the prologue of the fourth Gospel, the evangelist summarizes the mystery of our creation, salvation, and sanctification, not to satisfy our intellectual curiosity, but to lead us to a prayer of praise. When John unfolds the mystery of God's Word, he offers it as a doxology, a way of giving glory to God. In order to make his doxology our own, we need to situate our knowledge of God in the concrete circumstances of our own existence. That requires hard theological work but always "work" that brings us to a prayer of praise. When theology no longer serves God's glory, it easily becomes a form of vainglory.

The view that theology always has to be and remain doxology has led me to the conviction that studying the Word of God can only be fruitful when it takes place in the context of living the Word. This means that studying theology is first of all an event in the here and now. When theological understanding is sought primarily as a preparation for a future life or a future profession, it can no longer be doxology. Praising God always takes place in the present because the God we praise is always where we are. God is a God of the present. To God belongs glory, here and now. Any suggestion that real life and real work are taking place later makes theology into something it is not: a tool to be used in a work not yet done. The Word must always be lived in the place and the moment where we find ourselves.

The view that theology is in essence doxology forms the basis of these reflections. In the following pages I would like to explore the implications of this viewpoint for theological education and show how the development of theological understanding in and of itself must always be a development of prayer, community, and ministry. I am not saying that a program in theological training should include courses that focus on prayer, community, and ministry. That is nothing new. I am saying that prayer, community, and ministry should be integral parts of true theological understanding. I am aware that this seems a very unpractical and unrealistic viewpoint, but without stating this as explicitly as possible, the purpose of my reflections will remain ambiguous.

To show how prayer, community, and ministry are three aspects of theology as doxology, I will use Luke's infancy narrative as a point of departure, especially the annunciation, the visitation, and the magnificat. By using these stories I want to present Mary as a model for the theologian.

A. Theological Understanding and Prayer. When I say that theological understanding cannot be separated from prayer, I am not arguing for the importance of prayer during the time of theological study, but I am saying that the study of theology itself needs to have the quality of prayer. The story of the annunciation as recorded by the Evangelist Luke shows this clearly.

The first response of Mary to the Angel Gabriel's greeting: "Rejoice, you who enjoy God's favour! The Lord is with you" (Luke 1:28), is fear. Mary was "deeply disturbed by these words and asked herself what this greeting could mean" (Luke 1:29). Here all theology starts. God has broken into history and deeply disturbed Mary to the point of fear. But instead of running away, she starts asking what the meaning of this painful interruption might be. It is a faithful response to what at first seems a sudden, unexpected shaking up of her way of being. From this, a first insight emerges: "Do not be afraid. You have won God's favour. Look! You are to conceive in your womb and bear a son, and you must name him Jesus" (Luke 1:30-31). What was experienced as a moment of interruption proves to be a moment of revelation. The theologian responding in faith to the situation of the moment discovers God's active presence in the midst of the pain and, trusting in that presence, dares to raise a question.

Mary said: "But how can this come about since I have no knowledge of man?" (Luke 1:34). This question is not an objection but the expression of a desire to enter more deeply into the mystery that is being revealed. A theological question is not an attempt to disqualify what is present. It is a prayerful request to be more deeply led into the truth. When Zechariah questioned the angel who announced to him that his wife, Elizabeth, would have a son in her old age, he did not believe and was silenced. But Mary's question did not come forth out of doubt. She asked for a deeper understanding of the mystery of which she had become part. And from that faithful questioning a new insight emerged: "The Holy Spirit will come upon you" (Luke 1:35). A deeper understanding of the nature of God's "interruption" is being offered. The theological question that leads to a deeper theological understanding is a question raised in faith. As long as we keep raising objections and relating to theology as an intellectual discipline in which we can sharpen our mind by keen arguments, nothing truly new can happen to us. We, in fact, might lose our power to speak even when we keep talking!

This obviously raises questions about the value of critical analysis of historical texts, the exploration of complex linguistic issues, the careful comparison between different schools of thought, and the scholarly examination of the ethical

and ministerial implications of specific viewpoints. I am personally deeply convinced of the crucial importance of these methods. I would deny the value of my
own long theological and psychological formation if I would now speak about them
as dangerous for true theology. I have seen enough damage resulting from an un-
critical, ahistorical, and uninformed enthusiasm within different religious circles. Much
violence has been done to the gospel by neglecting a critical approach to the text.

Still I have to say that such critical scholarship can only bear fruit in the context of obedience. In any form of theological education that claims to have a spiritually formative significance, true obedience—that is, attentive listening—to the
truth must be our basic all-pervasive attitude. Therefore, criticism can only be
fruitful when it is criticism within the limits of obedience. If criticism is shunned
as dangerous or even demonic, theology cannot exist, and all that is left is a fickle
piety. But if criticism is no longer practiced as part of true obedience, theology
will quickly lose its character of doxology and degenerate into a so-called "value-
free" science subject to fruitless disputes and argumentations. St. Anselm's definition of theology: "Fides quaerens intellectum" (faith seeking understanding)
implies that critical thinking is an integral part of true doxology.

The final words of Mary show clearly what the aim of all theology is. Mary
said: "You see before you the Lord's servant; let it happen to me as you have said"
(Luke 1:38). True theology creates the inner space in which God's word can happen to us. The purpose of theological understanding is not to grasp, control, or
even use God's word, but to become increasingly willing to let the word of God
speak to us, guide us, move us, and lead us to places far beyond our own comprehension. Thus theology *is* prayer. It is a faithful standing in the presence of
God, receiving the word, asking to be touched by it on always deeper levels, and
becoming more and more available to its saving work in us. Mary's yes was a yes
to let the word become flesh in her. All true theology is a yes to God's word that
wants to find a home in us and renew our being to make it acceptable in God's
sight, and thus make it a new place of praise.

It has always struck me that the first time the word *theologia* was used within
the Christian tradition it referred to the highest level of prayer. The desert fathers
spoke about three stages of prayer: the *praktike*, the *theoric physike*, and the *theologia*. The *praktike* refers to the discipline of bringing the whole person with all
thoughts, feelings, and passion into the presence of God; the *theoric physike* refers
to the contemplation of God's creation and providential plan as it becomes visible
in nature and history; and the *theologia* refers to a direct intimate communion with
God. It took a long time before *theologia* came to mean the explicit reflection on
the faith experience and only recently (since the Enlightenment) did it develop into
an academic discipline that stands beside many other academic disciplines. Thus
theology has become more and more subject to analysis and synthesis and less and
less related to the experience of union with God.

It seems crucial to me that the original connection between *theologia* and prayer does not get lost, because outside of the context of doxology, the praise of God, theological questions no longer lead us deeper into the mystery of God's self-revelation, but, to the contrary, pull us into the temptations of intellectual curiosity.

As we look into the story of the Annunciation, we see how Mary's question raised in prayer leads her to a deeper prayer. The first as well as the last moment of the encounter with the angel is a form of doxology, a living for the glory of God. And Mary's final words to the angel: "Let it happen to me" are only the beginning of a whole life of always fuller abandon to God's will. All the events that follow are new sources for deeper questions and a more total surrender to the work of God in her. Twice the Evangelist Luke points to this on-going inner search. After describing the shepherds' visit, he writes: "As for Mary, she treasured all these things and pondered them in her heart" (Luke 2:19), and after telling the story of how the twelve-year-old Jesus was found by his parents among the teachers in the Temple, he comments: "His mother stored up all these things in her heart" (Luke 2:51).

Here we see how prayer and theological understanding can never be separated. The knowledge the theologian aspires to is a knowledge that is essentially relational. We cannot come to know God outside of a relationship with God. To say it otherwise: Knowing and loving are one in God. Those who do not desire to love God more deeply cannot expect to ever know God more fully.

B. Theological Understanding and Community. Not only can theology not be separated from prayer, it also cannot be "done" outside of the community. In contemporary theological education, theology has become a highly individual, yes, even private, affair. Theologians are thought of as scholars who think and write about God on their own. Famous theologians are often people who are admired for their great intellectual capacities and their ability to express their insights in brilliant lectures or impressive books. They are seen as lonely stars against the dark sky of theological ignorance.

During my years of teaching theology, I have seen how students related to their studies as a highly competitive enterprise in which grades and prizes became their overriding concern. Working together in common vulnerability was not only impossible but even discouraged.

But if indeed theological understanding can only grow in the context of an intimate encounter with God, this encounter has to become incarnate in a community of faith. Faith in God is always embedded in a life together and can only be maintained and deepened in such a life.

The story of the Visitation offers a beautiful model for doing theology in community. The Angel Gabriel, who spoke to Mary, connected her election directly with the election of Elizabeth: ". . . I tell you this too: Your cousin Elizabeth also, in her old age, has conceived a son, and she whom people called barren is now in her sixth month" (Luke 1:36). Thus the promise to Mary is not given to her in

isolation. It is a promise connected with the promise to Elizabeth. Thus the intimate relationship between Mary and God is given a human context: the intimate
relationship between Mary and Elizabeth. And here it becomes clear that the encounter with God asks for the encounter with Elizabeth. When the promise cannot
be shared and has to be lived in complete isolation without any affirmation of other
human beings, that promise cannot bear fruit and is destined to get lost in the world
of doubt, suspicion, skepticism, and unbelief.

Therefore we read: "Mary set out at that time and went as quickly as she could
into the hill country to a town of Judah. She went into Zechariah's house and greeted
Elizabeth" (Luke 1:39-40). Mary, who had been greeted by the angel, now greets
Elizabeth and calls forth in her the gift she had received: "Now it happened that
as soon as Elizabeth heard Mary's greeting, the child leapt in her womb and Elizabeth was filled with the Holy Spirit" (Luke 1:41). Elizabeth in turn affirmed and
deepened the promise given to Mary: "She gave a loud cry and said, 'Of all women
you are the most blessed, and blessed is the fruit of your womb. Why should I be
honoured with a visit from the mother of my Lord?'" (Luke 1:42-43).

Wherever God appears we are called to community. We cannot live the
promise on our own. As God interrupts our history and shows us a new way to
go, God always offers us companions to travel with. Those who cling to a promise
in isolation may go mad. It is precisely in the community of faith that the jealous
love of God, who is greater than our heart and mind, can be absorbed and integrated. Even hermits need spiritual guides. Without any spiritual companionship
they cannot be a sign of God's presence. They become eccentrics.

Theologians who want to enter more deeply into the mystery of God cannot
do so alone. They need each other to stay in touch with the promise of God. Without a community of faith their theological understanding cannot bear fruit in the
church and the world. They become interesting figures who can stimulate many
debates but cannot foster a life of faith.

Both Mary and Elizabeth are women of great faith. They shared in the long
tradition of Israel, hopefully waiting for the fulfillment of God's promise. When
that promise "erupts" in their lives in a completely unique way, they are brought
together to help each other to maintain that faith in the presence of such an incom-
prehensible event, and to encourage each other to trust that what they have experienced comes from God and is not a demonic delusion. Here we see true
community. The deeper understanding of God's promises takes place in the mutual recognition and affirmation of faith. Mary needed to go to Elizabeth and stay
with her for three months to let what had happened to her mature in her. Mary
needed the support of Elizabeth to grow in her faith. Elizabeth needed Mary's visit
to deepen her discovery that it "had pleased God to take away from her the humiliation she suffered among people" (Luke 1:25). Thus, these two blessed women
guided each other in the discernment of the ways in which God is active in human
history.

In the encounter between Mary and Elizabeth the promise each had received takes a true hold on them and not only becomes affirmed but is given a space to grow. In both women something new is happening. A greeting becomes a blessing, a dormant promise leaps up, the yes of a servant becomes a yes of God's daughter. Elizabeth says it so clearly to Mary: "Look, the moment your greeting reached my ears, the child in my womb leapt for joy. Yes, blessed is she who believed that the promise made her by the Lord would be fulfilled" (Luke 1:44-45). Elizabeth and Mary are calling forth in each other the hidden gift that they have received and thus are able to hold on to that gift in gratitude and with hope.

That is precisely what theological understanding is called to do: to affirm the promise and hold that promise up as a sign of hope to the world. Thus theology not only is to be a way of praying but also a way to community. Both prayer and community are part of theology as doxology.

C. Theological Understanding and Proclamation. The third aspect of theology as doxology is that it includes proclamation at its core. Often we think about the study of theology as a necessary part of the preparation for the proclamation of the Word. "Good preachers," we say, "need to know their theology." Theology, thus, is seen as one of the tools for good proclamation in the future. I am increasingly convinced that the study of theology can only be good preparation for proclamation if it is seen and lived as proclamation every step of the way. This proclamation cannot be separated from theological understanding because God's Word is a Word to be proclaimed at all times. Just as one cannot make music without it being heard, so one cannot enter into the mystery of God's presence among God's people without the desire to let the presence be known. The Word that has been spoken to us always wants to be spoken by us. Truly knowing God always means wanting to make God known. Theological understanding of Christ's birth in the world thus always includes giving birth to Christ in the world.

Mary's Magnificat offers a convincing model for the way proclamation and theological understanding are connected. Her proclamation of the greatness of the Lord was a proclamation of a new understanding that came about in the encounter between Mary and Elizabeth. It is a witness to the marvels of God's promises bursting forth from a shared faith. Thus the Magnificat is not only a joyful acknowledgment of God's favor but also a fuller discovery of the mysterious ways of God.

Mary's proclamation starts with the recognition of the most personal favor she has received: "My spirit rejoices in God, my Saviour, because God has looked upon the humiliation of his servant" (Luke 1:46-48a). This recognition, however, does not remain limited to Mary herself. Since it is God's work that is being done to her, it deserves the recognition of the whole of humanity: "Yes, from now on all generations will call me blessed for the Almighty has done great things for me" (Luke 1:48b-49a). Mary now realizes that God's faithfulness that she had come to know in such an intimate way is in no way limited to her. It is a faithfulness that extends to all people who are open to God's love: ''Holy is God's name and God's faithful love extends from age after age to all who fear God'' (Luke 1:49b-50). In her own soul, Mary comes to see that she is indeed the representative of Israel. The way God has touched God's humble servant Mary is the way in which God reaches out to God's servant Israel. Mary has come to know God's ways with God's people in the littleness of her own heart. Thus she can proclaim:

> God has used the power of God's arm.
> God has routed the arrogant of heart.
> God has pulled down princes from their thrones
>   and raised on high the lowly.
> God had filled the starving with good things
>   and sent the rich away empty.
> God has come to the help of God's servant Israel
>   mindful of God's love.   (Luke 1:51-54, author's translation)

Here Mary unfolds in her proclamation God's mysterious plan of salvation. The humble servant of Nazareth becomes the voice that speaks in God's name to all God's people. The encounter between the angel and Mary becomes the encounter between God and all of humanity. The hidden woman becomes the representative of all who suffer from oppression and starvation. The love that has touched one human heart becomes a love that embraces all who are waiting in hope. And those who did not accept the word of salvation are now unmasked as those who isolated themselves by their arrogance, their power, and their wealth. Thus the most intimate, hidden, and unspectacular event has been ''opened up'' as the event around which human history turns.

All of this, while new and surprising, is happening according to the promise, the age-old promise that belongs to the precious inheritance of the people. God's mercy to Abraham and his descendants is bearing fruit in Mary, Elizabeth, and all God-fearing men and women.

Mary's visit to Elizabeth was the bridge between the personal and universal. In community with Elizabeth, Mary was able to proclaim that what had happened to her was an event for all of God's people. In community with Elizabeth, she dares to proclaim with authority the mystery of God's salvation.

It is important to see that all of this belongs to the heart of theological understanding. Those who study theology are not studying to proclaim God's faithful love on some later day. Spiritual knowledge is always knowledge for the moment. When theological understanding is not directly connected with proclamation, it is not true theology. Once the glory of God (the *doxa*) has been seen, it is proclaimed. Once we see the kingdom of God appearing among us, it must be made known. This does not require any more extra effort than the expressing of emotions when they arise. In fact, not proclaiming it is what requires effort since the knowledge of God is known as a knowledge for others to receive. When God's glory appears to us, it appears so that the world can see it and rejoice. What we have received in prayer and shared in community must be proclaimed as Good News for all people.

Conclusion. It is not easy to make prayer, community, and ministry integral parts of our search for theological understanding. A prayerful understanding of the Word has often been replaced by a competition for knowledge, a communal listening to the Word by isolating individualism, and the proclamation of the Word by a disclaiming of the Word. Many students experience a great tension between what happens in their classes and their own spiritual needs. Their studies themselves seldom lead them to prayer, create community, and call forth a fearless proclamation of God's mysterious ways of salvation.

Still we know that the Christian life calls us to give glory to God through prayer, community, and ministry. These are not practices for later, after we have finished our theological studies, but they are essential to the process of theological understanding itself.

Theological schools, then, must be schools where we live the Word in the form of studying. This makes it obvious that theological understanding reaches far beyond the boundaries of the theological school. Once we have come to know it as a way to live the Word, we will never stop being theologians. In fact, we come to see that ministry is an ongoing process of theological understanding. Preaching, teaching, sacramental ministry, pastoral care and counseling, evangelization, liberation of the poor and oppressed, and other forms of ministry all are ways of coming to theological understanding.

If it is true that all theological understanding is in service of salvation, and if it is true that all ministries are for salvation, then there can be no ministry that is not also theology. Every form of ministry is a way to evoke, broaden, deepen, strengthen, and discipline the life of faith. But this is also the aim of the dialectic of theological understanding. Both the ministries of the church and theological understanding aim to discern God's active presence in the concrete realities in which we find ourselves. Therefore, they do belong together. In the schools, theological understanding must always include ministry. In the church, ministry must always include theological understanding.

It is most important to see theology and ministry in unity. Theology is not just preparation for ministry; ministry is not just the application of theology. They are both intimately connected ways of doxology: that is, ways of recognizing and glorifying the presence of God among us.

II. Studying Theology as Doxology

Introduction. I now want to raise the very concrete question: "How is it possible to study theology as doxology in our contemporary seminaries and divinity schools?" If prayer, community, and proclamation are indeed essential aspects of the study of theology, how then can such a study be realized?

Even though theological understanding has to be pursued at every phase of the life of those who want to minister in the name of Jesus, it seems important and even indispensable that certain periods of time are explicitly set aside for the study of the Word. It is of great value—especially in such an opportunistic and pragmatic society as ours—that those who want to dedicate their lives to the Word of God are given the time and space to make the reflection on the Word their primary concern. A climate of solitude, resources for research, competent guidance, and stimulating fellowship can all be very helpful for those who want to bend themselves with full attention over the Word of God. Therefore, schools for the study of theology are indispensable. There is much to learn. We want to become familiar with the Word of God as it is spoken to us in the sacred Scriptures, as it has been lived through the centuries in the community of faith, and as it has been ordered in systematic thought. We also want to know about the relationship of the biblical Word of God to other spiritual traditions such as Buddhism, Islam, and Hinduism.

In the first part of these reflections, I tried to show how studying the Word cannot be done outside the Word since we who study the Word derive our whole being from the Word. We are created through the Word and redeemed through participation in its fullness (John 1:3, 16). We are not masters over the Word, critics of the Word, evaluators of the Word. By placing ourselves outside the Word as its critics or judges, we place ourselves over and against the Word and thus are no longer its servants. Studying the Word, therefore, is only possible as an act of worship (doxology) in which we enter more deeply into the mystery of our own creation and redemption. When we enter more deeply into these mysteries, however, we have to enter them with our whole being, including our ability to think critically and to distinguish between pious applications and true spiritual insights. Therefore doxology can never be separated from truth-seeking scholarship.

In the following notes, I would like to explore the educational aspects of this vision of theological study. How can we develop disciplines in which we safeguard prayer, community, and proclamation as essential ingredients of the study of theology? I propose to look at four aspects of studying the Word: listening to the Word, speaking the Word, reading the Word, and writing the Word. All theological studies, whatever the subject may be, include listening, speaking, reading, and writing. In our search for theological understanding, we must be very concerned that we listen, speak, read, and write in ways that are appropriate to the nature of the Word we study.

Listening to the Word. Mary listened to the Word. Because of her listening to the Word, the Word could become flesh in her. Listening is the main attitude of the person who prays. Before anything else, prayer is listening to God, being open and receptive to God's influence. Listening thus is a very vulnerable stance. Mary was so vulnerable, so open and so receptive, that she could listen with her whole being. Nothing in her resisted the Word that was directed toward her. She was "all ears." Thus God could fulfill the promise in her far beyond her own understanding and control. She could "let it happen" according to God's will.

True listening has become increasingly difficult in educational institutions where students are mostly on their guard, afraid to expose their weak side, and eager to be recognized as being bright. In our contemporary competitive society, listening often is a way of "checking the other person out." It is a very defensive stance in which we do not really allow anything new to happen. It is a suspicious way of receiving that makes us wonder what serves our purposes and what does not.

Many theological seminars in which small groups of students come together to discuss a subject are not safe places for true listening. Instead of offering the space where people feel free to become vulnerable to the Word, they often prove to be battlefields on which one person wants to prove to the other his or her superiority in knowledge. Thus it often seems that the Word is being conquered instead of listened to. It, therefore, is not surprising that many students who enter theological education with a rather open mind and open heart find themselves increasingly closed to the Word they are studying. Trust gradually is replaced by distrust, love by fear, willingness to be vulnerable by power games, and hope for renewal by a despair about the future. Thus a prayerful listening gradually is replaced by a style of learning in which it seems that God is being called to accountability.

The psalmist warns against this hardening of the heart.

Today, listen to the voice of the Lord;
Do not grow stubborn,
    as your fathers and mothers did in the wilderness,
When at Meriba and Massah
    they challenged me and provoked me,
Although they had seen all my works.   (Psalm 95)

If we want to study theology as a way of giving praise to God and maintain the qualities of prayer, community, and proclamation, we must start listening again. When Peter, James, and John saw Jesus full of light on Mount Tabor, they heard a voice saying: "This is my Son, the Chosen One, listen to him" (Luke 9:35). Listening together to the Incarnate Word, that is the beginning of all theological understanding. Schools are precisely meant to be places where this can happen. They are meant to be places where true obedience can be learned. The word *obedience* has often come to mean doing someone else's will without really wanting to do it. But the deepest meaning of the word *obedience* is listening with quiet attentiveness (from the Latin, *ob-audire*). This obedience to the Incarnate Word is the basis of all true theological education.

When we look prayerfully at the life, passion, death, and resurrection of Jesus, it becomes clear that Jesus' whole mission was a mission of obedience to his Father. To believe in Jesus means to believe that all that Jesus says and does is said and done in complete obedience to the One who sent him. That is why St. Paul can write that just as by one person's disobedience many were made sinners, so by one person's obedience many will be made righteous (Rom. 5:19). This total unlimited obedience of the Incarnate Word forms the heart of the Christian faith. God's words to the friends of Jesus on Mount Tabor, "This is my Son, listen to him," ask for a listening response to the one whose whole being is listening. In Mary we see the purest response. That is why she is called blessed by her cousin Elizabeth. It is through her total obedience to the Word that became flesh in her that she becomes not only the Mother of God but also the Mother of all the faithful.

The theologian is called to this same obedience, a faithful listening to the Word in order to let the Word become flesh among the people of God. Without such obedience, theological understanding leads to power games in which the glory of God is replaced by the human need for affirmation, influence, and success.

Theological education is such a precarious enterprise precisely because without true listening the understanding it seeks easily leads to vainglory instead of the glory of God.

Speaking the Word. Mary spoke to the angel, to Elizabeth, and to all of humanity. Her words were words emerging out of her deep listening. They were articulations of a lived faith and thus became a form of prayer, a call to community, and a proclamation of Good News.

In our anxious times, speaking often is tainted with violence. Often it has the quality of an attack, an attack coming from a fearful heart that considers aggression the safest form of defense. In many theological schools debates, discussions, and arguments look like verbal combats in which the speakers try to protect themselves and try to maintain their once taken position.

But speaking the Word of God is participating in God's own speaking. It is a speaking that emerges out of silent love and thus creates new life.

All theological words need to be born out of silence and constantly return to it. That is the movement of Jesus, the Incarnate Word. Jesus is the Word coming forth from and returning to eternal silence. When our words are no longer connected with and nurtured by the silence from which they come, they lose their authority and degenerate into "mere words" that cannot bear fruit. But when our words carry within them God's eternal silence, then they can be truly life-giving.

One of the most important aspects of God's Word spoken by Jesus and his followers is that it always creates community. When the Word is spoken with deep reverence for the silence that it carries with it, a new space can be created where people can come together in safety and experience the love that embraces them.

There have been many occasions in my life during which I felt isolated and cut off from God and my fellow human beings. But every time the Word of God was directed to me by someone who spoke it with great humility and love, I had a sense that a new space was being offered where I could meet my God and my brothers and sisters anew. And every time this happened I felt a deep desire to let that Word grow deeper by dwelling in its silence.

Maybe one could say that it belongs to the main task of theology to find the words that are born in silence, words that do not divide but unite, that do not hurt but heal. Theological understanding cannot be doxology when what is being said is void of the uniting and healing silence of God.

There are fearful, shameful, and embarrassing silences, but the silence hidden in the Word of God is always a silence that brings reconciliation, unity, and peace. Let me offer a simple example. When someone says to a person in pain: "God loves you as the apple of God's eye and is always with you even when you feel most alone," such words can be little more than a pious phrase that does more harm than good. But when these words are spoken with a heart that has listened long to God's voice and has gradually been molded by it, then they can truly heal and bring new life because then these words are "sacramental." That means they carry within themselves the reality they express.

Theologians speak about God. They want to offer knowledge that is oriented toward salvation. Their words can lead to darkness or to light, depending on whether they are spoken in the service of God's Word or not. When they are spoken from a heart filled with anger, resentment, or the desire for recognition and success, they easily become instruments of the powers of darkness and destroy the heart instead of heal it. But when they are spoken from the silence of God, from the place where all is one and no words are needed, they can be words of light offering salvation.

Mary's words spoken in the Magnificat came forth from a heart that knew the silence of God and had come to understand in that silence the ways of God with God's people. Her words were free from all darkness and filled with life-giving light. Her words were void of any sentimentality, self-righteousness, or manipulation. They were very critical words, radically upsetting the ways of the world, cutting deep into the human condition of sin, and courageously announcing the new order of God. But they came from a humble heart deeply touched by God's love. Mary's words are pure prayer, pure proclamation, and a pure call to become a new people of God. Thus Mary becomes a model for all who want to speak God's Word.

Reading the Word. Reading and writing the Word are "educated" ways of listening and speaking the Word. They ask for special skills that require much training. Countless people in this world are not able to read or write. Their relationship to the Word is limited to listening and speaking. Those who do read and write have a special responsibility since these tools must be used in the spirit of true listening and true speaking. This requires a hard spiritual discipline since reading and writing easily become ways to exercise power and control.

Reading is a lost art in our contemporary education. Most students relate to reading as a method to collect information that they can use at some later time. It often has the quality of arming oneself for the battle that is coming. Books—the Bible included—then become sought-after resources to actively participate in the competition and rivalry of the world. I continue to be surprised how often books are read with a conquering mind-set. Usually there are time pressures, exam pressures, grade pressures, and peer pressures, and words written to peacefully dwell with are quickly received, summarized, remembered, and reproduced without ever having reached the human heart.

When the Word of God is read in this way it cannot fulfill its mission. Instead of leading us to salvation, it increases our resistance to it. The greatest tragedy of theological education is that students may end up using their theological sophistication in ways that prevent the Word that they "know" so well from leading them to conversion.

True reading involves the trust that in the words we read there is always the Word to encounter. It is an attentive waiting for the words that connect deeply with the Word and a careful discerning where the Word leads us. Reading thus is a form of listening to the Word in which we keep wondering which words are written as food for our own spiritual journey. *Lectio Divina,* spiritual reading, is the term that is often used for this way of reading. It belongs to the monastic tradition where monks were trained to read for their own and their community's spiritual growth. It is a reading not to master the Word, not to criticize the Word, but to be mastered and criticized by the Word. In short, one could say: Spiritual reading is a reading in which we allow the Word to read us.

I vividly remember a scene in which this happened in a very dramatic and unexpected way. I had asked a class of theology students to form little groups and to reflect together on the story of the Annunciation. The students gathered in different rooms and started to discuss the dialogue between the Angel Gabriel and Mary. Suddenly the door of one of the rooms was opened and a student came running out, screaming, "It is true, it is true." I ran after him, worrying about his state of mind. When I stopped him and asked, "What is true?" he said, "I never truly heard Mary's words: 'Let it happen to me as you have said.' I myself am always trying to plan, predict, and organize my future. I never want anything to happen to me without my being able to control it. Now suddenly Mary's words reached me in the center of my being. I am completely stunned by the new awareness of my need for a radical conversion."

This experience is very telling. Words that were often read suddenly found a new fertile ground and started bearing fruit. This happened when St. Augustine heard a child's voice say: "Pick up and read." When he took the Bible and opened it, he read the words that were meant for him most personally, and he found the strength to follow Jesus radically. Spiritual reading is a reading in which we are open to be captured by the Word of God and led to a new place.

Most important in our way of reading the Word is that we receive it with our whole being, our mind and our heart; our present condition, our past experiences, and our future aspirations; our individual selves and our social selves, including family members, friends, and acquaintances. When we thus expose all that we are to the Word, the Word can truly act in us and show us the ways of God for us, hidden for all ages but revealed here and now in our reading. When indeed theology is doxology, we cannot exclude any part of our life from giving praise to God. This is what all great theologians have lived so intensely. St. Augustine, St. Thomas Aquinas, St. Theresa of Avila, John Henry Newman, Bonhoeffer, and many others would have never been able to have such a profound influence if their words had not come from the center of their being where they had allowed the written Word to transform them. They all read the Word with a fervent desire to let the Word anchor itself in their own personal story, with their own most intimate pains and joys and with their own most personal struggles with God. This reading of the Word as a Word most personally for them allowed them to become true theologians whose words could be heard as words about God transcending time, place, and personal history.

Writing the Word. Studying theology always includes writing. The written word has a very important place in our society. Even though radio and television have become major forms of communication, the written word continues to remain the most formative and influential way in which thoughts are expressed and made known. Most of the audio and visual materials are dependent on the written word.

Writing, however, is often the source of great pain and anxiety. It is remarkable how hard it is for many students to sit down quietly and trust their own creativity. There seems to be a deep-seated resistance to writing. I have experienced this resistance myself over and over again. Even after many years of writing, I experience real fear when I face the empty page. Why am I so afraid? Sometimes I have an imaginary reader in mind who is looking over my shoulder and rejecting every word I write down. Sometimes I am overwhelmed by the countless books and articles that already have been written, and I cannot imagine that I have anything to say that has not already been said better by someone else. Sometimes it seems that every sentence fails to express what I really want to say, and that written words simply cannot hold what goes on in my mind and heart. These fears not seldom paralyze me and make me delay or even abandon my writing plans.

And still every time I overcome these fears and trust not only my own unique way of being in the world, but also my ability to give words to it, I experience a deep spiritual satisfaction. I have been trying to understand the nature of this satisfaction. What I am gradually discovering is that in the writing I come in touch with the Spirit of God within me and experience how I am led to new places.

Most students of theology think that writing means writing down ideas, insights, or visions. They are of the opinion that they first must have something to say before they can put it on paper. For them, writing is little more than recording preexistent thoughts. But with this approach, true writing is impossible. Writing is a process in which we discover what lives in us. The writing itself reveals to us what is alive in us. The deepest satisfaction of writing is precisely that it opens up new spaces within us of which we were not aware before we started to write. To write is to embark on a journey of which we do not know the final destination.

Thus writing requires a great act of trust. We have to say to ourselves: "I do not yet know what I carry in my heart, but I trust that it will emerge as I write." Writing is like giving away the few loaves and fishes one has, trusting that they will multiply in the giving. Once we dare to "give away" on paper the few thoughts that come to us, we start discovering how much is hidden underneath these thoughts, and thus we gradually come in touch with our own riches.

Theology requires a constant attempt to identify ways in which God is present among us. Regular writing is one important way to do this. I remember how, during a long stay in Latin America, daily writing helped me to discern how the Spirit of God was at work in all that I was experiencing. Underneath the seemingly fragmenting multitude of visual and mental stimulations, I was able to discover a "hidden wholeness." Writing made that possible. It brought me in touch with the unity underneath the diversity and the solid current beneath the restless waves. Writing became the way to stay in touch with the faithfulness of God in the midst of a chaotic existence. In these circumstances I came to realize that writing was indeed a form of prayer. It also brought about community since the written word helped me to create a space where different people, who found it hard to identify anything lasting among their passing impressions, could gather and come to trust their own experiences. Finally these words became a proclamation of God's faithful presence even there where least expected.

In theological education it is of great importance to rediscover writing as a spiritual discipline by which we can come to discern the active presence of God among us. In a fear-filled society that makes writing a very competitive activity, such a discipline is not easy to develop, but without such a discipline real theological education can hardly be possible.

Conclusion. Listening, speaking, reading, and writing in ways that are faithful to the Word of God are hard spiritual disciplines. If we study God's Word, not to master it, but to be mastered by it, we have to constantly make choices that go against the grain of our power-hungry world. To listen in the spirit of obedience, to speak out of the silence, to read while waiting to be addressed, and to write in search of the hidden wholeness beyond the fragmenting experience of our everyday life, these are not spontaneous responses in our contemporary society. But as we gradually develop these disciplines as expressions of our desire to become true disciples, we will start catching glimpses of the new heaven and the new earth we are searching for. And as we do so, we become increasingly aware that the final meaning of all theological understanding is to offer glory and praise to the One in whom God "wants all fullness to be found" (Col. 1:18). The spiritual disciplines of listening, speaking, reading, and writing are the concrete ways in which theology becomes doxology.

General Conclusion

With deep gratitude I remember the many years of teaching in theological schools. The times in which I experienced my teaching as another way to pray, to be in community, and to proclaim the Good News have stayed with me as timeless times. I remember these as times during which no energy was wasted and hard work was most rewarding. The moments that God's Word really broke through to my own and my students' hearts, during which we sensed how good it was to be together, and felt spoken to in a very healing way stand out as great teaching and learning moments. It seemed that the Word was happening then and became a true event in which the distinction between words and acts was transcended. Every time this took place it was an experience of pure grace, a gift from God who allowed us to catch a fresh glimpse of the great mystery of which we have become part.

I now realize that these theological moments were indeed moments of doxology in which knowing God, loving God, and praising God became one. It was these moments that gave birth to the insights that I have tried to articulate in these reflections. There are many questions facing teachers and students of theology: questions concerning the practical and theoretical aspects of theology, concerning the role of "experience" and "story" in theology, concerning the integration of theology in the daily life of those who study it, and not least of all concerning the theological curriculum. None of these I have directly touched upon in these reflections, but I hope that this "spirituality for theologians" can offer some inspiration to those who are doing the hard work of theological education.

6

On the Religious Education of American Rabbis

Neil Gillman

There are three commonly accepted dimensions to the education of an American congregational rabbi: the academic, the professional, and for want of a better word, the "religious."*

I

The first two are easy to define. The academic dimension refers to the bodies of knowledge and linguistic and textual skills that a rabbi must acquire to function as an authority on Judaism: the ability to speak, read, and comprehend modern Hebrew; the skills needed to understand a body of classical Hebrew and Aramaic texts—primarily biblical and rabbinic (the Babylonian Talmud, the anthologies of *midrash*, the liturgies, and the later codifications of Jewish law)—along with a knowledge of the contents of significant portions of these texts; and a basic general knowledge of Jewish history, Jewish theology and philosophy, and medieval and modern Hebrew literature. Whatever other roles the modern American rabbi may play, he or she is expected to be a master of the broad field of Jewish learning.

The professional dimension includes homiletical, pedagogical, counseling, pastoral, and administrative skills. There is a theoretical component to mastering

*The issues under discussion in this paper have been on my agenda for nearly a decade. It would be impossible even to begin to list the people who have helped clarify my thinking, but they would surely include my colleagues on the faculty of The Jewish Theological Seminary—particularly Chancellor Ismar Schorsch; Chancellor Emeritus Gerson D. Cohen; Professor Raymond D. Scheindlin, Provost of the Seminary; and Professor Gordon Tucker, Dean of its Rabbinical School—and generations of rabbinical students who have participated in endless discussions of these questions both in the classroom and out. My gratitude to all of these in no way diminishes my personal responsibility for the conclusions of this contribution to the inquiry.

some of these skills (for example, curriculum development, psychoanalytic theory), but it is clearly subservient to the practical.

The religious dimension is much more elusive. It may be taken as the cultivation and refinement of a perspective that views the world as manifesting a singular "order of existence," that understands that order as reflecting the presence of God, that is powerful enough to motivate the individual to shape his or her life experience in response to that presence, and that instructs the rabbinical student as to how to transmit that perspective to a congregation of American Jews.[1] In other educational circles, this dimension is referred to as "religious formation," but I have never heard that phrase used in regard to Jewish education.

Of these three, by any criterion of measurement, it is the academic dimension that monopolizes the curricula of modern rabbinical schools. There is nothing inherently new or surprising about this emphasis. Judaism has always prized learning, largely because it understands God's will to have become recorded in sacred texts. Jews must study these texts to ascertain what it is that God demands of us in any life situation. From the very outset, then, rabbinic authority has been rooted in intellectual and scholarly accomplishment. The impact of modernity on this model has been felt in the broadening of the curriculum beyond the mastery of sacred texts alone, by the introduction, in some circles, of new scholarly methodologies, and by the addition of the professional dimension to rabbinic education.

The introduction of this professional dimension was itself the result of the reshaping of the rabbinic role in the modern setting. Essentially, the American rabbi assumed the pastoral, clerical, and administrative functions of Christian clergy. For many years this professional dimension was accorded at best a grudging recognition by rabbinical schools. It was usually relegated to a few courses in the last year of study ("Why do we have to use class time to teach students how to conduct a funeral? The first time, they'll make ten mistakes, the second time, five, and by the end of their first year, they'll be able to do it in their sleep!"). More recently, it has come to be recognized as crucial to the student's sense of professional integrity and is now accorded a much more central place in the curriculum.[2]

---

[1]This is my own reformulation of Clifford Geertz's definition of religion in his seminal "Religion as a Cultural System," in *The Interpretation of Cultures* (New York: Basic Books, 1973) 90.

[2]In the 1988–89 curriculum of the Seminary's Rabbinical School, for example, students were required to register for (or be exempt from on the basis of prior, parallel course work elsewhere) fifty-four semester courses that were textual or academic in nature, and ten semester courses in "Professional Skills." Also required were an additional four semesters of "Synthesis" courses, i.e., interdisciplinary, theme-oriented courses that synthesized available bodies of knowledge on a particular issue and attempted to apply them to specific problems that confront the congregational rabbi. These were, in fact, experimental versions of the kind of course work this paper proposes as indispensable to rabbinical education. It should be added that that current curriculum was begun to be phased out

It is also clear that neither of these two dimensions presents a formidable educational challenge. We know, or can easily discover, how to conduct an advanced academic program and how to teach professional skills; we simply have to decide on our goals and shape our curriculum accordingly.

In contrast, the very existence of a "religious" dimension to rabbinic education is just coming into awareness and is a source of considerable bewilderment. To be more precise, the bewilderment applies mostly to the institutions on the left or "liberal" wing of the religious spectrum, to those schools that are committed to a critical or "scientific" approach to the study of Judaism. In the context of the contemporary American Jewish community, it applies to The Jewish Theological Seminary of America in New York (the fountainhead of the Conservative Movement in American Judaism), the Reconstructionist Rabbinical College in Philadelphia (the youngest of the three, the school that reflects the late Mordecai Kaplan's naturalist reading of Judaism), and the Hebrew Union College-Jewish Institute of Religion with its main campuses in Cincinnati and New York (which trains rabbis for American Reform congregations).

Of these three schools, this author has been associated, for more than three decades, exclusively with The Jewish Theological Seminary—as a student, administrator, and professor. The analysis that follows, then, inevitably reflects my personal experience. My sense is that it applies equally well to HUC-JIR and less to RRC, but I cannot claim to speak of their programs with any degree of authority.

The schools that represent the right, or traditionalist (commonly called "Orthodox"), wing of the Jewish religious spectrum—primarily a number of *yeshivot,* or academies, most of them transplanted to America from their Eastern European settings during the first half of this century, and, to a certain extent, the "modern Orthodox," or, as its leadership prefers, "centrist" Rabbi Isaac Elchanan Theological Seminary, affiliated with Yeshiva University in New York City— are not at all bewildered. They are spared because they share a number of theological and ideological assumptions: Both the "written Torah," that is, Hebrew Scriptures (primarily the Pentateuch), and the "oral Torah," as recorded in talmudic literature (which constitutes the authoritative interpretation of Scripture), were directly (either verbally or propositionally) revealed to Moses at Sinai.

---

in the academic year 1989–90 in favor of an entirely new structure that is informed throughout by an attempt to deal with the issues raised in this paper. For a somewhat dated, but still ground-breaking study of rabbinic education in the United States, see Charles Liebman, "The Training of American Rabbis," *American Jewish Year Book 1968,* vol. 69, ed. Morris Fine and Milton Himmelfarb (New York: The American Jewish Committee; Philadelphia: The Jewish Publication Society of America, 1968) 3-112. On the rabbinate as an institution, its evolution, and its role in contemporary America, see the collection of papers in *Understanding American Judaism,* vol. 1, *The Rabbi and the Synagogue,* ed. Jacob Neusner (New York: KTAV, 1975), in particular the contribution by Wolfe Kelman, "The American Synagogue," 69-89.

This body of teaching contains God's final and exclusive word for Israel on all matters of belief and practice. The study of this literature, then, is itself an act of worship, for its goal is to uncover the will of God for the infinite details of the Jew's life-experience at all times. This entire body of teaching—including the post-talmudic (that is, post-sixth-century c.e.) legal material that extends, elaborates, explains, and codifies the earlier material—retains a singular integrity, unaffected by historical, cultural, sociological, or economic considerations. In other words, it represents one internally coherent and consistent body of discourse. This body of material, then, can be taught only by instructors, and with the help of exegetical resources that share all of these assumptions.

Finally, these schools are clear on what constitutes a "religious" or authentic Jew, and hence, as to the goal of the entire enterprise. It is to create a Jew who is committed to fulfilling the explicit will of God as embodied in this sacred tradition, throughout his (but not her, for these schools will not ordain a woman) life experience, and who has the skills needed to persuade and enable his congregants to do the same.

To put this another way, in these traditionalist circles, the academic and religious dimensions of rabbinic education coincide. The academic program *is* the instrument of religious education. The entire enterprise is endowed with explicit religious significance.

This traditionalist model of rabbinic education has exhibited a singular resiliency; with relatively minor modifications, it has been in place from the talmudic era to this day. When it began to be questioned, it was not, at least at the outset, questioned because of its purely theological assumptions. That came later. What came first, during the nineteenth century European *haskalah* or "Enlightenment," was the application of those critical or scientific modes of scholarship to the study of Judaism. The primary result of this extended inquiry was to introduce the *fact* of history into the study of all Jewish texts and institutions. Everything Jewish was discovered to have had a history and thus to have been shaped by the ever-changing, broader cultural contexts in which the Jewish community has participated to the present. Even the Bible itself was now seen as embodying manifold reflections of its pagan, mideastern setting. The Talmud and its later elaborations were replete with borrowings from Hellenistic civilization, from medieval Jewish institutions, from Christianity and Islam. Every area of Jewish law, from the very outset in the biblical and talmudic eras, was viewed as influenced by and responding to economic, sociological, and cultural considerations.[3]

---

[3]A useful anthology of writings representing "The Science of Judaism" school is collected in part 5 of *The Jew in the Modern World,* ed. Paul R. Mendes-Flohr and Jehuda Reinharz (New York and Oxford: Oxford University Press, 1980) 182-213. See, in particular, the contributions by Leopold Zunz (1794–1886) and Moritz Steinschneider (1816–1907), both founding fathers of the school. For an elaboration of the implications of that

In short, Torah (in the extended sense as the entire body of Jewish religious instruction from the Bible to the present) was no longer viewed as a single, internally coherent, and consistent body of discourse, floating above time and history, but rather as deeply enmeshed in the life experiences of Jews in different geographical and cultural settings, doubtless shaping these experiences, but also responding to and being substantively affected by them as well. Torah, implicitly, came to be viewed as itself a cultural document. As such, it could legitimately be studied with all of the tools and resources available to study any cultural document. Effectively, the study of Torah became secularized.

II

The founding faculty of The Jewish Theological Seminary was deeply committed to this mode of study. They shared this commitment with the faculty of the (Reform) Hebrew Union College, which predated the founding of the Seminary by more than a decade. What precipitated the break with American Reform Judaism and led to the founding of the Seminary in 1886 (and eventually, to the Conservative Movement) was largely the respective positions of the two founding groups in regard to Jewish law, particularly to the ritual law. Reform Judaism, in its landmark Pittsburgh Platform of 1885, viewed all of the ritual law of the Torah as anachronistic, valid in the earlier, more primitive stages of Jewish national history but now an obstacle to the "spiritual" development of Judaism in a modern American setting. The founders of the Seminary, in contrast, viewed the law in its totality as remaining the preeminent form of Jewish religious expression. True, this body of law may well have evolved over time in response to changing historical conditions and should, in fact, continue to do so. But in principle, they affirmed the law as binding, and their approach to Jewish legal development was evolutionary, gradualist, cautious, or, in short, "conservative."[4]

approach for Jewish law, see Ismar Schorsch, "Zacharias Frankel and the European Origins of Conservative Judaism," *Judaism* 31/3 (Summer 1981): 344-54. Frankel (1794–1875) was the founder of the European movement that, in its American incarnation, became Conservative Judaism.

[4]On Reform Judaism's Pittsburgh Platform, see *The Pittsburgh Platform in Retrospect,* ed. Walter Jacob (Pittsburgh: Rodef Shalom Congregation, 1985). The intricate story of the emergence of a "conservative" reaction to nineteenth-century American Reform Judaism and the founding of the Seminary is traced in Moshe Davis, *The Emergence of Conservative Judaism: The Historical School in Nineteenth Century America* (Philadelphia: The Jewish Publication Society of America, 1963). It should be noted that in our own day, Reform Judaism has gone a fair distance in modifying the ideological perspective of the Pittsburgh Platform, including its views on the ritual law. See Eugene B. Borowitz, *Reform Judaism Today* (New York: Behrman House, 1983), particularly Book Three.

The generations of students who came to study at the Seminary, then, were exposed to a conflicting message. In the classroom they were taught, implicitly again, that Torah is a cultural document that can be studied with all of the tools available to Western scholarship. ("I teach Torah at the Seminary much as I might teach it at Harvard.") But concurrently, and programmatically, Jewish law remains binding in all of its detail, as if it were explicitly revealed.[5]

This conflicting message could be maintained because the Seminary's founding faculty studiously avoided doing theology. Solomon Schechter, president of the Seminary from 1902 until his death in 1915, wrote a masterful survey of rabbinic theology and at great length on the ideology of the Seminary and of the movement that it was in the process of creating. But he reveals almost nothing about his personal theology. Most important, he says nothing about his own understanding of revelation, that theological issue which deals explicitly with the question of religious authority.[6]

Of the early Seminary faculty, only Mordecai Kaplan (who taught at the Seminary from 1909 to 1963, when he left to found the competing Reconstructionist Rabbinical College) followed the educational assumptions of the school to their theological and programmatic conclusions and propounded a thoroughly naturalist view of the emergence of Judaism. In broad strokes, Kaplan taught that Judaism is not only a religion but the evolving religious civilization of the Jewish people. God is the process within the natural order that promotes salvation; revelation is the discovery, by a human community, of what makes human life more and more abundant, creative, and value-filled. In short, the authority for determining the shape of Judaism in any generation has always been, and continues to be, the caring and committed community. Thus, Torah is legitimately a cultural statement. Theology, ideology, and eventually, program (for what the community originally created, the community can continue to reshape) become aligned.[7]

---

[5]On the "founding myth" of the Seminary and its varied "mixed messages" see my "Mordecai Kaplan and the Ideology of Conservative Judaism," *Proceedings of the Rabbinical Assembly* (1984): 57-68.

[6]Solomon Schechter, *Aspects of Rabbinic Theology* (New York: Schocken Books, 1961). Schechter's statements on the Seminary and Conservative Judaism are collected in his *Seminary Addresses and Other Papers* (New York: The Burning Bush Press, 1959). An excellent anthology of papers, scholarly and otherwise, by the founding fathers of the school and representatives of its faculty can be found in *Tradition and Change: The Development of Conservative Judaism* (New York: The Burning Bush Press, 1958). The absence, in all of this material, of any attempt to do theology in the modern vein is striking.

[7]Mordecai Kaplan's first and most-systematic exposition of his thought is in his monumental *Judaism as a Civilization,* enl. ed. (New York: The Reconstructionist Press, 1957). An excellent appreciation of Kaplan's impact is in the anthology, *Mordecai Kaplan: An Evaluation*, ed. Ira Eisenstein and Eugene Kohn (New York: The Reconstructionist Press, 1952). See also n. 5 above.

But Kaplan was the exception. By and large, his colleagues remained pious Jews who pursued their scholarly inquiries in the modern style. If it occurred to them to ask why Torah should retain any authority whatsoever in their lives if it was accessible to secular tools of investigation, that question was never posed in the classroom.[8]

Essentially, then, for most of its first century (1886-1986), the Rabbinical School of the Seminary was such in name only. It was, in fact, an extraordinary graduate school for advanced Jewish studies. Long before doctoral programs in Jewish studies were in place in major American universities, and, in fact, long before the Seminary itself began to offer a formal doctoral program (1970), students who never had any intention of becoming congregational rabbis came to the Seminary because it was the only place where they could acquire a first-rate, graduate-level education in the broad field of Judaica. Many of these men were later to populate departments of Jewish studies in universities in America and abroad.

But with the questioning of the traditionalist model, and the eventual collapse, for many Jews, of its theological foundations, the nexus between the academic and religious dimensions of rabbinic education dissolved. What then was to become of that religious dimension? If Torah is indeed a cultural document, to be taught with secular tools, how is it to be taught in a religious setting? In fact, what, then, *is* Jewish religious education? Clearly more than texts, skills, and bodies of knowledge. But what is this "more"? And how are the culture and curriculum of a rabbinical school different from those of a graduate school?

III

It is stunning, in retrospect, that for the first eight decades of the Seminary's existence, these questions were rarely explicitly confronted.[9] But they eventually became unavoidable.

---

[8]Eventually the purely theological issues were addressed in a more traditional style than in Kaplan's writings by, among others, Abraham Joshua Heschel, who taught at the Seminary from 1946 until his death in 1972, and his students, the late Seymour Siegel, who taught theology (and Talmud) at the Seminary until his death in 1988, and still among us, Fritz Rothschild. Part of Heschel's *God in Search of Man* (Philadelphia: The Jewish Publication Society of America, 1956) is a masterful inquiry into the issue of revelation that avoids the extremes of traditionalist literalism and Kaplanian naturalism. My own "Toward a Theology for Conservative Judaism," *Conservative Judaism* 37/1 (Fall 1983): 4-22 is a survey of possible options on the issue and their legal and programmatic implications.

[9]To be fair, they were addressed on the rhetorical level. Seminary mythology includes an exchange that took place when Solomon Schechter (president of the Seminary 1902–1915) interviewed Louis Finkelstein (president and then chancellor of the Seminary 1939–1972) when the latter applied for admission to the Rabbinical School. To Schechter's question, "Why do you want to come to the Seminary?" Finkelstein answered, "To study the

First, on the most practical level, in 1970 the Seminary established its own graduate school, offering M.A. and Ph.D. degrees in Judaica. But the Seminary is a small (some 500 students) institution and its faculty teaches in all of its programs. What criteria, then, are to be used in the hiring of faculty? Is academic excellence sufficient? Are the instructor's personal religious commitments to be taken into consideration? But how are these to be measured? Can an instructor be hired only for graduate school courses? Only for rabbinical school courses? And what happens when financial considerations lead to cross-registration between graduate and rabbinical students in the same Bible or Talmud course, and when a number of graduate students are not even Jewish?

Second, Seminary instructors and students began to be aware of the possibility that Judaism could be taught as "religion." The study of religions had become a discipline in the academic world at large—primarily in Protestant seminaries, university departments of religious studies, and in the social sciences—but until the seventies these developments had had only minimal impact on scholars of Judaica. Jewish religion, it was now beginning to be acknowledged, is much more than texts, laws, theologies, liturgies, and institutions. A "religion"—any religion—is a unique and complex entity that can be studied as such, according to certain canons of scholarship that have won acceptance in the scholarly world at large.[10]

Finally, the Seminary administration and faculty began to acknowledge the existence of a persistent dissatisfaction, on the part of its rabbinic alumni and students, with the training they had and were receiving at the Seminary. Part of this dissatisfaction, it was felt, was endemic to professional education across the board and referred to the relative neglect of the professional dimension. But a good deal of it applied to the faculty's perceived failure to go beyond the purely academic demands of the curriculum.

A rabbinic graduate of the 1960s, in a personal conversation, put it this way: "On Yom Kippur [the Day of Atonement] I stand before a congregation of three thousand Jews. It occurs to me that I know everything *about* this holiest of days—

---

great books of the Jewish tradition." To this, Schechter is said to have responded, "To study great books, all you need is a library. The only reason to come to the Seminary is to associate with great men." There is no question, in my mind, that Finkelstein believed that association with great role models can provide an experience in religious education, and it probably does, but that aphorism hardly constitutes a conceptualization for a curriculum.

[10]Of this century's giants of Jewish scholarship, the late Gershom Scholem who, almost singlehandedly, created the field of Jewish mysticism, was the only figure who incorporated the emerging discipline of religious studies into his scholarly work. See, e.g., his earliest and most accessible work, *Major Trends in Jewish Mysticism* (New York: Schocken Books, 1941). More recently the scholarly work of Jacob Neusner and his students, particularly on Jewish religion in the talmudic era, has brought this entire agenda to the forefront of Jewish scholarship.

all the relevant biblical and rabbinic texts, all the liturgies, the historical background of the day, its theology, the laws that pertain to its observance, and reams of homiletical material. But what I don't know—what I was never taught at the Seminary—is what difference this entire experience is supposed to make for my congregants out there? How is it all supposed to affect them, transform them, make them different at the end of the day than they were at the beginning? How am I supposed to translate and to transmit the meaning of this experience in terms of their existential situation?''

To officiate at a funeral, then, is more than a matter of saying the right words and making the right gestures. It is to address the issue of our mortality. To officiate at a wedding is to address the issue of love, intimacy, and sexuality. To visit a hospital bed is to address suffering and pain. To preach on Yom Kippur is to speak of anxiety, guilt, and the possibilities of growth and rebirth. What does Judaism have to say about any of these existential issues? More important, what does it have to say to a community of modern American Jews? And how are these messages to be transmitted in the endlessly varied settings in which a rabbi participates?

No one questioned the Seminary faculty's mastery of the academic disciplines of Judaism. But it is one thing to teach the historical setting(s) of the book of Isaiah with minute attention to the textual variants, the higher critical apparatus, and the plain-sense or literal meaning of the text. It is quite another thing to distill Isaiah's message for a contemporary congregation of Jews. The faculty did the first superbly well, but it generally avoided the second. That task would have required instructors to step out of their academic role, to put themselves into the text, to speak out of their own existential situations, as one human being to another, or as one "religious" Jew to another. Whatever the original function of the strong textual orientation of the seminary curriculum, it was clearly serving a secondary, and (from the instructors' perspective) welcome, purpose as well: It allowed them to distance themselves from their material and from their students. The text came between the two.

But now a host of new problems arose.

First, what is a "religious" Jew? What model are we trying to create? Some years ago, this author, reacting against the careless use of the term "spirituality" in Jewish circles, suggested that we can discern three different models of Jewish spirituality: the behavioral, the pietistic, and the intellectual. Each of these was proposed as an answer to the question: What does God demand of a Jew above all? Is it a certain behavioral pattern (obedience to the law), inwardness or intense emotion (as in mystical or Hasidic circles), or is it the intellect, study, the mind (as in Maimonides)?[11]

---

[11]Neil Gillman, ''Judaism and the Search for Spirituality,'' *Conservative Judaism* 38/2 (Winter 1985–1986): 5-18. It is worth noting in this context that the original version of this paper was delivered at a conference on the Future of the American Synagogue, funded by the Lilly Endowment, with the generous encouragement of its senior vice-president, Dr. Robert Lynn.

In retrospect, that inquiry seems to me to have been mislabeled. I fixed on the term *spirituality* out of an impatience with the current interest in that particular form of religious expression. I suggested that most Jews who preach "spiritual" Judaism assume a univocal definition of that term, what I identified as the "pietistic" model, and I then proceeded to question the exclusivity of that model in Judaism. I would have been more honest had I simply insisted that "spirituality" as it is popularly understood is not a Jewish value in the first place. Among other problems, it reflects a dualistic view of the world and of the human person, which normative Judaism has generally decried.

What I was searching for in that inquiry was, more accurately, a phenomenology of religious "authenticity" in Judaism. Who is the authentically religious Jew? The Jew who meticulously observes all of the laws? The Jew who feels God's presence most intensely? Or the Jew who devotes his life to the study of God's will? Of course, ideally all of these should come together, but in fact, they are usually in tension, and any one Jew usually feels most comfortable with one of the three over the other two.

But each of these models demands its own curriculum, its own set of educational strategies and pedagogical techniques, a distinct faculty, and a school with a distinct culture. Is it possible to get a faculty to agree on any one of these models? My sense is that in the traditionalist academies referred to above, there is a general agreement on the supremacy of the behavioral model of authenticity. The other two models are not ignored, of course, but then alternative models of this kind rarely are. We are dealing with emphases, not exclusivities.

But without this agreement on educational goals, little in the way of Jewish religious education can take place. And it is quite clear that such a consensus will be much more difficult to arrive at in a faculty that is selected primarily for its academic excellence, not for its religious commitments, and particularly in a school that takes a highly nonintrusive stance toward its faculty's private lives.

What further complicates the issue, then, are three longstanding cornerstones of the Seminary's mission: its commitment to academic excellence, its insistence on measuring that achievement by the canons of the American academic community, and its commitment to an essentially academic model of the rabbinate.

It is well-nigh impossible to overestimate the power of these three commitments in the culture of the Seminary. On the first, a simple glance at the roster of names—Solomon Schechter, Louis Ginsberg, Alexander Marx, Saul Lieberman, Mordecai Kaplan, Shalom Spiegel, Abraham Joshua Heschel, and still among the living, Louis Finkelstein, H. L. Ginsberg, David Weiss Halivni, and Gerson Cohen, just to single out a few from the prior generations—confirms what was frequently repeated in Seminary circles: "The cardinal Seminary sin is shoddy scholarship."

On the second, not only the Hebrew Scriptures but also the Talmud was taught in rabbinical school classes with all of the methods of lower (textual) and higher (source or documentary) criticism.[12] The application of these methods to Scripture is hazardous enough, but their application to talmudic literature is even more potentially heretical.

In Judaism it is not so much the *peshat* or plain-sense of the biblical text that carries religious value but rather its talmudic interpretation. The Sabbath, for example, as it is concretized in the life experience of the Jew, is hardly a biblical institution. It is the Talmud that defines what constitutes the modes of work that are to be avoided, that stipulates the liturgies that are to be recited and the rituals that are to be performed, and that weaves the metaphorical web (Sabbath as Queen, Sabbath as Bride) that makes the observance of the day such a rich experience. To suggest that the talmudic elaboration of the Sabbath law from its biblical and early rabbinic sources is marked by serious gaps and ambiguities and that the later codifications of this legal material may well reflect misunderstandings of the earlier rabbinic sources themselves;[13] that specific laws may reflect sociological or economic influences;[14] that the very methods of talmudic exegesis of Scripture were

---

[12]To be precise, all of the Hebrew Scriptures *except* the Pentateuch were taught critically from the outset. From what I have been able to glean through a perusal of Seminary Registers, it was not until 1959 that the Pentateuch itself was taught in this manner as well. The issue is somewhat obscure, but my sense is that there was a generalized reluctance to apply critical scholarship to the Pentateuchal text, first, presumably because of its heightened sanctity (why is not clear since no one was willing to address the issue of revelation), and second, because the entire enterprise of higher biblical criticism was thought to reflect an implicit anti-Jewish bias. (It should not be forgotten that it was not until the middle of this century that Jewish scholars joined the enterprise.) E.g., in 1903, one year after assuming the presidency of the Seminary, Solomon Schechter delivered an address entitled "Higher Criticism—Higher Anti-Semitism," published in his *Seminary Addresses and Other Papers,* 35-40. Until 1959, either mastery of the Pentateuch was an entrance requirement, or the text was taught with the traditional, medieval exegetes. The turnabout, when it came—again, this is a matter of speculation—was due, possibly, to a growing sense of the incongruity of distinguishing between the Pentateuch and the rest of Hebrew Scripture, and also to the gradual dissemination of the work of the Israeli Bible scholar Yehezkel Kaufmann, whose multivolume *Toledot HaEmunah HaYisraelit* (Tel Aviv: Bialik Institute-Dvir, 1937–1956), trans. and abridged by Moshe Greenberg, *The Religion of Israel* (Chicago: The University of Chicago Press, 1960), used all of the higher-critical apparatus without its presumed anti-Jewish bias. Kaufmann quickly became required reading in all Seminary Bible classes.

[13]This is the thrust of the ground-breaking talmudic scholarship of David Weiss Halivni in his *Megorot UeMesorot (Sources and Traditions)*, 4 vols. (Tel Aviv: Dvir, 1968, 1975, 1982). Halivni's most recent and most thorough English exposition of his method is in *Midrash, Mishnah, and Gemara: The Jewish Predilection for Justified Law* (Cambridge MA: Harvard University Press, 1986). Ch. 2 of this book was published as "The Early Period of Halakhic Midrash," *Tradition* 22/1 (Spring 1986): 37-58. Some sense of the discomfort Halivni's method engenders for the traditionalist can be gleaned from Emanuel Feldman's "The Halakhic Midrash: A Rejoinder," *Tradition* 22/4 (Winter 1987): 65-74.

[14]This is the thesis of Louis Finkelstein, *The Pharisees: The Sociological Background of Their Faith,* 3rd ed. with suppl. (Philadelphia: The Jewish Publication Society of America, 1962).

borrowed from Hellenistic exegetes of Homeric literature[15]—all without engaging in the "reconstruction" of the text as sacred literature—can only play havoc with the religious sensibilities of students. And then, to insist that despite all of this classroom experience, rabbinical students and their congregants-to-be are expected to observe and teach the Sabbath law as binding simply compounds the confusion.

It should also be noted that the Seminary faculty has always enjoyed total academic freedom, as befits an American academic institution. Mordecai Kaplan, for example, whose naturalist reinterpretation of Judaism and its programmatic implications were very much at odds with the ideology of the leadership of the school and of just about all of his colleagues, nevertheless taught his own material to rabbinical students for more than five decades. When he left, it was at his request. It was not uncommon for the Seminary to invite a prominent, secularist Israeli scholar to serve as visiting professor in Rabbinical School classes, providing, of course, that his scholarship was beyond reproach.

The third of these cornerstone commitments—the commitment to an academic model of the rabbinate—flowed naturally from the first two. Almost to a person, the Seminary faculty embraced the intellectualist model of authenticity referred to above. In the culture of the Seminary, the model Jew was the scholar, the best of rabbinical students were to be encouraged to enter academia, and only those who could not make it in the academic world would enter the congregational rabbinate. The hierarchy was well nigh explicit, and on occasion, it even led to a sly disparagement of the accoutrements of the rabbinic role. Certain interpretations of biblical texts, for example, would be dismissed, in class, as "sermons." (Gratefully, this kind of innuendo has just about totally disappeared.)

But even the congregational-rabbi-to-be was expected to be a well-grounded generalist in Judaica. Thus the heavily academic texture of the curriculum, the relegation of professional skills courses to its periphery, the refusal to consider "soft-core" subjects such as the sociology of the Jewish community or congregational studies as worthy of course time. In fact, the Seminary's academic emphasis, particularly its emphasis on the mastery of the Hebrew language and of talmudic texts,

---

[15]See Saul Lieberman's "Rabbinic Interpretation of Scripture" in *Hellenism and Jewish Palestine* (New York: The Jewish Theological Seminary of America, 1950) 47-67. Lieberman was the dean of Seminary talmudists from 1940 until his death in 1983 and was generally acknowledged to be the outstanding talmudic scholar of his generation. For a broader application of the thesis that talmudic Judaism was shaped by its Hellenistic setting, see Elias Bickerman, *From Ezra to the Last of the Maccabees* (New York: Schocken, 1962). An extension of Bickerman's thesis through the rest of Jewish history is elaborated in Gerson D. Cohen, *The Blessing of Assimilation in Jewish History* (Boston: Boston Hebrew Teacher's College, 1966). Cohen served as chancellor of the Seminary from 1972 until 1986.

was one of the qualities that would distinguish it from the Hebrew Union College, whose graduates, it was believed, were never exposed to this intensive training.

If it is impossible to overestimate the power of these three basic Seminary commitments, it is equally clear how much they militate against any simplistic definition of what religious education might look like in a setting of this kind. It may be possible to claim that the faculty's commitment to scholarship in the scientific mode was, in fact, a modern transformation of the intellectualist model of religious authenticity and that these scholars' inquiries were as much a religious quest as those of the traditional exegetes,[16] but that understanding was rarely apparent to their students, hardly ever emerged in the actual classroom experience, and was never explicitly articulated or defined. Finally, the exclusivity of this model in Seminary faculty circles served to distance those rabbinical students who did not share that model.

Despite these obstacles, within the past decade the issue of the religious dimension of rabbinic education has become *the* Seminary issue, addressed in faculty meetings and in student forums, discussed at length in the self-evaluation material that was prepared for our 1986 reaccreditation process, and again and again in classroom settings. Most important, it has led to a thorough revision of the curriculum of the Rabbinical School, which began to take effect in the 1989-1990 academic year. There is also well-nigh universal agreement that these changes must never be bought at the price of sacrificing the schools' strong academic orientation, the academic superiority of its faculty, its commitment to critical scholarship, or its academic model of the rabbi. The school will never abide that, nor should it be asked to. The culture of the Seminary is firmly established and generally esteemed, and besides, if anything, the scholarly demands that the lay community is making of its rabbis today are higher than ever before. Almost all American lay Jews now have a college education; large numbers of them are competent professionals or academicians. They expect their rabbis to be masters of their field, as they are of theirs.

But this new model will make unprecedented demands of the faculty. It will lead, in particular, to a significant reassessment of the authority structure in the classroom. The classic curricular structure, particularly its strong textual emphasis, invested instructors with clear and unambiguous authority. Their mastery of their disciplines, of the texts and tools required to read them, served as their power base.[17] The educational enterprise that followed was inherently infantilizing. In

---

[16]I expand on this claim in my ''Judaism and the Search for Spirituality.'' See n. 11 above.

[17]William Bean Kennedy's ''Toward an Ideological Critique of Theological Education in North America,'' submitted to a Consultation on Doing Theology in Diverse Contexts, sponsored by the Programme on Theological Education of the World Council of Churches, Prague, 21-25 June 1988, and to be published in the report of that consultation, is a stunning dissection of the power structure of much of current theological education. I am grateful to Professor Kennedy for having shared his paper with me.

fact, one of the mysteries of the old style of rabbinic education is that it used an infantilizing educational experience to create an authority figure. Not unexpectedly, the graduates of this structure transposed it to the congregational setting, except that now, they did the infantilizing. Just look at the design of the large, suburban "cathedral" synagogue: The rabbi stands in front of and above the congregants who are literally imprisoned below in long, immobile pews, who sit, stand, turn to the proper page, read in English or in Hebrew, in unison or responsively—all in response to their rabbi's instructions—and who listen quietly and passively to the sermon that is preached "to" them.[18]

The new setting demands that instructors go beyond the explication of the text and expose their own personal struggle with its existential significance. There is no questioning the leveling of the authority structure that ensues whenever this takes place. The classroom becomes the arena for shared inquiry. To the extent that the faculty is transmitting the mastery of a discipline, its authority remains intact, but when it steps out of that traditional role and begins to wrestle with issues of meaning, its authority rests more in its prior engagement in a process than in any form of mastery. That enterprise is infinitely more hazardous. It requires a readiness to be personal, to put one's own agenda, feelings, achievements, and failures into the arena, to change one's mind, to explore, retreat, advance again, frequently without a clear vision of the outcome. It demands a good deal of charity and an ability to live with the possibility that there may be a number of equally tentative and legitimate outcomes to the inquiry. In short, it represents a new and anxiety-making experience.

This process does not have to take place in every class, nor should every instructor be expected to engage in it. But it has to take place somewhere, and the curriculum of the Rabbinical School, *from the outset,* has to be shaped around those settings where it is *designed* to take place—not as an appendix to a lecture, or as an afterthought, or in extracurricular discussion groups, but at the heart of the teaching process itself. That is what distinguishes the curriculum of a rabbinical school from that of a graduate school.

This transformation of the authority structure in the Rabbinical School will lead to a similar and parallel transformation in the congregation. In fact, this transformation is already taking place—for example in the emergence of the new *havurah*-style setting for worship (worship takes place in a library or classroom, seats are movable and all on the same level, intimacy and community are encouraged, the service is democratic and participatory) and in the replacement of the tradi-

---

[18]I elaborate on this thesis in my contribution to the symposium, "Entering the Second Century: From Scholarship to the Rabbinate," *Proceedings of the Rabbinical Assembly* (1986): 41-46. Of course, we should not be deceived about the rabbi's vaunted authority, for the congregation retains the authority to hire and dismiss its rabbi.

tional sermon with a question-and-answer session or discussion of the biblical readings, with the rabbi asking questions and *listening,* as well as speaking.

IV

Finally, on the substantive issue itself, I can do no more—or no less—here than what I attempt to do in the classroom, which is to trace how I myself struggle to resacralize my tradition without sacrificing the critical perspective that remains precious to me.[19]

My teachers in this enterprise have been Clifford Geertz, Paul Tillich, and James Fowler. Geertz's "Religion as a Cultural System" remains the single most impressive attempt to capture what a religious perspective on the world is designed to accomplish, namely, to formulate "conceptions of a general order of existence" through a system of symbols that engender "powerful, pervasive and long-lasting moods and motivations." Tillich's *Dynamics of Faith* opened my eyes to the structure of the act of faith and the indispensability and power of religious/theological symbols and myths. Finally, Fowler's *Stages of Faith* made it possible for me to understand my own theological journey—in particular, how I was able to move from his Stage 4 to Stage 5, from the Individuative-Reflective Faith of my Seminary years and after, to the Conjunctive Faith that I am now trying to teach, or, in Tillich's language, to affirm Torah as the classical and authoritative formulation of a broken, but very much living, myth.

This crossroad between Fowler's Stages 4 and 5, the focus of this entire inquiry, is precisely where most of my students are stuck. I understand my task as the attempt to get them over this hurdle, to convey to them the full exhilaration and liberating power of Paul Ricoeur's "second naivete."[20]

I am most clearly aware of this sense of liberation when I deal with the issue of God in Jewish theology. For reasons that should be obvious by now, the discomfort that most Conservative rabbis feel when asked to preach or teach the Jewish concept(s) of God is amply justified. Looking back at my own teaching experience, I now understand that though I have always taught the classical Jewish literature on God, that is all that I did. I taught it at a distance: the classical

---

[19]For other attempts to address this issue, see the contributions of my colleagues Barry W. Holtz, Joseph Lukinsky, and Ivan G. Marcus to *The Seminary at 100: Reflections on The Jewish Theological Seminary and the Conservative Movement,* ed. Nina Beth Cardin and David Wolf Silverman (New York: The Rabbinical Assembly and The Jewish Theological Seminary of America, 1987) 195-204, 205-14, and 215-22 respectively; and Lawrence A. Hoffman, "Jewish Knowledge: Redrawing the Map," *Conservative Judaism* 38/2 (Winter 1985–1986): 36-43.

[20]For Fowler's discussion of Stage 5 and Ricoeur's "second" or "willed naivete" see *Stages of Faith* (San Francisco: Harper & Row, 1981) 184-98.

proofs, the experiential and existential approaches; Maimonides and mystics on God; Heschel, Buber, and Kaplan on God; and the rest. It was a safe, academic exercise.

More recently, I have begun to teach the Jewish concept of God as a complex system of symbols that changes and evolves before our very eyes— I have used the metaphor of a kaleidoscope—as we move from Genesis through the prophets, the Psalms, Job, and the rest of the Bible, the talmudic *aggadah*, the classical liturgy, and the later philosophical and mystical literature to our very day.

To speak of God as an evolving symbolic system permits me to ask a host of new questions: Why these symbols and not others? Why one God and not two or more? Why the masculine imagery and not the feminine? Why is God portrayed as creating? as revealing? as redeeming? Why do some of these symbols persist and others die? Why does the system change? Why, for example, is the God of the early Genesis narratives so quick to punish while the God of the prophets is so patient and eager for repentance? And why is God so vulnerable, so caring, so frustrated, so incapable either of achieving God's goals or of abandoning them, despite God's vaunted power? Why the difference between the harshness of the Samuel-Saul encounter in I Samuel 15 and the pathos of the last verses of Jonah? Why is Job in the canon? What books did not make it, and why? What of the silences? And all of these questions increase and multiply as we move beyond the Bible to the later tradition.

Once the Jewish image of God is portrayed as a complex and evolving paradigm, not as what God is in some "essence" but rather as the way my ancestors read their experience or mapped their world, all of these questions become legitimate. And then I can also ask: Which of these symbols are alive for me today, which are not, and why? What can I appropriate and transmit, and what do I reject? Effectively, I do for myself what the authors of Job and Jonah did with their received tradition, and I invite my students to do the same. In that spirit, I no longer ask my students to write research papers. Instead, I require personal position papers on a variety of theological issues: God, revelation, eschatology, the problem of evil and the rest, and then subject these position papers to class discussion. The format demands that they be as personal in their writing as I am in my teaching.

This inquiry draws upon the best of modern critical scholarship. It retains its academic character. But it is also imbued throughout with issues of personal meaning, and the teaching experience itself becomes a model of doing theology.

Fowler claims that Stage 5 is "unusual before mid-life." That was true in my case, and it may account for the resistance of some students. We are all too painfully aware of the seductive quality of absolute systems and of our need for authoritarian models, whereas this approach puts a premium on individualism, pluralism, the inherently relative nature of all religious claims, personal responsibility, and extended periods of indecision as the process of appropriation and rejection works itself out. But many students have been able to emerge from the experience with a renewed sense of personal integrity and to begin their rabbinical careers with the confidence that their religious and intellectual commitments are at one. That integration, long the hallmark of rabbinic education in traditionalist settings, now reappears within a radically different and novel mind-set.

V

This exposition of Judaism as a complex symbolic/mythical system forces us to confront the twin issues of authority and authenticity in Judaism. Once we deny any literalist understanding of revelation and acknowledge the community's substantive role in shaping its content, these two issues acquire a new urgency. For, first, what criteria does the community invoke in determining if a particular reading of Judaism is, or is not, authentic? Obviously not fidelity to the original revelatory content, for that is also the creation of a community of Jews. But then what? And second, since we have no ultimate authoritative body to pass on contemporary theological statements, who decides? Even more pressing for this conceptualization that accepts the inevitability of theological individualism, how does the community exercise its function?

I now address these issues in class by using the classroom inquiry model that I have sketched above as a paradigm for how Jews have dealt with them in the past. My theological assumptions are grounded in some well-established traditions that acknowledge the indeterminacy of meaning of the revelation at Sinai. According to one of these, at Sinai the divine voice was split into seventy voices, one for each of the seventy nations of the world;[21] according to another, mystical tradition, the divine voice was heard differently by each of the 600,000 Jews present at the foot of the mountain.[22] An even more radical suggestion is conveyed by Gershom Scholem in the name of Rabbi Mendel of Rymanov, who claimed that all that was revealed at Sinai was the *aleph*, the first letter of *anokhi*, the first Hebrew word of the Decalogue. Scholem notes that the *aleph* is nothing more than the position taken by the larynx when a word begins with vowel. "To hear the *aleph*," Scholem continues, "is to hear next to nothing; it is the preparation for all audible language, but in itself conveys no determinate, specific meaning. Thus . . . Rabbi Mendel transformed the revelation on Mount Sinai into a mystical revelation, pregnant with infinite meaning, but without specific meaning."[23]

But despite this indeterminacy of meaning, as the process of canonization worked itself out, what emerged from Sinai was one sacred text. Certain readings

---

[21]*Midrash Exodus Rabbah* 5:9.

[22]Quoted by Scholem, *On the Kabbalah and Its Symbolism* (New York: Schocken Books, 1965) 65.

[23]Ibid., 30. The first two chapters of this volume constitute an extended discussion of the authority of Torah in Jewish mystical circles.

of revelation were accepted, others rejected; certain documents were considered authoritative, others not; certain books were canonized, others not. The dynamics of the process are lost, but if it was not the work of God, then it had to be the work of the community. Of its "leadership"? Perhaps—but then it is the community who vests its leadership with the authority to make these decisions.

Still later that sacred text itself becomes subject to multiple interpretations. Paradigmatically, look at a page from the *Migraot Gedolot* (literally, the "large Scriptures"), the authoritative, published version of the Hebrew Scriptures. The layout of each double page includes a few verses of the scriptural text, and surrounding them, two Aramaic translations, five medieval commentaries, and another five supercommentaries. Effectively, then, we read Scripture through the eyes of our ancestors, and we can choose from among them— either the eleventh-century Frenchman Rashi (acronym for Rabbi Solomon ben Isaac) for the literal meaning mingled with an anthology of rabbinic homilies, or Rashi's student, the twelfth-century Samuel ben Meir, or the twelfth-century Spaniard Abraham Ibn Ezra for a philological perspective, or the thirteenth-century Spaniard Moses ben Nachman for more mystical or philosophical insights, or the late fifteenth-century Italian Obadiah ben Jacob Seforno for a more scientific or critical perspective. All of these varied voices are on the page, all in dialogue with one another, all offering different perspectives on the text—which remains one and singular. But again, who determined which of these exegeses made it onto the page, if not the community—simply by the process of deciding who it would read and who it would ignore?[24]

Catch the tension, then, between individual and community, between unity and diversity: one God, one prophet (Moses), but multiple revelatory voices; one Scripture but multiple interpretations; one community but multiple understandings of the text.[25]

And if the criterion for authenticity is neither fidelity to God's will nor to the original revelatory content, then we have no alternative but to appeal to the criteria we use to determine mythic truth. A myth is true if it does the things that great myths have always done: open up levels of reality that are otherwise closed to us, unlock hidden dimensions of our own being, explain how our experience of the world "hangs together," help us cope with the predictable and unpredictable crises of living, stimulate loyalty to our community, give us a sense of rootedness or belonging in the world.[26] A vital, living community in an almost intuitive way will

---

[24]I am grateful to my colleague Professor Edward Greenstein for this insight into the layout of the published text of the Bible.

[25]I am echoing here a striking rabbinic homily on Eccles. 12:11, in Bab. Tal. Tractate *Hagigah*, 3a-3b.

[26]My expansion of Tillich's discussion of the functions of symbols in religion in *Dynamics of Faith*, 42-43.

screen out those readings of revelation that fail to accomplish these purposes and retain those that do. The process is subtle, complex, messy, anxiety-filled, and it may take generations to work itself out—and the committed traditionalist will shun this portrayal like the plague—but for many of us, it is the only way.

Finally, who decides? Everyone—that is, every Jew who has a stake in the outcome, which is nothing less than the continued vitality of Judaism as a religion.[27]

The classroom inquiry is a microcosm of that process. On any one issue, I begin by teaching what I consider to be the most significant options available from within the tradition, and then proceed to teach how I deal with these options in working out my own position. Students then write their own personal statements, and the inquiry comes to a focus in those sessions where a number of these papers are circulated to the entire class for open class critique. In the course of the discussion, positions are clarified, modified, reformulated, and sometimes abandoned. My goal is to enable each student to emerge from the course with a coherent, defensible, personal theology. The interplay between the individual student and the class becomes the paradigm for what transpires in the community at large.

I have been urging my students to use this model as a way of teaching Jewish theology in their own congregational settings. My sense is that our lay people have theological concerns and are capable of serious thought, provided they are given the resources and a modicum of encouragement and legitimation. That sense of legitimacy is absolutely crucial to Fowler's Stage 5, but rabbis will never be able to transmit it to their congregants unless they have it themselves. That achievement remains the key test of an effective rabbinic education.

---

[27]A more extended discussion of all of these issues is in my "Authority and Authenticity in Jewish Philosophy," *Judaism* 35/2 (Spring 1986): 223-32.

7

The Tragic Dilemma
of Church Education

Edward Farley

However different their approaches, church educators agree that religious education is formative. The formation (nurturing, socializing) of Christians is education's primary aim. While this consensus appears to be a modern and Christian version of education as *paideia,* its offspring in contemporary Christian congregations is unimpressive. Formation and socialization are formal traits of the total effect of a tradition and an institution on its participants. Once church education emptied itself of rigorous and ordered learning by handing it over to clergy or "theological" education, it had to settle for education as a mere shadow and distant reflection of ordered learning.[1] The reigning consensus that education is Christian formation helps the churches hide from themselves the uncomfortable fact that they promote an education that does not educate. Church education, in other words, occurs in a never-never land between a program of ordered learning (for example, public schools, clergy education) and the general formative influence of everything the church is and does. Thus what it is and does has little distinctive character. Present-day church education is entrapped in another way as well: in its attempt to serve and promote both the demands of popular piety (and with that, the social vitality of the church) and the reality of faith. This dilemma of church education, which creates a tension that is constant but rarely remarked, is the focus for this essay.

Church Education in Service of Popular Piety

There appears to be an open and shut case for church education's primary aim. This aim is to promote and maintain the popular piety (or religiosity) that is the necessary condition for the vitality of actual religion. Prior to and through the early

---

[1]Education as ordered learning means a process over time whose cumulative effect is to produce or discipline a skill or an already existing way of interpreting something. See the author's "Can Church Education Be Theological Education?" *Theology Today* 42 (Summer 1985): 158-71.

twentieth century, the mainline Protestant denominations, the "Protestant Establishment," had social vitality because they embodied a living, serious popular piety. Drawing on a similar store of piety, present-day "evangelical" movements have moved from a marginal to a central position in the United States.[2] In both cases, church education has existed to serve, not challenge, popular piety. It has assisted the transmission of the mythology, belief-system, casuistry, and even emotional ethos of that piety. Embodied in and promoted by the educational programs have been the convictions and messages that sent impassioned missionaries to the North American frontier and to various parts of the world. Education has reinforced the sentimental popular hymns, the Jesusolatry, the verse-quoting biblicism, and the prescientific cosmology that carried these convictions. The lesson seems clear: The very vitality of a religious faith is endangered if church education does anything other than support and confirm the passions of popular piety.

This open-and-shut case becomes more evident when we consider the shift now taking place in North American Protestantism. The decline of the mainline denominations in population, vitality, and national influence coincides with the demise of the popular piety that had been their very heart and soul.[3] This erosion seems to have something to do with what some would regard as a desirable trait of these denominations, their openness to cultural influence, to the world of public schools, to the sciences, to democratic values, to nonauthoritarian forms of sociality, and to a more pluralistic posture. These traits appeared in these denominations in the form of ecumenism, commitment to theological education, and socially liberal bureaucracies. The result was that popular piety (nonecumenical, nonpluralistic, nonrelativistic) was pushed to the margins of these churches, the so-called "evangelical wings" of the denominations. Among the leadership and general population of these churches, popular piety was displaced by a commitment to religion in general and a syncretistic culture-religion mix.[4]

---

[2]See Dean Kelley, *Why Conservative Churches Are Growing: A Study in Sociology of Reliion* (San Francisco: Harper & Row, l972; ROSE ed., Macon GA: Mercer University Press, 1986) and W. C. Roof and W. McKinney, *American Mainline Religion: Its Changing Shape and Future* (Rutgers NJ: Rutgers University Press, 1987).

[3]In a small, popular work written about twenty years ago, I described a shift in popular piety or religiosity going on in American mainline denominations that was toward what Dean Kelley calls "leniency." This shift is a decay of vital piety. See *Requiem for a Lost Piety: The Contemporary Search for the Christian Life* (Philadelphia: Westminster, l966).

[4]From the 1960s to the present, religious and culture historians and social analysts such as Gibson Winter, Martin Marty, Peter Berger, Robert Bellah, and Phillip Rieff have described the rise of an amorphous, culturally syncretistic religion in North American that is other than but that pervades Judaism, Catholicism, and Protestantism. See, for instance, Peter Berger's *The Sacred Canopy: Elements of a Sociological Theory of Religion* (Garden City NY: Doubleday, 1971); Martin Marty, *The New Shape of American Religion* (New York: Harper & Row, l959); and Robert Bellah, *Beyond Belief: Essays on Religion in a Post-Traditional World* (San Francisco: Harper & Row, l970).

This mix of civil and therapeutic religion may be the "Arminianism" of to-day. Powerful forces of modernity have been at work in the larger culture for centuries. As mainline Protestantism became culturally open rather than culturally closed, its popular piety merged with and was displaced by the quasi-religious civil pieties of the larger culture. Along with this displacement came a change in the function of church education. Church education shifted at the level of its basic aim from promoting traditional, popular piety to promoting civil and therapeutic piety.[5] This shift exemplifies what looks like a sociological principle. A religious faith loses its social vitality when its popular piety erodes or is displaced. Thus, the open-and-shut case for church education's primary aim is clear. That aim must be to transmit, promote, and support the popular piety of actual religion. To borrow from Martin Luther, church education "can do no other."

Popular Piety and the Vitality of Religion

The recent decline and displacement of mainline Protestantism by forms of Protestantism in which traditional popular piety survives indicates a relation between vital piety and social vitality. The social "weakness" of mainline Protestant denominations and the social "strength" of evangelical movements add up to a historical case for church education's primary aim, the promotion of popular piety. The phenomenology and sociology of religion tend to corroborate the open-and-shut historical case that a religion's educational programs must promote its popular piety. At work in our historical example is something structural and perennial in religion itself.

What is popular piety? We must be clear that what is under consideration is not what recent studies are calling "popular religion."[6] This term names a reli-

---

[5] Some curricular efforts in mainline denominations were heroic attempts to place a nontherapeutic content at the core of church education. One thinks of both the *Faith and Life* curriculum of the Presbyterian Church, U.S.A., and the *Covenant Life* curriculum of the Presbyterian Church, U.S. These efforts were relatively short-lived and did not stem the tide of therapeutic religion beginning to shape the mainline denominations.

[6] In most of the recent literature popular religion names an "extra-ecclesiastical symbolic activity . . . carried on outside the formal structures provided by most societies for such activity." Peter Williams, *Popular Religion in America: Symbolic Change and the Modernization Process in Historical Perspective* (Englewood Cliffs NJ: Prentice-Hall, 1980). Popular religion, in other words, refers to an underside of official or conventional religion and its existence is an indication of the inability of conventional religion to be an adequate framework of religious expression for a certain group of people. Examples of popular religion in this sense are the popular Catholicism of present-day Latin American countries, the Jesus movement of the 1970s, and the electronic church of the 1980s. Latin American popular Catholicism seems to be one of the first such movements studied in recent decades. Conferences were held on the subject at Medillin in 1968 and in Quebec in 1970. For the

gious movement that occurs in dependence on, yet in tension with, official or established religion. The Jesus movement of the 1960s and the charismatic movements in the mainline denominations occurred over against the institutions, literatures, leadership, and programs of the established denominations. Popular piety is a feature, I would say, the driving dynamism, of any actual religion, established or not.[7]

Quebec conference, see B. Lacroix and P. Boglioni, eds., *Les Religion Populaires* (Laval, Quebec: University of Laval, 1972). For an early study of popular religion in America, see Louis Schneider and S. W. Dornbusch, *Popular Religion, Inspirational Books in America* (Chicago: University of Chicago Press, 1968). Nor should popular religion be taken as a synonym for *folk religion*. For various meanings of folk religion see P. Vrijhof and J. Waardenburg, eds., *Official Religion and Popular Religion* (The Hague: Mounton, 1979), "Introduction." If folk religion is used to define the religion of a nonliterate people (Vrijhof and Waardenburg) or religion of a discrete people (Kuenens), then popular religion names something else. Abraham Kuenen's Hibbert lectures of 1892 argue and explore the difference between national religions (*Volksreligionen*) and universal religions. The matter is confused by some authors who use the terms *folk religion* and *popular religion* interchangeably. For instance, Segundo Galilea, "The Theology of Liberation and the Place of 'Folk Religion,' " in M. Eliade and D. Tracy, eds., *What Is Religion: An Inquiry for Christian Theology* (New York: Seabury, 1980).

[7]The recent literature on popular religion is somewhat confusing on this point. Many of the features that describe popular religion, features of a vital, rebellious, antithetic movement within or on the margins of conventional religion, also describe any vital religion. Thus, for instance, Michel Meslin characterizes popular religion as a relation to the sacred in the mode of simplicity, immediacy (with little institutional machinery), and with a focus on utility and effectiveness. See "Le phenomene religieux populaire" in Lacroix, *Les Religion Populaires*, 5. Other traits proposed in the literature are certitude, concrete mediations, the primacy of feeling, group loyalty, and commitment. In the light of such a list, one wonders what a phenomenology of *religion* itself would yield. Either popular religion is religion itself, in which case it is not a contrast term to official religion, or it is a form of religion that rebels against but is dependent on conventional religion in which case these features are not distinguishing marks. Without denying the distinction between popular religious movements and "conventional religion," I find more adequate an approach that not only acknowledges that the traits of popular religion are traits of any vital or strong religion as such but discerns a cycle at work in the origin and duration of a religion. Thus, a religion's originating movement or period of creation (Christianity, Mormonism, Wesleyanism, Pali Buddhism) shows a certain kind of vitality and has the traits of popular religion. This is the case because a religion is always a correction of some sort, a new vision, a polemic against an existing and encrusted religious institutionality that has become conventional, corrupt, "socially weak" (Kelley). If the movement survives at all, it will itself become institutionally and socially established, thus inviting new invigorating corrections. This happened to Christianity, Buddhism, Wesleyanism, Mormonism, etc., and I would think that it will also happen to those present evangelical and charismatic movements that show signs of social vitality. Dean Kelley is instructive here. What some students call the features of popular religion, he sees as traits of socially strong or vital religion in contrast to "weak" religious movements. For the cyclic view, see Linda K. Pritchard, "Religious Change in Nineteenth-Century America," in R. Bellah and C. Glock, eds., *The New Religious Consciousness* (Berkeley and Los Angeles: University of California Press, 1976)

An actual religion—whether native African religion, diaspora Judaism, or medieval Christianity—originates, endures, and spreads as a piety. There is a redundancy here, for piety simply means a specific religiousness. It names religion as a way of life rooted in deep commitments that reach the emotions and determine loyalties and convictions. To say someone is religious is to say these things. To say that a corporate phenomenon is a religion is to say that its participants relate to each other in and through these convictions. Popular piety or religiousness forms as the perpetual problematic dimensions of human life (suffering, mortality, evil, societal ordering, cosmic meaning) are experienced as shaped by sacred power. What is at stake is not the trivial, the contingent, the ephemeral, but the condition or set of conditions of what is perceived to be most important: life itself, the fulfillment of deep desires, salvation. Religion, in other words, is always a kind of passion.

This is what is behind the foremost subjective feature of popular piety, the posture of *certainty*.[8] The language of qualification, degrees, tentativeness is not the language of the religious cultus. Jews do not say that approximately five-ninths of the Torah comes from God. Christians do not confess that Jesus probably died to save them from sin.

A second feature of popular piety is *cosmologizing*.[9] The realities that popular piety voices are not only *the* realities. They constitute the real world, and they unify the world. However metaphorical and narrational their form of expression, they come together into a way of grasping the temporal and spatial structures of the world. Resurrection, cross, creation, heaven, soul-body, angels, Satan, and God may be metaphors, but in popular piety they are also cosmic realities.

The third feature of popular piety is *casuistry*.[10] In addition to cosmologizing the way in which the sacred shapes the world, religious persons need their every-

---

298. See also Ernst Henau, "Popular Religiosity as Christian Faith," in N. Grenacher and N. Mette, eds., *Popular Religion* (Edinburgh: T. & T. Clarke, 1986), who sees religion as the "indispensable stage on the way to the formation of the Christian sense of the sacred" (74).

[8]Robert Towler offers a strong case for certainty as central to popular religiosity or piety. His approach is to study the place and role of certitude in various types of religion and his thesis is that certitude as the absence of doubt is the "corporate style" of popular religion. *The Need for Certainty: A Sociological Study of Conventional Religion* (London: Routledge and Kegan Paul, 1984) 108.

[9]Drawing on the work of Alfred Schutz and using methods of sociology of knowledge and social world analyses, Peter Berger sees religion as a specific instance of what all societies do, engage in world construction. This imposition of an order of some sort, a meaning-framework, he calls "nomizing" (cf., the Greek term for law, *nomos*). Religion, then, is "the human enterprise by which a sacred cosmos is established." *The Sacred Canopy*, 26.

[10]According to Dean Kelley, one of the features of a socially strong or vital religious movement is the presence of "controls" by which conformity to the group's aims is assured. *Why Conservative Churches*, ch. 5. These are the sanctions and reinforcements that

day lives ordered by and under the sacred. The covenant code, taboos, halakha, cases of conscience, and the *Didache* all express piety's casuistical element.

Finally, popular piety requires specific vehicles of authorization for its cosmological and casuistical content. It calls for specific textual, event-ful, personal-charismatic, hierarchical *authorities* as trustworthy bearers of reality.[11] Jesus, the magisterium, the Bible, the Church Fathers, the Reformers, creeds all function in varying ways as authorizing. Certainty is the primary posture toward the religious cosmology, casuistry, and authority. And the authorizing authorities reinforce the posture of certainty.

In its individual mode, popular piety is a human *posture*, the way the self is directed toward things. In its collective mode, popular piety is a set of *institutional conditions* for the creation and perpetuation of piety. Thus, as a corporate reality, actual religion transmits and preserves its cosmology and casuistry in oral traditions or written texts and through institutional authorities responsible for their continued reinterpretation. Thus sedimented, institutionalized authority is the corporate counterpart of certainty.

What I am describing here is actual religion as an effective and vital movement. If actual religion as a popular piety does have the traits just described, it should be evident why these are conditions of strong social vitality. "Vitality" to

---

the religion requires of and communicates to its members. It is the element of discipline or behavioral rigor in religion. That period of the Christian movement that especially reflects the church's creation of a moral rigorism is the last part of the first century and the beginning of the second. This creation is one aspect of early "Catholicizing" of the Christian movement. The clearest example of the casuistical and rigorist accomplishment of this period is *The Teaching of the Apostles* or *Didache*, which is a manual for life in the church and in the world. A monumental study and history of the rigorist element in Christianity is Kenneth E. Kirk's *The Vision of God: The Christian Doctrine of the Summum Bonum* (London: Longmans, Green, 1931). Those religious movements in North America that are vital, growing, popular are also those able or willing to specify to their adherents concrete prohibitions and obligations. They are able and willing to require specific behaviors in relation to sexual activity, abortion, church attendance, Bible reading, prayer, the role of the wife and mother in the family, etc.

[11]Dean Kelley describes this feature under a more general category, communication. Thus, a religion can be socially vital only if communication is successful. I would make the point more specifically. From the perspective of individuals whose salvation is experienced in modes of passion and certainty and that orders their world and clarifies their obligations, there is a need to understand the basis of all this. The cosmology and casuistry are "true" because of their source in the sacred itself. But this is rarely if ever experienced as a direct mediation. Rather, it is experienced through an authorized representative of the sacred; a theophanous messenger, a sacred king, a prophet, a charismatic leader, a social-political structure (the papacy), a text (the Bible), etc. And while it may be the case that popular religious movements lay claim to a more direct mediation than what is transmitted through the authority structure of established religion (Meslin), they never eschew authorization and authority. However, their authority may be other than the official organization and its mediations. Thus, a new charismatic leader or new text replaces the conventional ones.

be sure is an imprecise notion.[12] Applied to a social entity or movement (a political party, an organization of hobbyists, a religious denomination), it refers to a certain high degree of loyalty and commitment the participants have toward the cause or movement, the success the movement has in fulfilling its own aims, the social "toughness" of the movement to survive in its larger historical situation, and its ability to grow where that is possible and appropriate.[13] Applying these criteria, we can say that second-century Christianity was a vital social movement and that the "religion of Numa," the ancient religion of Lares and Penates, was losing its vitality.

What is necessary to create the features of passionate commitment to the (religious) group or cause? It is only partly the presence of a passionate piety whose existential *certainty* discovers cosmological and casuistical expression. For these things themselves must successfully create their social counterparts; the deposit of casuistry in the corporate memory (texts, oral traditions), the structuring of the life of the group through a regulative *nomos,* and the ordering of that life under an authoritative leadership. On the other hand, these features of corporate life are not in themselves sufficient for a vital religious movement. Sedimented corporate memory, a casuistical tradition, and an established authority may all exist in a decaying religious movement. In a vital religious movement there is a close mutual influence between the passion and loyalty of the participants, between their "certainty" and the way the social features function.

Idolatry of the Sacred as the Condition of Religious Vitality

The following thesis will at first sight seem outrageous: *All actual religion is idolatrous.* Or this thesis can be seen as simply a banality. It can be taken as an acknowledgment that religion is not immune from human evil, that religion too should be added to the list of idolatrous human endeavors.[14] This approach can

---

[12]As I am using it, the term *vitality* is virtually identical with Kelley's concept of socially "strong" religion. *Why Conservative Churches.*

[13]Some social and religious movements may have vitality yet do not grow because the historical context does not permit growth. Thus, a tribal religion in Kenya or in Polynesia may not be a growing religion if there is no larger environment or population to grow into. Yet it may have all of the traits of social vitality.

[14]Two Protestant theologians of the first half of the twentieth century come to mind as proponents of the idolatrous character of religion. For Dietrich Bonhoeffer religion is a human framework, a trait of long-term historical epochs, and as such is not only surpassable but is not a necessary presupposition of faith and revelation. *Letters and Papers from Prison* (Glasgow: Fontana Books, 1959) 91ff. See also E. Bethge, *Dietrich Bonhoeffer* (New York: Harper & Row, 1970) 773ff. Karl Barth's case is stronger. Religion is a faithless human work, an unbelief, to be abolished by revelation. It has an explicit idolatrous character. See *Epistle to the Romans* (Oxford: Oxford University Press, 1933), ch. 4, vv. 9-12; and *Church Dogmatics* (Edinburgh: T. & T. Clarke, 1956) I, 2, #17, "The Revelation of God as the Abolition of Religion." See esp. 2., "Religion as unbelief and as idolatry."

then distinguish between the innocent "essence" of religion and its inevitable corruption. In the banal interpretation, idolatry is an accidental distortion on the margin of religion.[15]

Against this, it seems clear that the very vitality of religion requires in a necessary way an idolatry of the sacred. What does this mean? The thesis assumes the anti-idolatry tradition, versions of which we find in Israelite prophetism, the *via negativa* of Christian Neoplatonism, and German transcendental theology (Schleiermacher). According to that tradition, there can be no *identity* between the sacred and the realities (creation) subject to or dependent on the sacred. The sacred can be understood as related to, pervasive throughout, even incarnated in these realities but never *as* them.[16]

It goes without saying that all actual religions are historically and culturally specific. But what originates the idolatry of the sacred is not simply the inevitable cultural specificity of religion but rather what happens when the existential passion evoked by the sacred attaches itself in the mode of certainty to the cultural vehicles it requires. Thus, cosmologizing is not simply an attempt to order experience but is an ordering of space and time by means of appearances and acts of the sacred. The sacred is said, literally, to have "caused" or brought about the event (creation, flood, plague, vision). The identity posited here is not between the sacred and the caused entity but is rather in the concept of causality (intervention) itself. This literal causality draws the sacred into the world system and ren-

---

[15]The "essence of Christianity" tradition as it originates and is given shape by Schleiermacher promotes essence (*Wesen*) as something that occurs on the gradations of historical embodiments. Thus, religions where the sensible self-consciousness dominates the representation of the sacred occur as lower grades; religions moving beyond this are higher grades. The distinguishing element of all religion is piety (*Frommigkeit*) which is an "essential element in human nature," the dependence aspect or structure of the immediate self-consciousness (*Gefuhl*). The qualification (distortion) of this in actual religion is Schleiermacher's version of the idolatrous character of religion. However, the essence of the highest monotheistic religions has eliminated the idolatrous element. Hence, a tradition is created according to which Christianity as a religion is a fulfillment of essential piety. *The Christian Faith* (Edinburgh: T. & T. Clarke, 1928) #7-11. Feuerbach, on the other hand, de-idealizes the essence of Christianity by arguing that as history proceeded from an "objective" to a "subjective" understanding of religion's object, its development is toward idolatry, that is, worship of human being. And this is the fate and common nature of all religions. See *The Essence of Christianity* (New York: Harper Torchbooks) 13.

[16]In the Hebrew prophets this nonidentity is rooted in what Schleiermacher calls the teleological or moral character of the relation between God and the world. As righteous, God alone is the source and measure of the life and actions of all creatures. In Christian Neoplatonism and medieval theology, nothing can be identified with that through which it is or has its being. Schleiermacher argues that the referent of utter or absolute dependence experienced at the heart of the self (and which dependence is expanded to the total world system) can never be itself an aspect or entity in the world system to which our relation is always one of reciprocal influence, not absolute dependence.

ders it an "entity." Cosmologizing attaches the sacred to an experienced world phenomenon unanalogically and unmetaphorically, making it appear a caused intervention. We must be clear that what is under consideration here is the cosmologizing of popular piety, not the critical theological reaction to this that works to remove the posited identity. Similarly, a casuistry requires an identity between the world order and the sacred. Casuistry that occurs in the mode of subjective certainty and absolute institutional authority asserts that the sacred requires or forbids specific acts. Again, the posited identity is not between the acts and the sacred but between a content in the "mind" or "will" of the sacred and discerned mundane contents. For this certainty to be effective, the sacred must be thought of as psyche, as a type of intersubjective entity we experience in the mundane social order.[17]

These acts of idolatry follow popular piety into its social support system. Certainty about both cosmology and casuistry reaches beyond these things to that which makes them certain. This is not simply "revelation," "grace," or "the Spirit," but the specific historical and cultural locations and authorities that mediate them: texts, the Book, the hierarchical leadership. Here, too, an identity is posited, not between the sacred and the Book as such, or the sacred and the magisterium as such, but between the willful act and its content of the sacred and the functions, effects, and contents of these mediations. An identity is required between the sacred's agenda and the authority's agenda, if the authority does in fact locate and mediate the other (causal) identities. In popular piety certainty characterizes relation to all the things salvation depends on, and therefore the act of doubt cannot be simply piecemeal. To doubt a specific text, authority, or piece of cosmology (the cosmic sacrifice of the Son, the Second Coming) is to invite something into the house of popular piety that introduces decay of vitality.

To summarize, under consideration is *actual* religion, not religion ideally described or critically refined. And actual religion is always a specific cultural and social incorporation of the sacred, a social movement. This movement can be vital only to the degree that its participants' existential certainty of the sacred's edifying power (salvation) is so cosmologized and rendered into specific codes for living that it can endure and spread over time. And these acts of cosmologizing and casuistry, occurring under sedimented authorities and in the mode of certainty, re-

---

[17]Familiar are the criticisms of this or that aspect of popular piety as idolatry. Thus, we hear about "Jesusolatry," "bibliolatry," triumphalism, etc. These polemics mislead us into thinking that rendering the sacred into entity language and positing identities between the sacred and world system realities is an exceptional or rare act of actual religion. On the contrary, the idolatry of the sacred pervades all major themes of cosmologizing. Thus, identifying the sacred and the world order occurs in popular piety's way of understanding divine creating (a specific willed event a long time ago), God (a very comprehensive and powerful gathering of mental processes), providence (a series of intervening causes directed to illness, deaths, thunderstorms, etc.), revelation (a specific act of communicating information held originally in divine mental processes), and so forth.

quire a number of acts in which the sacred and something in the world order are identified.[18] In other words, vital, successful religion must *absolutize* the world order in order to experience and attest to the sacred.[19] Or to reverse the expression, all vital religion requires an idolatrous *mundanizing* of the sacred in order to take cultural root, survive, and grow. Lacking this, in other words, lacking popular piety, individual and social, no actual religion can exist. This is why idolatry is not marginal to an essentially innocent religion but is intrinsic to its very vitality.

If this is so, religion like other historical and human things has a tragic character.[20] Insofar as an account of religion stops with the theme of idolatry, its tragic structure will remain hidden, for there is nothing essentially tragic about idolatry. The tragic refers to something whose very being and existence requires interdependent elements that are in conflict with each other in such a way that the entity can realize its ideal and good aims only by promoting at the same time opposing and corrupting aims. Innocency and corruption are tragically interdependent.

What is religion's nonidolatrous side? If the sacred is itself not a world-order power or entity but that on which the world order depends, there is something at work in any experience or discernment of the sacred that resists all claimed identities between the sacred and anything else. If in fact these acts of identification do deeply corrupt the human being as Israelite and other prophets attest, redemption or salvation in its most general sense names a liberation from the effects of this corruption. Accordingly, salvation is always, whatever else it is, salvation from religion and from the idolatry necessary to vital religion and its popular piety. That which salvation in this sense evokes—we could say what the sacred as the sacred evokes—is faith. Faith, then, is an element in religion that transcends, opposes, and criticizes the idolatrous character of religion.[21]

This means that there is always a tension, a conflictual relation, between faith and the posture of certainty; and there is, therefore, conflict between faith and cosmologizing, casuistry, and their mundane authorizings. Through faith, religion opposes and surpasses itself. The most fundamental critical element in religion is

---

[18]For a detailed analysis of the principle of identity as it functions in the way authoritative texts and institutions are interpreted, see the author's *Ecclesial Reflection: An Anatomy of Theological Method* (Philadelphia: Fortress, 1982) 34-41.

[19]Dean Kelley comes close to this position when he argues that "strictness" is necessary to a socially "strong" religious movement and then claims that one trait of strictness is an *absolutizing* cognitive posture. *Why Conservative Churches.*

[20]The term *tragic* refers here not simply to suffering or misfortune but to realities whose "good" and fulfillment necessarily require an alliance with something that corrupts or opposes that good. The human condition is tragic insofar as human creativity, freedom, and imagination require as their conditions or in some way produce suffering, anxiety, grief, and so forth.

[21]For an account of faith distinguished from and over against religion, see H. Richard Niebuhr's interpretation of what he calls "radical monotheism" and "radical faith." *Radical Monotheism and Western Culture* (New York: Harper & Row, 1943).

not introduced by "reason" or "empirics," but by faith, that which refuses *all* identities between the sacred and the world order. Actual religion, then, is tragic because its vitality depends on idolatrous postures and idolatrous social structures, yet the sacred, which is its subject and existential concern, evokes postures that undercut and oppose that very vitality.

We must be clear that this distinction is not between types of religion or between levels of actual religion. I am not positing a distinction between popular religion and academic or critical religion. The thesis is that *all* actual religion requires a set of idolatrous identifications and that the one thing that surpasses and opposes this is faith.[22]

Church Education Between Religion and Faith

We turn now to the subject of this essay, church education. There are certain standard approaches to church education. One seeks to appropriate learning theory, developmental psychology, and theories of educational process. Another struggles with alternative general approaches to church education. A third probes curricular resources and explores better ways to teach the Bible. I am pressing another issue still, one that occurs at the level of a "deep structure" in the life of the church. What is education's relation to popular piety, the conditions of the vitality of actual religion, and to faith that opposes and surpasses the idolatrous character of popular piety? Three questions conduct us to the final step of this exploration. (1) Is the open-and-shut case for education's promotion of popular piety a final

---

[22]Two widespread interpretations in the church and its theologies tend to hide the church's own idolatry of the sacred from itself. The first represses the absolutizing elements of the popular piety of actual religion by assigning or reducing absolutizing to an aberrant and marginal phenomenon of "fundamentalism." Fundamentalism is an aggressive and socially inflexible movement that would if it could impose its absolutizing cognitive and moral commitments on the life of the church (and larger culture). But there is continuity between this easily criticized extreme movement and the "softer" and less politically aggressive absolutizing of popular piety.

The second interpretation is characteristic of liberal Protestant theologies that define the "essence" of Christianity as a suprahistorical ideality, not an actual religion. "Christianity" thus names a religion of love, or grace, or universality, etc. But it is the case that any religion, Christianity included, may have as part of its actual historical reality elements that oppose and surpass the idolatry of the sacred. But there exists no other "Christianity" than the one that has an actual history and the vitality of that Christianity has always been fueled by popular piety and the idolatry of the sacred. The identification of the sacred (or something about the sacred, its will, knowledge, etc.) and worldly entities characterizes the first century spread of Christianity and its literatures, the Catholicism of the High Middle Ages, the Protestant Reformation, European pietism, the spread of Christianity on the American frontier, revivalism, etc. In the sense of sociological realism, popular piety and the idolatry of the sacred *is* the essence of Christianity.

word? (2) Given the legacy of history, is it possible for education to be anything other than a servant of popular piety? (3) What obstacles and risks face the church when it introduces an education that serves faith's opposition to popular piety?

(1) The open-and-shut case for restricting education's function to the promotion of popular piety is based on a certain sociological realism. Popular piety along with its idolatrous identifications is the fuel that runs the engine of religion. Its cosmologizing, casuistry, and authority are necessary to the social vitality of actual religion. Hence, anything that opposes, weakens, or qualifies popular piety reduces at the same time religious vitality. But if popular piety, the idolatry of the sacred, is the necessary condition of religious vitality and faith is opposed to such, the conclusion is an almost unthinkable one. Faith destroys or weakens religion. And one promotes faith only at the risk of the vitality of religion.

Two considerations should create some uneasiness about this open-and-shut case. The first connects with the very self-interest that prompts the church to protect popular piety; that is, its legacy of cosmology, casuistry, and authority. The present vitality of religious movements that embody and promote popular piety may be misleading. Such movements may be on a collision course with the formidable social and cultural movements now set against actual religion across the globe. These countervailing movements include Marxism, scientific and historical worldviews whose cosmologies and ways of thinking are incompatible with religious worldviews, and technocratic, therapeutic, and bureaucratic cultures. Although these movements are not without idolatrous elements, they do present severe criticisms of the identity claims and absolutizations of popular piety as both cognitively implausible and socially oppressive. Having taken centuries to originate, these global movements are the context for recent claims that this is a "postchristian" era. Nietzsche's parable of the death of God is cited as expressive of a massive shift in Western history in which a serious and unclosable fissure has arisen between the taken-for-granted ways of understanding reality in the larger culture and the absolutizing of popular piety. The message of this literature from Bonhoeffer to Altizer is: The game is up. The message could be wrong. But the fact of radical cognitive disjunction between the world of modern history, physics, and microbiology, universities, global politics, and multinational corporations on the one hand, and the world of popular piety, on the other, is not to be dismissed lightly. It prompts us to ask whether popular piety in the forms we know it can survive such a world. Exacerbating the uneasiness is the fact ever before us that popular piety has not survived in vast populations and subcultures of North America and Western Europe. As a way of thinking and experiencing, religiosity is marginal to most of the institutions in which our culture is now embodied: government, corporations, leisure activities, science, aesthetics, the military, and education. Gnawing away at the apparent vitality of conservative religion is a question. Can Christianity or any religion survive the modern world merely as popular piety?

A second consideration is theological. It is raised by the faith element in actual religion and with the church's commitment to the truth of its message and experience. Once actual religion becomes aware of the idolatrous element in piety and vitality, can it look the other way? To the degree that it experiences faith, the redemption of religion itself, can it simply withhold faith's opposition to the idolatrous identities of popular piety? Of course not. Only a religious cynicism that is neither faith nor passionate piety could promote such a repression of faith and a use of piety. Actual religion can *self-consciously* promote its own idolatry only in the mode of a self-conscious cynicism. From these considerations, we conclude that the case for education's servanthood of popular piety is not so open-and-shut, sociological realism notwithstanding.

(2) Even if there originates in the church a self-conscious intention to permit faith's opposition to and surpassing of popular piety to inform the aim of church education, can this intention ever be implemented? The historical legacy of the past presents formidable obstacles to such a possibility. It simply seems to be the case that actual religion has always resisted education in the sense of an endeavor that confronts and criticizes popular piety. This resistance appears to be at work in the vast difference between clergy and congregational education. Not only is clergy education ordered learning (a disciplined, accumulative, and testable program of study), while congregational education is not, most clergy education is also historical and critical, while most congregational education is not. Even so, the elements of clergy education that might oppose idolatrous cosmology and casuistry tend to remain locked up in ministers' files. In other words, Protestant clergy do not carry their own ordered learning and other resources for critical confrontation of popular piety into their function as church educators.

Behind this fact of recent history is a long-term historical legacy. As the primary way in which the sacred is experienced and communicated, popular piety's cosmology, casuistry, and authority have now a normative character in the church. These features of popular piety officially define the church's message of salvation. And the normative status of these things is institutionally embodied and thereby promoted and protected. Two features of the modern church support the continuation of normative popular piety. First, critical and historical theological education is limited to one stratum of church life (the education of clergy) and is sealed off from congregations. Second, the noncritical, nonhistorical way of thinking about reality (human beings, history, truth, authority, social world, nature, etc.) remains dominant in popular piety in spite of the fact that it has largely disappeared from public, higher, professional, and graduate education.

The situation is, of course, more complicated than this. Mainline denominations now exist somewhere between uncritical/unhistorical and critical/historical ways of understanding religion. The certainty, cosmology, and casuistry of popular religion are no longer dominant, but what has displaced them is a general moralism and therapeutic religion. In other words, popular religiosity has waned in mainline denominations (hence their recent decline), but what has displaced it is not education in service of faith's correction and surpassing of popular piety but a kind of therapeutic quasi-religion. This is the historical legacy and present situation that the churches face even if they would introduce an education in the service of faith.

The church's past, however, shows us a face other than simply the protection and promotion of popular piety. An explicitly self-conscious confrontation with the idolatry of popular piety has occurred in a number of movements of the church's past. Neoplatonic and medieval mysticism is one example. We do such mysticism an injustice when we think of it as merely abandoning the world for otherworldly visionary experiences. Much of this literature is an account of the *disciplining* of the "mind" (Bonaventure). The metaphor of a ladder or scale (Walter Hilton) describes a series of steps that expose and purge the many levels of the identification of the sacred with mundane reality. A virtual restructuring of human consciousness is proposed precisely because of the idolatrous way the human being initially apprehends and experiences the sacred. Nor was this restructuring something meant only for priests, monks, and nuns in a privileged educational process. It was this epoch's version of what it meant for any Christian to advance in the Christian life.

We should not idealize this example from Christian mysticism. As actual religion, it retained its own version of popular piety and, therefore, of idolatry. Its importance as an example is that it displays the tension between idolatrous popular piety and faith's discernment of the nonidentity of the sacred. Further, it embodies this discernment in a program of discipline. This program is not recoverable by most contemporary Christendom. It does show, however, that popular piety is not the only historical legacy of Christianity, that the tension and struggle between faith and piety has been a recurring part of history. It also shows that the idolatry of popular piety can be confronted and opposed in the midst of a vital religious movement. Today there are other resources and conceptual frameworks for the "disciplining of the mind." Both the praxis hermeneutics of liberation and the historical-critical hermeneutics of the academy offer powerful tools that education can and should appropriate in the service of faith.

(3) The exploration has arrived at a dilemma. To confront and oppose popular piety is to tamper with the conditions of religious vitality. For mainline Protestant churches, to take up education in the service of faith is to risk further decline and more displacement by types of Christianity that aggressively embody the idolatry of the sacred in a still vital popular piety. But to continue the older patterns of quasi-education, education in the service of therapeutic piety, incurs the longer-term risk of mythological religion in a nonmythological age and the bad faith present in repressing faith's opposition to popular piety. Thus, the tragic character of actual religion creeps into and structures church education itself. For church education can never simply choose a side but, at best, must combine a promotion of popular piety and the service of faith. That is, church education cannot simply re-

pudiate the cosmologizing (doctrine), casuistical (life codes), and authority (Scripture, tradition) contents of popular piety. No genuinely Christian *paideia* can occur apart from interpreting the church's past, tradition, primary symbols, doctrines, etc. On the other hand, church education is called into the service of faith's opposition to and surpassing of the idolatrous element of actual religion's way of transmitting these things. Church education is, accordingly, a tragic endeavor because it requires the idolatrous legacy of popular piety as the substance of its critical surpassing.[23]

What is meant by an education in the service of faith? Education is itself neither religion nor faith but an undertaking in a community whose aims are the disciplining of various modes of interpretation already occurring in the life of that community. Because it is not faith, education is not itself a term for redemption. We expect too much of church education if we expect it to redeem religion. We expect too little of any ecclesial undertaking, however, if we isolate it from the workings of grace and redemption. What education can do is to recover and continue to hold before the community the contents of its tradition; it can bring discipline to ways of interpreting those contents; and it can make available tools from a variety of human sciences in this undertaking.[24] Thus it can move beyond the place where education to promote popular piety stops short. It can help believers to become self-conscious about idolatrous elements in cosmology, casuistry, and authority by using appropriate methods to expose the relativity and historicity of these things. Contemporary church education must embrace its own tragic character, serving both piety and faith. It must decide whether it will be *education* in the full sense of the word.

---

[23]The tragic tension at the heart of church education, the opposition between faith and commitment to popular piety, may be a specific version of what Paul Tillich called Catholic substance (cf. popular piety) and the Protestant principle. In spite of this language, Tillich did not restrict the substance side to Catholicism nor the critical side to Protestantism. See *Systematic Theology* (Chicago: University of Chicago Press, 1963) 3:245.

[24]The introduction of such things into the life of the church will inevitably be on collision course with popular piety, with its orientation to feeling rather than thinking, immediate problems of life rather than long-term issues of truth, action and activity as evoking simple techniques rather than dense and complex policies. This, too, shows the tragic character of education (ordered learning) as something that would serve yet challenge the popular piety and therefore the vitality that calls it into being.

8

"All the Way Down": A Spirituality of Public Life

Parker J. Palmer

Among the many voices calling to the Christian community these days, two seem especially important to me. One calls individual Christians to ground themselves more deeply in spiritual reality, to deepen their lives of prayer and contemplation, to become more intentional about the inward journey toward the wellspring of faith. The other voice calls the institutional church to become more fully engaged with the world, to move beyond the confines of personal and corporate spirituality and engage both the problems and potentials of our pluralistic public life.

I. Introduction

Of course, these voices are not new. Their calls are perennial and the tension between them poses a classical paradox, variously named as the problem of prayer and politics, of contemplation and action, of faith and practice, of being and doing. Christians have never had an easy time hearing these two voices in concert: We have tended to listen selectively to one or the other as if the two taken together made wild cacophony. In our day and place, hearing the harmony between them seems especially difficult for several reasons.

First, the constitutional separation of church and state, that fundamental doctrine of American civic piety, seems to prohibit the mingling of spiritual and political impulses. This has inhibited the institutional church from listening with both ears. Second, our unconscious dualism, that habit of the Western mind that sees contradiction instead of paradox everywhere it looks, persistently categorizes our experience by the logic of either/or. This has inhibited individuals from listening with both ears. These factors, among others, have created a divided culture and divided hearts. While there are individuals, and even some congregations, that manage both prayer and public life, seldom does the church give compelling witness to the unity of the two.

Here, I want to make a case for unity. I begin by exploring the nature of the spiritual life, focusing on some of its neglected features, features that create natural links between the spiritual and the public realm. Then I explore the nature of the public life, finding here, too, neglected features that provide links to the life of the spirit. Next, I examine the privatization of American culture, a third factor that, added to our church-state squeamishness and our dualism, has diminished our capacity to live at the intersection of the spiritual and the public life. I shall argue that the private has become a "black hole" in our national life, swallowing up both the spiritual and the public and destroying the very instincts and impulses that would allow us to live out their unity. Finally, I suggest some ways that Christians and congregations who care about this problem can resist the gravitational pull of privatization and help restore both the spiritual and the public to their rightful mutuality in our lives.

II. The Nature of Spiritual Life

Among all the learned definitions of spirituality, there is a story about the philosopher Alfred North Whitehead that offers a humorous but compelling image of how "the spiritual" is experienced. It seems that Whitehead had just finished his opening lecture in a basic course on cosmology when an agitated young man took issue with him.

"I'm sorry, Professor, but everything you said about the structure of the universe is wrong, dead wrong."

The great philosopher patiently asked the young man to explain his own views on the subject.

"Well, the fact is that the entire universe sits on the back of a gigantic turtle."

Whitehead, taken aback but believing that he might at least teach this student something about the logic of assumptions, asked, "And what does that turtle stand on?"

Without blinking the young man said, "Another turtle."

"And what . . ." Whitehead began.

But before he could complete his question, his young challenger exploded with frustration: "I know exactly what you're going to ask, Professor, and the answer is it's turtles all the way down!"

The humor of this story points toward at least two truths about spiritual experience. First, the spiritual life moves metaphorically downward, not upward. It is not a movement toward abstract generalizations but toward those common-ground experiences that make us human. Both theology and spirituality use words, but they use them in different ways: Where theology offers logically consistent ideas about God, spirituality offers images of our experience of the spirit. Second, everyone has some sort of image, implicit or explicit, for the dimension of depth in his or her life—an image for what it is "all the way down." For some, the image is of chaos, randomness, the absence of meaning, the void. For others it is of determinism, predictability, lawful relationships. For still others it is an image of compassion, mercy, grace. Whether the image is turtles or otherwise, everyone has a controlling metaphor that points to the heart of his or her spiritual experience.

The downward movement of our spiritual lives and some important images of what we might find in the depths are explored by Annie Dillard in a passage I find both provocative and apt. Properly understood, Dillard's words not only open up the spiritual life in new ways but—as I shall suggest in the next section—allow us to see its intrinsic connections with the outer public world:

> In the deeps are the violence and terror of which psychology has warned us. But you ride these monsters deeper down, if you drop with them farther over the world's rim, you find what our sciences cannot locate or name, the substrate, the ocean or matrix or ether which buoys the rest, which gives goodness its power for good, and evil its power for evil, the unified field: our complex and inexplicable caring for one another, and for our life together here. This is given. It is not learned.[1]

Implicit in these words are several insights into the inward and personal spiritual journey—and its relation to outward and corporate public life. The first has to do with the route toward community, toward what Dillard calls "our complex and inexplicable caring for one another." Where we often image community as an external social structure, Dillard sees it as an interior reality. Where we often believe that the most direct route to community is through outward action, Dillard claims that the best route is inward and reflective. Her suggestion is that if we are to retrieve our sense of a common life, of what Thomas Merton called our "hidden wholeness," we must begin not with external activity but with a commitment to contemplation. The assumption behind these reflections is both radical and liberating: Long before community can be built as a social and political reality, it must be perceived and received, as a spiritual fact.

When Annie Dillard says that our sense of community "is given . . . not learned," she is pointing toward a crucial truth. Put negatively, the truth is that no law, no ethic, can create community from the outside in. There is no external form or force that can compel us to feel the sense of relatedness on which our common life depends. Put positively, the truth is that community is our created condition. All of the great creation myths speak of a time before time when humans lived in harmony with all beings. The memory of that original blessing is driven deep into our backbones. So our first task is not to create community but to *re-member* it, in the primitive sense of that term: to re-member means to put the broken body back together, while to forget where we came from is to dis-member

---

[1] Annie Dillard, *Teaching a Stone to Talk* (New York: Harper & Row, 1982) 94-95.

ourselves. At bottom, the spiritual journey offers us the chance to remember where we came from and who we really are—beings bound to each other by common caring.

But the second insight Dillard offers is a darker one. In the downward movement of the spiritual life, we will not reach the core of unity until we pass through layers of division, fear, conflict, confusion, and death. Before we can recover the selves we were created to be, we must confront the selves we have become—and this means confronting our own inward warfare with its threats to our comfortable images of identity.

Our challenge is to overcome the common notion that a person is, or ought to be, a singular, monolithic, homogeneous self, and to acknowledge the fact that each of us is a congeries of many forces, a home for many selves. Most of us live by selecting one self from among the many—often the best and the brightest self— and pretending to ourselves and others that this is the whole of who we are. Ironically, people who are spiritually inclined may be especially prone to this kind of distortion since they often live under the press of traditions that seem to value only the light and condemn the shadow side.

But at the crisis points in our lives, when we are consumed by pain or disappointment or defeat, other aspects of our inner complexity are revealed. We learn then that we are cowards as well as heroes, gluttons as well as ascetics, sinners as well as saints. We learn that our own spiritual ecology includes monsters, and we are faced with a question that has momentous implications for our lives: How shall we relate to those parts of ourselves that we experience as alien forces, that are utterly foreign to our image of the kind of people we "should be"?

This question takes us to the third and most pivotal insight in Annie Dillard's description of the inward journey. She suggests that the best—perhaps only—way to make the journey through danger toward personal and communal unity is to "ride the monsters" all the way down. Paradoxically, if Dillard is right, those fearsome forces within us may turn out to be our closest companions and most knowledgeable guides on the spiritual journey. Those seemingly alien monsters may be the only parts of ourselves that know the way toward the unity we seek to re-member.

If so, it is a paradox that makes common sense. It takes only a moment's reflection to realize that the "best and brightest" parts of ourselves are the parts that tend to separate us from each other, not join us together. Our successes and distinctions are what they are precisely because they set us apart; they name our specialness, our differences, our distinctions. But the more "monstrous" aspects of our lives offer us a chance to know ourselves as common, ordinary members of the human family. These are the places where we are most wounded, most fearful, most broken—and therefore most in need of others, most open to connectedness.

For example, what might happen if we could abandon our need to appear completely successful and "ride" our failures, and our fear of failure, "all the way down"? What might we discover if we could follow this particular monster all the way to the source? Since failure is a universal fact of life, my failures unite me with others, and in my failures I need consolation in a way that gives others access to me. Deeper still, my fear of failure reveals another way I block community. For behind that fear is my inability to receive life as a gift, my cockeyed conviction that I must somehow make a life all by myself—an appalling illusion that must be penetrated if I am ever to sense my utter reliance on "the substrate, the ocean or matrix which buoys" us all. Any monster, ridden all the way down, will reveal both how we dismember community and how we can re-member it in our lives.

But why would a person choose to ride the monsters? They are, after all, fierce and dangerous creatures. Every instinct in us cries out that we should flee from them. They can easily overpower us, and if that happens, we may be doomed. So why would anyone choose to travel with such beasts?

A story from my own experience may suggest an answer. It happened on an Outward Bound "wilderness challenge" course on the coast of Maine. I, at age forty, full of my fear of heights, had been placed on the edge of a 110-foot cliff with a thin rope tied around my waist and told to lean back over God's own emptiness and make my trembling way down the rock face step-by-dreadful-step to the base of the cliff.

The word "terror" barely describes what I felt. But slowly I began, and slowly I realized that I was actually doing it. Then, about half way down, just as I was starting to gain some confidence, I suddenly realized that the rock face was angling away from me, disappearing beneath my feet. Realizing that I would have to assume an even more unnatural posture to negotiate this position of the cliff, I did what came naturally: I froze. For a long time I stayed frozen there, paralyzed by the certainty that I could not possibly cope with this terrifying turn of events, that my demise was only a matter of time.

The instructor, who had been tracking my terror, shouted up, "Is anything wrong, Parker?" Instantly I responded from some long-dormant, child-deep part of myself: "I don't want to talk about it!" The instructor, after a pause (and, surely, a professionally suppressed laugh), then yelled, "I think it's time you learned the motto of this Outward Bound School . . ." "Wonderful," I thought, "I am about to die, and she is feeding me bromides." And then she called out words that had an amazing impact on me: "If you can't get out of it, get into it."

Somehow, those words rang so true to me that I was able to follow them with my body. I saw that the only way out was in and through, so I began to move and eventually made it to terra firma. That, I think, is the one and only reason a person would choose to ride the monsters: There is no way to move around them or against them so one must move with them. When one is able to do that, the paralysis of fear is broken and the very thing that had one paralyzed becomes companion and guide. If Annie Dillard is right, "getting into" our fears because we can not get

out of them will lead us eventually to the inward terra firma of our common and
public life.

III. Links Between the Spiritual and Public Life

The remarkable fact about that quotation from Annie Dillard is not only that
it evokes crucial features of the inner life but that it does the same for the public
life. And as it does, it shows us relationships between two realms that are often
regarded as hermetically sealed. But before I apply Dillard's images to an interpretation of the public life, I need to explain that I am using the term *public* in a
sense more classical than contemporary.

In our time, *public* often refers to the formal functions and institutions of government: A public school is one supported by taxes, a public policy is a legislative
enactment, a person in public life is an elected official. But the term has a deeper
and richer meaning if we trace it back to its ancient Greek origins. Here, the term
can be taken to refer to all those processes, occasions, and settings in which cit-
izen-strangers meet, interact, and have a chance to identify themselves as a company of people who share common space, common resources, common problems,
a common destiny, a common life. "The company of strangers" is my metaphor
for the public, and with it I mean to portray a community of interaction and engagement that is essentially prepolitical: Public life existed before formal institutions of government were invented, and those institutions (at least in their
democratic forms) depend on the public's health for their own well-being.

The public life constitutes a realm of comparative chaos that lies between two
realms of comparative order—the private and the political. The private realm
(which I explore more fully later) consists of my family, my friends, my posses-
sions. It is a realm from which the stranger qua stranger is excluded. The political
realm consists of mechanisms by which strangers do business with one another—
adjudicating disputes, allocating resources, making other corporate decisions.
Between these two is the life of the public, the ebb and flow of the company of
strangers, which happens in relatively unstructured and unorderly ways: on the
city streets, in parks and squares, at festivals and rallies, in shopping malls, neighborhoods, and voluntary associations. In these places the stranger is both expected
and encountered (unlike the private realm) but the encounter is governed by a minimum of formal procedures (unlike the political realm).

The importance of this messy "middle layer" called public life is easily seen
when we ask what kind of society exists once the public life is eliminated. The
answer, of course, is a totalitarian society, a society of strict order in which there
is no realm of comparative chaos to buffer the relations of the private and the political. On the one hand, the absence of a public life means that there is no private
life worthy of the name since political power now has direct and unmediated ac-

cess to the fragile private person; the private person is deprived of the protections offered by public gatherings and public outcry. On the other hand, the absence of a public life means that there is no political process worthy of the name; individuals and potential groups have no access to public forums that could amplify their voices. This is why totalitarian movements always outlaw such key features of public life as congregating on the city streets, holding rallies and debates, meeting in voluntary associations.

At first glance, the inner or spiritual life and the outer or public life would seem to have precious little in common. But the images of Annie Dillard gather up their profound commonalities. Both the inner and the public life are realms of relative chaos through which we must move if we are to find the most fundamental order of our lives, the "unified field" Dillard speaks of. Paradoxically, that order is not only found in the midst of chaos, but the chaos itself somehow generates and protects that order. The inner and the public are both realms of genuine creativity in the deepest sense of that word: realms depicted in the great creation myths where order emerges from disorder and yet the two remain intimately entwined. This sort of creation is not a once-and-for-all event, but a continuing process, and any individual or society that banishes chaos from its midst also kills creativity.

Both the inner and the public life are vast, uncharted realms of power where we encounter a strange and alien pluralism; life in both realms involves considerable threats and danger. The monsters of the inner life, those powers of the night that we encounter as we journey toward the source, have their obvious counterparts in the monsters of public life. We are most likely to think of the public monsters associated with drugs, random violence, and calculated crime which lurk in the back alleys of our cities. But there are other monsters in the public realm, sometimes elected to office, who hold massive and unaccountable powers of destruction, who are armed not with switchblades and handguns but with indifferent bureaucracy, insensitive policy, and even the push-buttons of Armageddon.

Both the inner and the public life involve risks, challenge, radical uncertainty. When we venture into them, our lives are always in some peril. But since this is a peril we cannot get out of, we need to get into it. It is simply the peril of being fully human and fully alive, and it can be "avoided" only by choosing to be neither. We can temporarily withdraw from both inward and public engagement, and for a time we may feel we have escaped. But sooner or later the reality of our humanness will catch up with us. Sooner or later the pluralism of the public will impinge on our lives, and sooner or later our own inner pluralism will rise up to claim us. Instead of trying to retreat, we are well advised to enter thoughtfully into these realms of power and find our relation to the powers that live there. Only so can we participate in the continuing creation of the world and of ourselves.

The fact is that the inner and the public worlds cocreate each other, so to withdraw from either is to opt out of a life-making dynamic. The clearest examples of this mutual creation are found in the psychological concepts of "projection" and "introjection," projection being the means by which the inner world helps shape the outer, introjection the converse. Walter Wink has described both of these phenomena with uncommon brevity and clarity. Writing about "enemies," he says:

> My enemy is my mirror. I project onto my enemy everything in myself that I cannot stand, tolerate, acknowledge, or accept. My enemy returns the compliment. My enemy also stirs up in me those very aspects of myself that I cannot stand, tolerate, acknowledge, or accept. We are locked into a very tight embrace, my enemy and I.[2]

When our inner monsters remain unknown to us, we project them out onto the world, finding someone or something to bear the monstrousness we cannot bear within ourselves. For some whites, blacks carry the projection; for some Americans, it is Communists; for some adults, teenagers play the part. But there are objective monsters in the public world as well, and when we do not relate to them consciously, we can easily introject them into our souls. As Wink writes, "Are we not unconsciously attracted to the very evils we most stridently denounce? . . . No one can escape this, for we are all so much a part of the human community that every crime elicits a secret fascination in some corner of our hearts."[3] Even our attraction to evil is a sign of the underlying community of which Annie Dillard writes!

Of course, there is goodness as well as evil in us and in the world, and the dynamics of projection-introjection work for good as well as for ill. The unrealized or unfulfilled vitalities within us are sometimes projected onto another person, and the result is that classic human experience we call "falling in love." The vitalities of the public world are introjected as well. One of the great functions of the chaotic and creative "company of strangers" is to offer us a life-force that can open our narrow ego-boundaries to the fuller joy of being human. In a thousand ways the inner life and the public life continually create each other.

The ultimate link between the inner and the public life is in the simple fact that, together, they comprise the natural habitat of the human being. We reside in ourselves, in our spirits and souls and psyches; and we reside in the unformed flux and pulsing energies of the company of strangers. Ultimately, it is only in the inner and the public life that we have a chance of finding home, ground to stand on, the home ground some have named God.

In the great spiritual traditions, we are told to look for God in one of two places—either in the secret recesses of the human heart, the tunnels of the inward journey, or in the great events of human history, the social, political, and economic realities that come when souls are incarnated in space and time. The wisest of traditions, it seems to me, have pointed to God in both places. They have under-

---

[2]Walter Wink, "My Enemy, My Destiny," *Sojourners* (February 1987): 30.
[3]Walter Wink, "We Have Met the Enemy . . . ," *Sojourners* (November 1986): 18.

stood that to search deeply for God in either realm is to find one's self searching in the other realm as well.

Within each human heart there is a deep impulse to seek home, ground, God. The question, then, is why so few of us enter upon the inner life or the public life as pathways toward that home? The answer, in part, is that another pathway has been offered to us, one that seems more like "home" than the inner or the public but one that quickly leads to a dead-end. This is the pathway marked "private." I want now to show how our turn toward privatism has dulled our home-seeking impulse, has diverted us from both inner and public experience, and has prevented us from finding the common ground we instinctively seek.

IV. The Privations of Privatism

Inner life and public life, because they involve continual encounter with the strange and the alien, always arouse fear, that most paralyzing of human emotions. Whatever threatens our own version of truth and goodness is fearsome to us, and such threat is a common occurrence in both public and inner experience.

One strategy for dealing with that fear is to try to gain enough power to enforce our own standards on the alien experience. In public life, for example, we have seen the dominance of a white male version of truth and goodness, or the myth of the "melting pot" that would render all our diversities homogeneous. In spiritual life the same leveling occurs. Outwardly it takes the form of religious institutions and hierarchies controlling the definition of "orthodoxy" and suppressing all signs of "heresy"; inwardly, it takes the form of simple denial that we have a shadow side.

But our main strategy for dealing with our fear of the alien involves the evolution of "private life," which, if Americans did not invent it, we have elevated to unsurpassed status. Our fear of the strange and the stranger has manifested itself in a compulsive commitment to the private realm, in an unparalleled investment of material and psychic resources in private well-being. Instead of encountering, engaging, and growing from the diversity within and outside us, we have tried to avoid it altogether by building high the walls of privatism.

By *private* I mean the realm of family and friends, of personal property and prerogatives. Within this realm the stranger has no place; indeed, we have wide-ranging legal rights to exclude the stranger from our private lives. In private we have the best chance of controlling the degree of contradiction and conflict in our lives. Here, we can surround ourselves with people who look and think and act like us—and if they refuse to conform, we can banish even them from our private lives. To hear Americans talk about their history, one could easily conclude that its most important thrust has been toward the fortification of the private.

In and of itself, the private is not pathological. We do have a fundamental right to privacy. We do have the right to pick and choose our closest associates.

We do have the right to a *sanctum sanctorum* in which we can express ourselves in ways we would not or could not (or should not) in public. The pathology arises when the private becomes our dominant mode of experience, when it begins to function like a "black hole" in space, pulling everything into its gravitational field and compressing the whole of our lives into private terms. When this happens, when the inner and the public life are swallowed up in the private, not only are those two realms destroyed but the private is diminished as well. The health of private life depends upon the health of the inner and the public life.

The private life swallows the spiritual life by replacing the adventure of inward journey with the continual reinforcement of personas within the circle of family and friends. When this happens, we destroy the personal uniqueness that the private realm is intended to protect by capping off the inner well from which uniqueness springs. Observers often comment that in American society, with all its insistence on private prerogatives, it is possible to go from one pocket of privatism to another and see this freedom being exercised in exactly the same way. Why is there so much homogeneity between these private enclaves despite our ferocity about the right of personal choice? Because the inner life—the life that nurtures the uniqueness of the individual—has been gutted by privatism, leaving us easy prey to the leveling forces of mass culture.

Similarly, when our obsession with the private leads us to withdraw our energies from the public realm, the private suffers as well, for it takes a healthy public to protect the health of the private. For evidence of this fact one need only look at a totalitarian society where no real privacy exists because no public life is tolerated. Where "the company of strangers" is destroyed—by design or by default—that crucial buffer is removed between the fragile private person and the massive powers of government. No true privacy exists in such a society: Neighbors and friends may turn out to be informers, and "the disappeared" have no one to speak for them.

Our own society has been relatively free from autocratic attempts to strangle the public life. Our threat comes, instead, from a culture that defaults on the public in its obsession with the private sphere. The thing we need to fear, and fight, in our society is not a totalitarian takeover but the diminishment of the public realm through a process called privatization. Privatization is a phenomenon with many facets, and it touches nearly every area of our lives. To make it clear what I mean by the term—and especially to make it clear that I am not attacking private property, private rights, or the value of family and friends—I want to give several examples of how privatization is at work in our lives.

A major example of privatization is the mind-set that insists we can solve public problems by private means, a mind-set exemplified in popular responses to the public problem of crime. There are, of course, a variety of political responses to crime, which range from hiring more police to enacting new laws. But our most popular "solutions" take the form of private measures financed by private dollars, and they simply do not work. We buy "pet" dogs bred with killer instincts. We lace our homes with electronic alarm wires. We stock our nightstands with deadly handguns. We build entire communities surrounded by fortress walls.

Not only have these private measures failed to reduce the level of public crime, but they have probably increased the level of private mayhem. Statistics show that if you are going to be murdered in America, the killer is more likely to be someone you know (or are even related to) than a random stranger—and those handguns in the nightstands are one of the reasons why. Furthermore, those statistics generally count only premeditated killings, not the accidental shootings of family members who come into the house late at night and are mistaken for burglars by some other member of the household. The private realm in our society has become a dangerous realm—witness the frequency of spouse- and child-abuse. We have built such high walls around the private that too much violence and injustice is completely hidden from public view. And the ultimate irony is that this sort of privatization makes the public realm more dangerous as well as diverting concern and resources from public life.

There *is* an effective response to the public problem of crime, one that involves not private protections but public awareness. Many high-crime areas of our cities have experimented successfully with various versions of the "neighborhood watch." Here, people are brought out of their privacy and encouraged to become aware of what is happening in the community around them. If they see something suspicious down the street, they are taught to be curious, to alert others, to call the police—in a word, to care, to act like public citizens and to call on public resources. Measures like these can stop crime, for they seek solutions to public problems where they are to be found, in the public realm.

The broad range of the phenomenon called privatization can be seen in a second example, this one from the world of education. Several years ago the Carnegie Commission on Higher Education surveyed the most recent crop of college graduates. The survey asked, among other things, how the graduates viewed the future of the world. With few exceptions they were profoundly pessimistic. Environmental pollution, nuclear proliferation, economic collapse, political impotence— the respondents were able to give great and gory detail on the world's demise. Then the researchers asked these men and women to reflect on their *personal* futures. With few exceptions they said, in effect, "No problem. My future is rosy. I have a good education, made good grades, and I'll get a good job and make a good life for myself."

There are various ways to interpret these data, but the most compelling way I know is to see them as another form of privatization. This time it is a form inculcated by our schools. Year after year these students were taught about a world that exists "out there" somewhere, a fictional world created by an educational philosophy called "objectivism" that keeps all subjects of study at arm's length so that our knowledge of them will be "pure," allegedly without subjective bias.

Unfortunately—quite apart from the fact that such purity is impossible—this approach allows students to develop the fantasy that the world they are studying has no relation to themselves and their lives. In the objectivist strategy of education, the life-stories of the students are utterly unrelated to the subjects being studied. The result is one more form of privatism—namely, the conviction that it is possible to inhabit a niche of personal sanity in the midst of public calamity. Here, privatism takes the form of a mind-set that refuses to relate the fate of the public world to one's own private fate.

A third and final example of privatism goes directly into the nature of American religion (though much of what I have been describing can be called the tacit spirituality of our culture). In this arena, examples of privatism are abundant. I might explore the immense popularity of those forms of faith that promise private rewards of success and well-being in return for personal commitment. I might examine the fact that 11 A.M. on Sunday is still the most segregated hour of the week, with churches gathering into private circles of the like-minded (while "secular" society undertakes the Monday-through-Friday task of weaving together the company of strangers). But the true privatization of American religion lies deeper than these sociological illustrations suggest.

The deeper reality is that our underlying fear of the strange and alien has led our churches to domesticate God or, to put it more pointedly, to make even God an inmate of the private realm. Gone is the strangeness of God, the wild and alien quality of holiness that was so well known to primal peoples (witness the Hebrew Bible). In its place is an image of God as a member of the church family circle, a God who is like a kind and comfortable old friend, a God who comforts and consoles us—and even reinforces our prejudices—but in no way challenges or stretches our lives. Among Christians this tendency to domesticate the Deity has sometimes involved replacing God with Jesus, a Jesus who is so sentimentalized and even sanitized that he loses all the outrageous outlaw qualities of the Jesus of history. The ancient image of Immanuel, "God with us," which properly serves as a source of solace and strength, has somehow been translated into a self-serving image of "God like us."

I do not mean to suggest that an authentic experience of God excludes that which is intimate and familiar. But when we exclude the strange and alien side of religious experience, we are succumbing to the temptation to conform and control God for our own purposes. I do not know which is cause and which is effect, but there is a clear link between the mentality that wants to make God wholly familiar and the mentality that wants to avoid the threats of both inner and public pluralism by staying within the safe confines of the private realm. A spirituality focused on that which is intimate and safe will invariably join forces with social and personal strategies that arise from fear of the strange and the stranger.

V. What Can the Churches Do?

I have argued that the spiritual life and the public life are intimately related and, if we live them at all, we will live them into one another. But I have also argued that a long-term and multifaceted process called privatization has crippled our capacity to live authentically in either the spiritual or the public realm. If the church is to help us recover this capacity, its first concern must be to resist the gravitational pull of privatization. As long as the church is merely one more place where the private overwhelms both self and world, then the church will make no contribution to the recovery of those two related realms of meaning.

I have often heard it said that the sociological makeup of the typical congregation is already so homogeneous that the church can do little to resist privatization until congregations become more pluralistic—a change not likely to happen soon. True, 11 A.M. on Sunday is still the most segregated hour of the week, but demography does not decide everything. As valuable as it would be for congregations to fight privatism by encouraging diversity in their midst—and they should encourage it in every way possible—even the most homogeneous congregation can join that fight today. It can do so by strategies that take people beneath the surface of their sociological sameness where they will discover a diversity of attitudes, experiences, psyches, and spirits of such dimensions that even the most homogeneous congregation can have first-hand experience with "the company of strangers." Indeed, without such an approach, even congregations with great demographic variety will offer only a privatized experience.

The factor that keeps most congregations on the surface of their own lives is, of course, fear—fear of the fragmentation that might follow if they descended to the level of their inner diversity. In most congregations a tremendous amount of energy goes into maintaining the appearance of homogeneity, energy intended to keep people away from those flash points where conflict might occur. If some of that energy could be spent on freeing people for creative conflict, on creating settings where diversity can enrich rather than diminish our lives, the congregation could become a vital training ground for both inner and public encounters with the strange and the alien.

There are numerous practical ways to create such a training ground within the congregation, and I shall consider two of them before I bring this essay to a close. But the essential prior task is not programmatic; it is theological. If the church is to help people move out of privatism and embrace the alien, it must recover the alien quality of the sacred in its own theology; it must recover the experience of God as stranger. As long as the God who gives us life is equated largely with the intimate and the familiar, then all that is not familiar will be experienced as threatening to life itself.

Of course, the strangeness of God *is* threatening. But the threat is not to life itself; the threat is to our limited conception of life. The key to understanding the alien dimensions of God is to understand that the sacred, by its very nature, continually pushes and probes our taken-for-granted image of reality, our standard frame of reference, our conventional mind-set. In this respect God is the great iconoclast, continually smashing every concept we construct to capture ultimate reality. But this God threatens only our picture of life, not our actual living. Paradoxically, when our finite concepts of life are broken, life itself is enhanced since those concepts too easily limit and obscure the wonder-beyond-words that real life always is.

One way for churches to help people acknowledge and embrace the strangeness of God is, of course, through formal teaching and preaching. At very least, these ministries can honor the fact that at the very heart of Christian tradition, at the core of the Scripture itself, God and God's actions are often portrayed as utterly alien to conventional expectations. In the Hebrew Bible God is portrayed as One who created both weal and woe; who causes seas to open, bushes to burn, manna to fall from heaven; who gives the prophets messages that continually challenge the dominant versions of goodness and truth. In the Christian Testament, God and God's actions are no less strange. Here are accounts of the blind restored to sight; of a few loaves and fishes feeding thousands; of a Messiah who came as outcast rather than King; of the dead raised to life. Whether one takes these accounts as literal history or poetic interpretation of experienced truths, their cumulative meaning seems clear: God does not conform to conventional expectations.

But beyond formal teaching and preaching, there is an even more compelling way for the church to resist privatization and encourage the company of strangers. This is the way not of words alone but of actions as well. As educators know, the deepest things people learn in an educational setting come not from the formal content of lectures and discussions but from the "hidden curriculum." That curriculum consists of the rules, roles, and relationships that are played out as people interact in that setting. One can teach a course of democratic values, but if it is taught in an authoritarian way, the students are learning not to be citizens but subjects. Likewise, the church can praise diversity with words from now until doomsday, but if the lived experience in the church is one of diversity suppressed, then the church is merely another institution where privatism is nurtured.

One place where many congregations could helpfully reform their "hidden curriculum" is in the practical pedagogy of their teaching ministry. Far too many congregations continue to teach in ways that unconsciously assume that the parishioners are "empty vessels" to be filled up with theological content by the trained clergyperson or the lay teacher who has had special study. Far too many parishioners are "preached at" and "taught to" rather than engaged in a life-giving conversation between their own experience, a responsive teacher, and a given subject.

The top-down teaching methods still used in many congregations suppress diversity and encourage privatism in a variety of ways. They put complete control of the subject matter in the hands of the preacher or the teacher. One person's interpretation of things reigns supreme, and "learning" becomes a matter of students conforming to this "expert" view. In this way, the content being learned becomes privatized rather than open to public scrutiny and debate. Conversely, these top-down teaching methods keep the cap on the diversity of experience that exists within every congregation by prohibiting people from speaking a public word about how things look from where they stand. The public silence that exists in many congregations is not necessarily the result of people agreeing with what the teacher or preacher is saying. Instead, it results from the fact that people who are not encouraged to speak in public are reluctant to do so—and from the fact that a long experience of public silence tends to turn off the questioning mind altogether.

There are many alternatives to the teacher- or preacher-dominated mode of teaching, and this brief essay is not a good place to try to detail them. But a few general points can be made here. First, these alternative methods require a teacher who is comfortable with diversity and has moved beyond the need for control. The person who has not dealt with his or her inner pluralism cannot teach in a way that allows outward pluralism to emerge; the person who has not embraced his or her inner contradictions cannot teach in a way that allows outward contradictions to unfold. So congregations who wish to move toward alternative modes of teaching must be concerned with the spiritual development of those who preach and teach, for the qualities that allow a person to evoke and cherish pluralism are the qualities of a spiritually mature soul.

Second, these alternative modes of teaching and learning rest on the assumption that people are not empty vessels but bearers of personal truth. Here, the experiences and insights of ordinary people are received and respected before it is assumed that they must be examined and corrected. People contain within themselves an amazing depth of knowledge and wisdom. But often, they do not know it—precisely because so many of our institutions make the "empty vessel" assumption. In some respects, the key task of educators in the church is to help people learn what they already know—to help them touch, and name, and voice that knowledge. As the church is able to do this, it will also help people honor and grow from the amazing diversity of human experience, a diversity that does not necessarily cancel itself out in a warfare of subjective opinions, but weaves itself together in a tapestry that may even begin to resemble the rich complexity of the marvel called "truth."

Third, these alternative modes of teaching and learning do not stop with the public expression of personal truth, which can be no more than a pseudopublic display of privatism. Instead, they bring those personal truths into encounter with one another for purposes of dialogue and debate, conflict and consensus. In this sort of education the individual is honored but so is community, and the two are seen not in opposition but in living paradox. I said earlier that we need to respect personal truth before we inspect it and correct it, and that is the order in which things should come. But in that context of respect, inspection is always necessary, and correction is sometimes necessary—not at the hands of some solitary authority, but in the context of the learning community itself. Churches that bring this kind of community to life by using alternative methods of teaching and learning will make a significant contribution to the diminishment of privatism and the encouragement of inner and outer pluralism.

Another place where many congregations could helpfully reform their "hidden curriculum" is in the way they make decisions. Here the church has a special opportunity to encourage our capacity to deal with diversity; instead, the typical church stifles that capacity. In too many congregations, issues that might be divisive are settled either by an elite working backstage or by a majority vote in which the minority is simply overpowered. Behind the use of force in decision-making there is always fear, fear that things will get "out of control," fear that a pluralistic community cannot cohere for long unless it is coerced. As long as that fear dominates, and as long as church decision-making reflects that fear, the "hidden curriculum" will teach people to flee from diversity into privatism rather than to embrace creative conflict.

But there is a practical, time-tested alternative to elite rule and majority vote. It is called consensus, and it is designed to help us honor and grow from our differences rather than fear and flee from them. Consensus does not mean that everyone in the decision-making group must enthusiastically affirm a choice before it can be made. But it does mean that a decision can be taken only when there is no one in the group who strongly opposes it for significant reasons that he or she can articulate to the group. Consensus refuses to accept the premise that a majority is more likely than a minority to possess the truth; instead, consensus assumes that one person may possess more truth than the rest of the group combined. But deeper still, consensus assumes that the best way toward truth is for a group to be compelled to work together—to honor their differences, to listen to contradictions, to speak unpopular insights, and to allow this searching to move the group toward insights it did not have before the process began.

In a majority vote situation I am forced to listen for the worst in what my opponent has to say so that I can use it to ridicule his or her entire case. This is an adversarial process that more often leads to posturing, rhetoric, and cheap shots than to a true spirit of inquiry. But in a consensus situation—where the group cannot move until everyone in it is willing to go along—I must listen for the best in what others are saying, for those insights I can appreciate or affirm and perhaps even adopt as my own. If I do not, everyone suffers, including me.

When we move from malevolent listening to benevolent listening, a remarkable thing can happen: We can develop a collective wisdom that exceeds the wisdom of any single person in the group. We seek out our differences rather than flee from them, for it is in our differences that we are challenged and stretched toward that new truth the group needs to move forward. Using consensus, people begin to appreciate the constructive potentials of pluralism and conflict, an appreciation that can help move them out of privatism into the diversities of both the inner and the public life.

When people first learn about consensus, and begin to feel some enthusiasm for it, their enthusiasm is often dampened by memories of outrageous and obnoxious people who never want to go along with the group and simply must be overridden, voted down. But I believe that such people are made, not born. They are made by disempowering modes of group life in which the only way to be noticed and taken seriously is to act outrageously. When people begin to understand that consensus decision-making takes everyone seriously and empowers each individual in the group, they often grow into persons who can speak their own truth, hear the truth of others, and become a part of something larger than themselves.

This capacity to honor one's own uniqueness and the uniqueness of others while honoring the deep things we have in common as well—this capacity is the finest fruit of "a spirituality of public life." It is a capacity that should be the aim of the church in all aspects of its life—its theology, its preaching and teaching, its decision-making, and other aspects of its life too numerous to mention here. By developing this capacity the church empowers people to be at home in their inner selves and in the public world. Words fail when we try to name that home. But perhaps it is best evoked by the name of that God whom the church worships, follows, and witnesses to amid all the complexities of the inward life and the public realm.

9

"Experiments with Truth": Education for Leadership

Sara Little

Perhaps this essay is not so much a call for leadership as it is for a renewal of moral commitment, of care for the public good, of clarity about the purpose and conceptual structures that provide direction and framework for belief and action. It may be based more on anxiety about the fact that things seem to be "coming apart" than it is on a conviction about leadership development as a strategy for meeting those anxieties and redirecting the future. On the other hand, whenever crises have been met or clear vision has pulled people together with a sense of collective identity and an articulated purpose that replaces fumbling hopelessness, it seems that often, almost always, some leader—a prophet, a martyr, an organizer who knows how to give form to vision and words to yearnings of the heart, a person embodying courage—has had a hand in what happened. Thus this essay, which presupposes a kind of national and religious crisis of purpose, morality, and identity, moves in the direction of asking whether leadership can help. If so, what kind of leadership? And how can that leadership be fostered?

What is said here will not be an abstract formulation of principles, nor an objective analysis of theories then to be "applied" in detached fashion to a crisis situation. Like social scientist David Loye, I *care* about our world, and like him, think there may be some possibility of reclaiming the role of leadership as an instrument for the social good. In his book *The Leadership Passion* Loye poses two questions: "Where are we headed?" and "Can we shape the future to desirable ends, or are we helplessly adrift?"[1] His concern with the stability and well-being of individuals and of nations is approached through a survey of 180 years of research on leadership. James MacGregor Burns, historian and political scientist, in his monumental volume *Leadership* also sees the call for leadership as "one of

---

[1]David Loye, *The Leadership Passion: A Psychology of Ideology* (San Francisco: Jossey-Bass Publishers, 1977) ix.

the keynotes of our time.''[2] Burns's work is historical and biographical, in contrast to Loye's. Both men contribute significant insights, as do many others, but there is clearly no consensus about the concept of leadership nor the meaning of research findings as a way for finding and developing leaders.

Why, then, attempt an essay on leadership? One reason is that out of much reading, including confusing and invigorating entanglement with competitive concepts, I came across an idea that began to bring order out of chaos for me (note that the word is "began"). One writer mentioned Gandhi as one of the greatest of all modern leaders, referring to his own view of his life as "experiments with truth." I am not sure who that writer was because in a moment of insight my own conviction that leadership has to do with morality and religion and education found a compelling metaphor that took on a life of its own. In Gandhi's *Autobiography*, I saw clarity about ends and means focused in belief, and embodiment of those beliefs in a life of integrity. Gandhi said that, for him, "Truth is the sovereign principle," pointing to God as Absolute Truth, whose "manifestations are innumerable."[3] Life therefore could be viewed as consisting of "nothing but those experiments" where truth could be experienced and manifested. Gandhi did not become the source or norm for an understanding of leadership, but the fact that he was concerned with truth and faithfulness did come to serve as a point of reference for ordering a wide assortment of ideas and research.

Reflections on "experiments with truth" in conjunction with a wide selection of readings led to two theses, offering directions or clues to answers for the two questions about the kind of leadership that is needed and ways in which such leadership can be fostered:

> *First, the leadership needed for these times calls especially for a sense of vocation, commitment to truth expressed as moral courage, and a desire to serve.*
>
> *Second, the major avenue to the development of those who can offer such leadership rests in that kind of education for responsible membership that brings our conceptual inheritance to bear on our understanding and enactment of being and doing the truth in our care for the public.*

The procedure here will be to explore these two theses in order. Focal qualities cited as characterizing the kind of leadership especially called for in these times will not be analyzed directly or specifically. Rather, a broader presentation of approaches will suggest the context in which such qualities can be understood.

---

[2]James MacGregor Burns, *Leadership* (New York: Harper & Row, 1978) 451. He also admits that "we do not really know just what leadership is," and agrees with John Gardner that "many of the public statements about it are utter nonsense." Ibid.

[3]Gandhi, *Gandhi's Autobiography: The Story of My Experiments with Truth*, trans. Mahadev Desai (Washington DC: Public Affairs Press, 1948) 6.

With respect to the second thesis, dealing with education, reference will be made primarily to congregational education, although most statements have obvious implications for public education.

Leadership

When we speak of the kind of leadership needed for these times, are we implying that there is no normative definition? Probably. At least, I am not willing to venture a formal definition but rather look to that form or process of empowerment directed toward a worthy purpose offered by a person in various ways in configurations that differ from one period of time and one challenge to another. Moses, a political leader, with all the complexities of shifting configurations, at one time or another did exemplify such a description and did manifest all those qualities listed in the first thesis. He also *learned* how to be a leader. After exploring that statement about Moses in more detail, we shall move on to look at other persons or other perspectives, seeking to interpret the first thesis. Inevitably, such interpretations deal also with education, which emerges from almost any analysis as a first step toward doing something about the need for leaders.

First of all, then, what about Moses? Having complained about being a "nursing father" (Num. 11:12), he was able to express his religious calling by becoming a leader. Aaron Wildavsky, a political scientist who disclaims scholarly biblical competence, nevertheless writes a provocative analysis as he turns Moses' complaint into a book, *The Nursing Father: Moses as Political Leader*. His investigation informs the current conversation about leadership as well as offers new avenues for understanding the Bible. He presents Moses as able to become a political architect, sometimes deliberately designing a regime "to be compatible with his religion and personality," sometimes simply blundering "into a regime without fully understanding the consequences, either for his religion or for his style of leadership."[4]

Moses *learned* how to be a leader through interrogating experience, past and present. This "Mosaic" method "thrust him into becoming a participant in his own education," in a process during which he demonstrated several models of leadership. "Regime" is a key term. By that, Wildavsky means "political cultures, the shared values justifying the political practices that uphold different ways of life."[5] In responding to and shaping the regimes, Moses moved with his people from slavery to anarchy, then to a regime of equity, and finally to the institutionalization of leadership and the regime of hierarchy. The complex process of shap-

---

[4]Aaron Wildavsky, *The Nursing Father: Moses as a Political Leader* (University AL: University of Alabama Press, 1984) 19.
[5]Ibid., 5.

ing and being reshaped by the regime, for both leader and followers, is at the heart of the learning process that Wildavsky describes for Moses. This is quite different from the situational leadership theory of the social sciences, he says, which becomes a kind of collection of "kitchen-sink" variables. Wildavsky says that for him, the concept of leadership as a function of regime has to do with relating a people to God's intention through transformation of culture, understanding, and behavior. Obviously, this involves the "situation," but the elements of religion and moral leadership bring a new dimension. Moses learned how to be a founder of the nation, a revolutionary, a lawgiver, an administrator, a storyteller, a teacher, a student, and a politician. Somehow he changed the form of regime to what he was capable of doing and to what he thought must be done. He learned the dangers of the abuses of power. Finally, he taught the people that he was not God and that the future was in their hands.

The argument as developed by Wildavsky is far too complex to be presented here. It is a conversation with biblical meaning, Bible study, and interpretation in response to the questions brought to it, Wildavsky says—in this case, questions about what leadership is and how it develops and what the implications are for the future. The close relationship between learning, especially through failure, and leadership is a key to Wildavsky's view. And as for the future, no easy answer is available.

> Moses' interrogation of his own experience as a leader and as a teacher leaves us with the challenge of learning for ourselves. In learning how to make sense of the past as part of an effort to create an intelligible present, past instances and present problems merge to become a common body of evidence. As a rabbinic legend tells it . . . Moses himself goes on learning about the teaching he first imparted. The tradition has become autonomous. Once it is out of his hands, once his teaching becomes Torah, Moses has to learn from it like everyone else.[6]

Turn from the many models of leadership found in Moses to one model advocated by James Burns in *Leadership,* which he calls "transformative leadership," as over against "transactional leadership." His survey of literature on the topic from Plato to the present leads to the conclusion that society both needs and has the "makings" of an intellectual breakthrough through the rich literature that now encompasses many disciplines. At the heart of Burns's theory is the concept of *moral leadership,* which, he says, "concerns me the most."[7] Relationship between leaders and followers is always crucial for Burns's theory. Thus, for him, moral leadership "emerges from, and always returns to, the fundamental wants

---

[6]Ibid., 179.
[7]Burns, *Leadership,* 4.

and needs, aspirations, and values of the followers."[8] Such leadership is not a wielding of power or control but an authentic achievement of morally acceptable purpose. His explanation of the two basic types of leadership helps explain his theory:

> The relations of most leaders and followers are *transactional*—leaders approach followers with an eye to exchanging one thing for another: jobs for votes, or subsidies for campaign contributions. Such transactions comprise the bulk of the relationships among leaders and followers, especially in groups, legislatures, and parties. *Transforming* leadership, while more complex, is more potent. The transforming leader recognizes and exploits an existing need or demand of a potential follower. But, beyond that, the transforming leader looks for potential motives in followers, seeks to satisfy higher needs, and engages the full person of the follower. The result of transforming leadership is a relationship of mutual stimulation and elevation that converts followers into leaders and may convert leaders into moral agents.[9]

At the heart of his view of transforming leadership is its *teaching role*. He means here that the leader is so tuned to followers that separate interests are united in a collective pursuit of higher goals, which they come to understand as related to human purpose on the deepest possible level. This transformational leadership is therefore concerned with *end-values*, "such as liberty, justice, equality." Transactional leadership, in contrast, has to do more with *modal values*, "that is, values of means—honesty, responsibility, fairness, the honoring of commitments—without which transactional leadership could not work." On the other hand, Burns wants to be clear that leaders committed to a transformational theory must be alert to transactional styles since, as he says, "insufficient attention to means can corrupt the ends."[10] This kind of leadership, which is linked to collective moral purpose and to the realization of purpose in ways where ends and means are congruent, has the potential, Burns says, for building occasions where "persons *engage* with others in such a way that leaders and followers raise one another to higher levels of motivation and morality."[11] His appealing theory of leadership ends with Woodrow Wilson's call "for leaders who, by boldly interpreting the nation's conscience, ... could lift a people out of their everyday selves."[12]

A third approach is presented by David Loye, what he calls a "middle-position" between focus on conservation and on change. Concerned that "the lead-

---

[8]Ibid.
[9]Ibid.
[10]Ibid., 426.
[11]Ibid., 20.
[12]Ibid., 462.

ership passion'' may be dead or dying at the moment it is most desperately needed, he explores ways in which personality theory and approaches to social change interact with each other to produce persons capable of leading. The functioning of leaders, he says, has always fluctuated between those who viewed their role as norm maintaining and those who view it as norm changing. Heretic Pharaoh Akhenaton was a '' 'liberal' order shatterer'' who instigated radical change in Egypt. Charlemagne was a '' 'conservative' order reimposer'' who turned broken Rome into a Frankish empire.[13] Both were leaders. That is to say, innovation is not a norm for Loye, any more than liberal or conservative is. People of either orientation take risks, according to interesting research that contradicts the prevalent idea that only the liberal activist is a risk taker. Indeed, the increasing fragmentation and specialization of research has led to a loss of that passion for either stability or change that characterized past leaders. What happens, he says, in these times ''of rootlessness and ideological drift'' is that the dispassionate leader becomes the norm, a person of ''unmitigated expediency'' immersed in means and blind to ends, one who makes decisions on the basis of acquiring power and influence.

What is the way out of this dilemma? Loye points to certain directions, with promise of later development of ideas. For one thing, his ''middle-position'' advocates respect for ''the integrity of the passionate poles of left and right within the moderating periphery of liberalism and conservatism.'' There would be a balancing of ''the requirements for controlling and managing the system with the need to nurture and encourage its capacity for venturing.''[14] Along with this kind of view of the needed social leadership function is an image of leaders as ''reasonably *whole* people, with fully functioning hearts and minds.''[15] In fact, much of Loye's work has to do with the psychology of personality. He draws on motivation theory, on research on the authoritarian personality, on the interrelations of the social and personal dimensions of leadership. What emerges is a view of leadership as ''a functionally interrelated right and left,'' a style used for thousands of years in childrearing as well as in all ages and cultures, including the political work of the ''stellar company'' who developed the Declaration of Independence and the Constitution of the United States.[16] Can such a ''middle'' view evoke passion on the part of leaders and commitment on the part of followers? Loye sees no alternative for these times. For him, it is the best possibility for leaders to function in a way that relates personal commitment to social ends.

One final source for ideas feeding into the first thesis about leadership is Robert Greenleaf, both in his thought and through his life. A businessman who has

---

[13]Loye, *The Leadership Passion*, 3. Loye gives an excellent overview of research, especially in personality theory as related to social functions.

[14]Ibid., 223.

[15]Ibid., 222.

[16]Ibid., 222-24.

brought his concern into many realms of public life, especially as a consultant since retirement, he holds to the vision of servanthood as focal, a vision articulated in his *Teacher as Servant, Servant Leadership, The Servant as Religious Leader,* and other works. Greenleaf's interest in leadership began in his last term in college, when the professor, an "old man," in a "rambling lecture" pointed to the increasing dominance of large institutions. He called for some of the class to become "a force for good," leading those institutions "into better performance for the public good."[17] That was the beginning of Greenleaf's lifelong interest in leadership. Even in that beginning, the orientation was clearly toward servanthood.

In the course of a long life, Greenleaf says that without being able to give a logical explanation, he found himself increasingly moving toward concern with "religious-leading." For him, "leading is so dependent on *spirit* that the essence of it will never be capsuled or codified. Part of that essence lies beyond the barrier that separates mystery from what we call reality."[18] Reflection on research and theories gives rise to an uneasy feeling of a gap or incompleteness in what is needed to interpret leadership. Greenleaf brings a sense of rightness and confidence when the key term for him becomes *servant*. We are reminded of John Calvin's repeated statement, "We are not our own. . . . We are God's." Therefore, Calvin says, let us "abandon ourselves, and devote the whole energy of our minds to the service of God."[19] Surely the inner essence of leadership relates in some way to religious commitment and to a sense of vocation, a thought focused in the term *servant*.

I share Greenleaf's discontent with other terms often used to describe a leader; words like innovator, enabler, decision-maker, risk-taker, manager, organizer are somehow inadequate. Most of them deal with means more than ends; few of them seem even to suggest the importance of drawing on our conceptual inheritance to link past and present with the future; and they do not pick up the theme of the teaching role of the leader, as suggested by both Wildavsky and Burns. Of course, in general discussions, leadership may have as its frame of reference political or institutional or moral or religious spheres, or a host of other options. Moreover, leadership may refer either to a "natural" or to a "designated" leader. The person with a charismatic quality that inspires others seems to be endowed with a kind of personal power that enables him/her to help a group meet an urgent need or crisis, or function with high morale in ordinary circumstances. Such a "natural leader" may seem of a different order than the "designated leader," the corporate

---

[17]Robert Greenleaf, *Servant Leadership: A Journey into the Nature of Legitimate Power and Greatness* (New York: Paulist Press, 1977) 1-2.

[18]Robert Greenleaf, *The Servant as Religious Leader* (Peterborough NH: Windy Row Press, 1983) 6.

[19]John Calvin, *Institutes of the Christian Religion*, trans. Henry Beveridge, 2 vols. (London: James Clarke & Co., 1949) 3.7.1.

executive, the committee chair, the pastor, the school superintendent. But many functions—of interpretation, of building a common language and set of values, or organizing—cut across types of leadership. It does not seem possible to identify a set of personal traits that characterize a leader, in spite of the effort of numerous researchers to do exactly that.[20] But it does seem to be the case, whatever the setting, that leadership has to do with the moral and spiritual qualities of those persons of integrity who are able to share meaning and purpose, as well as to have and use the requisite skills for the tasks.[21] And whatever the task may be, in religious or secular spheres, it must be undertaken for the common good, not for personal aggrandizement. Thus Greenleaf's image of servant seems to hold up against competing images, as well as to give focus to some otherwise isolated research and concepts. It points clearly in the direction of the sense of vocation called for in the first thesis, as well as to the desire to serve.

Leadership is always both a mystery and a gift. The Lilly Endowment, with a long history of interest in leadership, expresses such a view in its 1984 report *Penetrating the Mystery of Leadership.* Having expressed the hope that the forthcoming bicentennial celebration of the U.S. Constitution would become the occasion for recalling the nation's "first principles," the report quotes the words of the English political philosopher Edmund Burke, written just a year after George Washington took office: "To be attached to the subdivision, to love the little platoon we belong to in society, is the first principle (the germ as it were) of public affections."[22]

The "little platoons" include those countless men and women, "dispersed leaders," who work in neighborhoods and community agencies and churches to make life better. There is no assumption that only the great and powerful are lead-

---

[20]See Matthew Miles's summary of research in his *Learning to Work in Groups,* 2nd ed. (New York: Teachers College Press, Columbia University, 1981) 17-18. He quotes R. M. Stogdill as saying in 1948, after having analyzed twenty-nine traits appearing in 124 studies, that there seems to be some slight relationship to leadership of "IQ, scholarliness, dependability, social participation, and socioeconomic status." Even then, he found that leaders in one situation were not necessarily viewed as leaders in another. And in 1974, after reviewing more than 3,000 books and articles, Stogdill concluded that the mass of findings was only bewildering and did not produce "an integrated understanding of leadership." C. M. Gibb was even clearer that there was no "consistent pattern of traits which characterizes leaders." Miles's own constructive synthesis is suggestive.

[21]Warren Bennis comes to this conclusion in his analysis of his interviews with ninety public and corporate leaders. His findings are reported in the tape, "Leadership in America," produced by Planet Tapes in 1984. Such persons brought leadership to workers and institutions in widely different settings. They were also able to rise to difficult tasks, as has been true historically. Bennis quotes Abigail Adams as saying to Thomas Jefferson, "These are the hard times . . . great necessities call for great leaders."

[22]Quoted by Robert Wood Lynn in *Penetrating the Mystery of Leadership* (Indianapolis IN: Lilly Endowment, Inc., 1984) 7.

ers. But faithfulness in small affairs prepares persons for broader responsibilities. In fact, at the root of individual commitment and of institutional service is "a shared sense of vocation, or, if you will, a common calling." The report goes on to say:

> In both the Jewish and Christian traditions, the presence of calling is embraced as a gift. The consequences of that gift are evident in a corporate sense of identity and in a unifying loyalty to a set of purposes. If that root sense of mission either has died or is decaying, the whole institution will sooner or later be affected in every respect. Nothing can be more subtle or serious an ailment that this sort of root disease. But whenever an institution undergoes renewal, its new life often springs from a deepened commitment to its vocation.[23]

Such statements lead inevitably to the question of how such values can be nurtured. Even though education cannot be suggested as *the* answer to such a question, it has at least some *beginning* answers, and in any case, there are implications for both religious and public education in the views expressed here, although most suggestions to follow spring primarily from the frame of reference of Christian education, most specifically, in its congregational setting.

Education for Responsible Membership as the Foundation for Leadership

What is the assumption behind the idea of approaching education for leadership through education for responsible membership? For one thing, much educational and administrative literature blurs the picture by references to "shared leadership" as the only appropriate way for a committee or class or institution to function.[24] References most often can better be designated as illustrative of responsible membership. It seems to be the case that membership is the matrix out of which leadership emerges, particularly when moral issues are at stake. Therefore any specific leadership education must presuppose a more basic education. This is not to say that there is no room for specialized "leadership" educational training. Rather, such processes are situation-specific (task, setting, institutional mission), probably quite temporary in form and procedure, and related to the support of the community served by its leaders.

---

[23]Ibid., 8.

[24]Literature on group process, coming from several fields, may be the source of the idea that everyone is a leader or that leadership is a function that shifts within a group. There is a truth in such statements, of course, but the tendency to make leadership mean simply *everything* blurs specific usefulness of the term. More important, inadequate attention is given to the concept of what characterizes responsible membership. To offer support to one another, to listen with care, to run the risk of proposing action, to offer moral insight—all of these responsibilities are as important for the member as for the leader.

Explore the idea of education more directly. If we are seeking to develop leadership for the church in a way that will motivate energies and unify loyalties around purpose, what is necessary? Clarity of understanding of the "roots" out of which that purpose comes, with ability to interpret the stories and beliefs and liturgies that shape and reshape the community. Ability to employ a common language and to build on a common memory for the whole community. Awareness of what is believed to be true, and ability to recognize the hints of truth to be observed in small and large decisions day by day. In quite practical terms, the curriculum that is planned, including printed and other resources and intentional structured activities, must be directed to *everyone,* else there can be no shared purpose. In most of its early history, the Protestant Church in the United States had built into the fabric of its congregational life, in preaching and education, concern for the public good. How have we lost that concern? Possibly through diffusing the concept of education to include simply influence from many sources, but more likely, through neglect of the work of direct teaching about our conceptual inheritance. But because truth must be "done" as well as "understood," we are calling for an education for faithfulness, for obedience, one that draws on heritage as the source for the value we place on care for the common good. If public institutions were asked about education for responsible membership in the public domain, or education for citizenship, the answer would be almost the same. What would be required, in addition, would be the right of all persons to know about the religious heritage of the nation, not as the source of eliciting commitment, but rather for understanding and affirming those "habits of the heart" that have shaped the American people up to this point. Such a view rests on the assumption that we value our national heritage, or to put the matter in other terms, that we cherish our membership in our nation, even that we cherish our membership in the human community. The member has the right to be critical, to call for reform. And the member works on problems, all the way from refusing to use certain pesticides to joining a research group working on conservation of the earth's resources. He or she does that because responsibility goes with membership. Thomas Green, educational philosopher, proposes that formation of conscience may well be the approach to moral education for these days, not as a private matter, but as a way of linking individual responsibility to the office of citizen and thus to public life. He says this:

> In other words, the proper unit of consideration in the conduct of moral education is not the individual, not even the individual conscience. Rather, *it is the member.* Conscience as membership is the fundamental reality that moral education must take as its object.[25]

---

[25]Thomas Green, *The Formation of Conscience in an Age of Technology* (Syracuse NY: Syracuse University and the John Dewey Society, 1984) 8. The whole of Green's lec-

Green reminds us of the close relationship between education and citizenship in Greek philosophy. For example, think of Plato's three classes of citizens in the *Republic*: artisans, warriors, and philosopher-rulers. The intention is not to promote class distinction but to enable each person to find a place in society that fits his or her abilities and to engage in an education that would develop those individual gifts in such a way that one's function in society could be fulfilled. Aristotle was equally explicit in his view that citizens did not belong just to themselves, and therefore were to be educated for the good of the state. Such an understanding reappears periodically, and links education and morality, membership and leadership.[26] If such a stance is to be taken toward the foundational nature of education for responsible membership, what are the emphases especially appropriate for the kind of leader we have been describing? Out of many possibilities, four present themselves as most critical for this moment in history.

1. Commitment to Truth. When Jesus, near the end of his earthly life, in the interchange with Pilate, said that he came to "bear witness to the truth" (John 18:37), he was surely talking about something different from the kind of intellectualist view of truth jestingly tossed aside by Pilate. In the biblical view, truth not only belongs to God, but God *is* truth—in essence and in attributes, in what has been made known as Self-revelation in Jesus Christ, as hope and demand for human beings. The person who is committed to this kind of truth is "held" by that truth and shaped by it.

Such an understanding seems compatible with Gandhi's view of his life as "experiments with truth." It does involve moral courage and sacrifice but does not exclude the necessity for thinking, seeking understanding. Gandhi's autobiographical accounts of his intellectual wrestling with those who sought to convert him to Christianity or to a particular political position demonstrate his unwillingness to accept or act on what he did not believe to be the case, that is, to be true. And in these days, when we seem to rely more on what can be made believable or expedient or titillating than on what is true, we are in trouble.

Think about the implications of such a view for congregational education. On the one hand, it means that we will educate in such a way that we come to know what we believe and why, in order that we might be able to help one another understand our identity and our calling as a people to serve God. On the other hand,

---

ture relates to this essay. In fact, in ways that he might not recognize, many of his concepts inform what is said here, especially those related to *membership*. In his discussion of "conscience as craft," he links the skills and habits developed with respect to small affairs to developing skills for living, a concept closely related to the vocabulary of ethics in Greek philosophy. His additional consideration of conscience as sacrifice, as memory, and as imagination contributes to an evocative presentation when one thinks about leadership and education.

[26]Cf. the symposium on "Philosophers and Kings: Studies in Leadership," *Daedalus* (Summer 1968).

it means that in our life together, including our outreach in service and in action, we engage in that kind of embodiment of faithfulness that enables us to know the truth by participating in it. Education, therefore, entails certain intentional activities related to understanding, but it utilizes for reflection, and in fact is dependent upon, "doing the truth" in individual life, community work, and worship. Although there are differences, much of what has been said here is applicable to education in the public domain.

   2. *Equipping the Saints for the Work of Ministry.* Throughout this essay there has been both a direct and indirect appeal to reclaim the idea of vocation, of calling. One of the things we Christians have lost, or almost lost, is that part of our heritage where in higher education, for example, we view ourselves as educating leaders for public responsibility, politicians and doctors as well as preachers. To be a Christian is, in fact, to be called to serve. Loss of meaning may be related to the loss of a sense of call. To educate for responsible membership in church or nation is to build toward self-understanding as individual calling.

   Take Dag Hammarskjold. He wrote for a radio program of Edward R. Murrow's that he "inherited" from his father a belief in "selfless service" to his country, and from his mother, a belief that in the "very radical sense of the Gospels," human beings were to be served "as children of God," a belief that he says gave direction to his life.[27] Although he did not publicize his religious commitment, and most persons knew only of his disciplined service as United Nations Secretary-General, Hammarskjold is an example of one whose life was an exemplar of his sense of calling.

   Again, think of a congregation. What if the annual worship service commissioning church school teachers were to develop into a commissioning service for leaders in public life? For business ventures that express risk and call for moral courage? What if we were to develop the idea of lay academies or schools of theology? Somehow those possibilities have never achieved their potential. Groups of persons, by occupation, meet together to consider ethical issues and forms of faithfulness. Some congregations are large enough to organize study groups as short-term electives within their own programs. The list could go on. We are limited only by lack of imagination and belief in the importance of vocation.

   3. *Discipleship and Citizenship.* For several years (1982-86), it was my privilege to be a part of a Lilly Endowment-funded interdisciplinary National Faculty Seminar, meeting at Christian Theological Seminary in Indianapolis. As a kind of venture in education for leadership, it dealt with issues in church education and centered on the question, "How might our activities of interpreting the Christian faith educate for the future good of the world?" Investigation unfolded in what we called an "organic process," dealing with many questions. The emphases se-

---

   [27]Dag Hammarskjold, *Markings,* trans. Leif Sjoberg and W. H. Auden (New York: Knopf, 1964) vii-viii.

lected here for consideration—discipleship and citizenship, and the one on bilingual education—come from that Seminar. They are mentioned primarily in the hope that readers will want to move to the far more detailed presentations by the authors who first offered them.[28] What they have to say is directly related to education for religious and public life.

Sociologist John Coleman, in his "The Two Pedagogies: Discipleship and Citizenship" agrees with Robert Bellah and associates, who, in their *Habits of the Heart,* found a remarkable relationship between individual character and society. Family life, religious traditions, and participation in local politics helped shape the kind of person who could support and maintain free institutions. But Alexis de Tocqueville was concerned even in the 1830s as to whether American individualism would become excessive and lessen commitment to the common good, thus eventually undermining the very conditions of freedom. Coleman says he shares the judgments of Bellah and associates that "a renewal of both discipleship and the more secular notion of republican virtue in the classic concept of republican citizenship would be necessary for any vital public philosophy in America today," although, as he says, he "does not give to the two notions the equal weight they give."[29] Agreeing with de Tocqueville that Christians are bound together with a vision of a universal world community going beyond all nations and boundaries, he sees that Christians could easily neglect citizenship. Here we see again the theme of responsible membership. Is it the case that disciples seek to "serve" the public but do not have an adequate view of what it means to *belong,* to be a part of the nation?

Coleman works at the relationship. He sees discipleship and citizenship as "both semi-autonomous (neither reducible to nor subordinate to the other), yet interrelated" zones of life, and is clear that the task for the future is to educate for both. Because of the interrelated nature of the two, people must work on both, with conversations that deal with both. Historically, Christians have been more directly concerned with discipleship, and yet, in a sense, education for discipleship is incomplete without education for citizenship. Citizenship, according to Coleman, adds to discipleship three qualities: "a wider solidarity, a humbler service, a more taxing reality-test for responsibility." The first step to developing the two pedagogies is to be clear about the meaning of discipleship and citizenship, and their relationship. That is the focus of Coleman's article.

When the subject matter of congregational education focuses exclusively on discipleship, we come to neglect our membership in the human community, with a re-

---

[28]Full reports of the work of the National Faculty Seminar are to be published in the near future. The two essays mentioned here are from *Education for Citizenship and Discipleship,* ed. Mary C. Boys. The second related volume is *Tensions Between Citizenship and Discipleship: A Case Study,* ed. Nelle Slater.

[29]See manuscript, Coleman, "The Two Pedagogies," esp. 51-54.

sponsibility that is more than a by-product of our faith. One should be a citizen, whether or not she or he is a disciple. But to be a citizen motivated and empowered by the faith of a disciple does indeed bring a new dimension to living. We have much work to do here in terms of implications for congregational education.

4. *Bilingual Education.* This second idea from the National Faculty Seminar is related to the first. Old Testament scholar Walter Brueggemann presented a paper entitled ''The Legitimacy of a Sectarian Hermeneutic,'' based on a study of 2 Kings 18-19.[30] He describes the dramatic encounter between the Assyrians and Judah, with the Assyrian army at the gate of Jerusalem, ready to receive the surrender of the city, which had been under siege. Brueggemann describes the drama in two parts—the conversation at the wall of the city and the conversation behind the wall.

At the wall the Assyrian negotiator tauntingly shouts the terms of surrender, saying that Yahweh is no more powerful than the other gods of the Near East, who have not been able to protect their people. King Hezekiah's emissary answers: Do not speak to us in the language of Judah, that is, Hebrew. Speak to us in Aramaic, that is, the language of international diplomacy. If the people hear the negotiations, they seem to be saying, in the language they can understand, they will be terrified, and we cannot negotiate. Of course, the negotiator does exactly what he has been asked not to do; he speaks in the language that makes negotiation impossible. But then there follows another conversation behind the wall where, out of sight of the Assyrians, the king does what Brueggemann calls ''grief work.'' He goes to the house of the Lord; he prays; he summons Isaiah to pray for the king and city. There, the power of Yahweh is assumed. And confidence in that power is validated at the end of the narrative with the deliverance.

Dramatically, it is important to note that these two conversations ''go on at about the same time.'' As Brueggemann says, ''. . . people of faith in public life must be *bilingual.* They must have a *public language* for negotiation at the wall. And they must have a more *communal language* for processing behind the gate, in that community.'' He urges that church education ''nurture people to be bilingual.''

The basic language for Christians is the language behind the wall: their community, the community that forms and is shaped by that language. The community must learn the language there, must sustain each other, wrestle at the deepest level of discipleship. But the community has no right to impose its language on others or to expect either motivation or perception that springs from that language. Nor should this sectarian community regard itself as having a monopoly on truth. In fact, the truth held by the community behind the wall is also subject to reform. But above all things, that faith community must not allow the larger community to impose its views of reality, its norms, on the judgments made by the faith group.

---

[30]Excerpts here come from selected passages in Walter Brueggemann, ''The Legitimacy of a Sectarian Hermeneutic.''

Both languages are legitimate. Neighbor-love, not just Christian love, becomes operative now. The requirement, therefore, is for bilingual education.

One conclusion to draw from such a view is that we Christians cannot escape involvement in public education. We become informed not in order to control it but with respect to our membership as citizens and to the care for the public that characterizes us as disciples. But then, in our church education, we help one another as we learn better how to use *both* languages, how to become bilingual. That, too, is the challenge for the future.

* * *

In summary, what is to be said about the kind of leaders and of education needed for the emerging twenty-first century? Leaders, those responsible persons who through their own moral courage and wisdom express their calling in ways that bring other persons together around purpose, are understandably sought for these days. They are not "educated" separately but as members.

Concerns expressed earlier in this essay—about our seeming to be "hopelessly adrift," about what has been called "homelessness of mind"— call clearly for moral leadership. In fact, every writer considered refers to the need for such leadership. Skills are important; it is not enough to hold out a moral vision and do nothing. Leaders need to hold out hope in a situation that is increasingly approached pessimistically.[31] And the source of such hope, ultimately, lies in God, not in human ability. For Gandhi, God *was* Absolute Truth. And however one understands God, or whatever doctrinal affirmations one makes, the path chosen by Gandhi still seems relevant. That is, the lifelong seeking to know, to be related to Truth, calls for action and being that are consistent with one's understanding. Believing and doing belong together. The subtitle for Gandhi's *Autobiography, The Story of My Experiments with Truth,* points to a unity of vision and form, of commitment and ways of being in the world. Again, we have no prescriptive guidelines, no criteria, but only an image and a direction. Somehow one must hold together reference to means and ends, to educational form and content. Dedicated minds work out "with painful thought" their faithful service of formulating purposes and processes. That may be what responsible membership in faith community and nation is like. If it becomes leadership, in one's expression of vocation, it is all the more a call to servanthood.

---

[31] "Futures," *Daedalus* (Summer 1987), is a case in point when such pessimism is mentioned.

Three

Paideia
for Higher Education

10

Protestants, Paideia, and Pioneers: Protestantism's First Great Cause

Glenn Miller

Werner Jaeger's monumental work *Paideia*,[1] published twenty-five years ago, set a new standard for educational historiography. Carefully weaving themes from the varieties of Greek culture with accounts of Greek literary and philosophical developments, Jaeger pictured a society dedicated to the training of body and soul for virtue and public life. For Jaeger, the various religious, social, and cultural components of Greek life had been smelted into an educational alloy stronger than any of its parts. The book did more than illumine the history of classical Greece. It also provided a possible model for the study of Protestant education that might reveal a similar amalgamation of ideals and institutions. Such a venture might be promising for contemporary American Protestants, often on the "margin" of present-day discussions about education.[2]

Thinkers writing about Protestantism have long sensed connections between Protestantism and education. Such nineteenth-century scholars as Ernst Troeltsch, Max Weber, and Adolf von Harnack[3] believed Protestantism had upset and eroded

---

[1]Werner Jaeger, *Paideia: The Ideals of Greek Culture*, 3 vols., trans. Gilbert Highet (Oxford: Blackwell 1947–1954).

[2]For the marginalization of Protestantism in education, see Robert W. Lynn, *Protestant Strategies in Education* (New York: Association Press, 1964).

[3]See Max Weber, *The Protestant Ethic and The Spirit of Capitalism*, 2nd ed., trans. Talcott Parsons (New York: Scribner's 1958); Ernst Troeltsch, *Protestantism and Progress: The Significance of Protestantism for the Rise of the Modern World* (Philadelphia: Fortress, 1968); Adolf von Harnack, *Thoughts on the Present Position of Protestantism*, trans. Thomas Bailey Saunders (London: A & C Black, 1899). For a sound discussion of the relationship between

the traditional European order and thus inspired (wittingly or unwittingly) new movements in economics, science, and government. H. Richard Niebuhr, although somewhat chastened by neoorthodoxy, recast the work of these earlier cultural analysts. Niebuhr believed that Protestantism, particularly its Calvinist form, was an embodiment of a theology that saw Christ as the transformer of culture. As Niebuhr understood Protestantism, the church reconstructed or reformed the ordinary affairs of life by imposing on the believer an acute sense of responsibility. As a consequence, Protestants were made aware that creative cultural change was always possible.[4] Keith Thomas in *Religion and the Decline of Magic*[5] provided a very graphic illustration of Niebuhr's theses. In the seventeenth century, he maintained, Protestant practices and teachings discredited ancient folk-beliefs and opened the way for validation of scientific explanation.

Protestantism's cultural power was mediated through religious practices that encouraged education. All religions combine ritual, ethics, and beliefs in different proportions, and their surrounding cultures reflect the varying weight given to each ingredient by the dominant faith. By emphasizing the sole authority of Scripture, Protestants accentuated the doctrinal or teaching component in the Christian tradition. Further, Protestants in Germany, England, and Scandinavia replaced the traditional ecclesiastical mysteries with new liturgies, printed in "prayer" or service books, that required the worshiper to read or memorize the appropriate responses. In Calvinist churches, worship was yet more austere and intellectual.

Wherever (and whenever) Protestantism has triumphed, Paul's admonition that faith comes by hearing was heeded. The Protestant sermon[6] combined exegesis, doctrine, and exhortation, forcing the hearer to attend to organization and detail. Further, Protestants first revived the ancient Christian art of catechetics and later experimented with Sunday schools. To this already substantial educational program, some Protestants, especially eighteenth-century pietists (evangelicals) and their successors, added regular individual biblical study.[7]

Troeltsch and Harnack, see Wilhelm Pauck, *Harnack and Troeltsch: Two Historical Theologians* (New York: Oxford University Press, 1968). Much of the analysis, of course, was based on the belief that Protestantism was a necessary antechamber to the Enlightenment.

[4]H. Richard Niebuhr, *Christ and Culture* (New York: Harper & Row, 1951).

[5]Keith Thomas, *Religion and the Decline of Magic* (New York: Scribner's, 1971).

[6]While there were some anti-intellectuals among American revivalists, the sermons were by no means devoid of content. Methodist and Baptist exhorters, for example, wrestled with the substantial issues of grace and free will with a high degree of precision, and such evangelists as Charles Finney adopted styles of preaching related to the rhetoric of the law courts. In the twentieth century, Protestant conservatives, who often assumed a seeming anti-intellectual stance in the evolution battles of the 1920s, have been important contributors to education and have established many schools, colleges, and universities.

[7]Virginia Brereton described the nineteenth-century pietist/evangelical understanding of biblical studies as

. . . a biblicism that included such elements as a reverence for the Authorized or

Yet, what was most remarkable about Protestants was not the educational elements in their culture. Until comparatively recently, Protestants made education, religious and secular, a "cause" or "movement." Schools were Protestantism's first great crusade—the great assault on the powers of darkness—and Protestant rhetoric linked learning with the future of church and society. In simple terms, to be Protestant was to favor educational advance. Although Protestants later espoused many other causes, education was a constant feature of their strategy of social change.[8] Schools were the means of reform.

But why an educational crusade? Since religions most often change cultures by slowly penetrating their adherents' understanding of the world, why did Protestants not trust their religious reforms to change society? What happened to the crusade when Protestants arrived in the comparatively free American environment? And what has happened to the crusade today?

The Making of a Crusade

Unlike Jaeger's ancient Greeks, who developed their educational strategy by the slow processes of evolution, the early Protestants were reformers. Martin Luther (1483-1546), a monk and professor at the small University of Wittenberg,

---

King James version of the Bible, for every word as the actual utterance of God; an intimacy with Scripture so constantly cultivated that the biblical rhythms became part of daily speech; the conviction that knowledge of the Bible makes a decisive and practical difference in the whole range of the individual's life, from the critical matter of the salvation of one's soul to smaller questions of how to conduct one's daily affairs.

"The Public Schools Are Not Enough," in David L. Barr and Nicholas Piediscalzi, *The Bible in American Education* (Philadelphia: Fortress; Chico CA: Scholars Press, 1982) 54-55.

[8]The First Great Awakening in America demonstrates this inherent link very well. Convinced New England revivalists, experiencing some opposition from Yale, joined with New Side Presbyterians to establish the College of New Jersey. When Eleazer Wheelock (1711-1779), inspired by the revival and by the Indian Christian, Samson Occom, felt called to carry the gospel to the Indians, he established Moor's Charity School in 1743 to train young Indians and, after that enterprise was condemned by the authorities, he moved to frontier New Hampshire to repeat the experiment at Dartmouth College. Recently, William Hutchison has noted the power of the ideal of the mission school on nineteenth-century Protestant missionaries, even when the prevailing missiology in the supporting boards wished another approach. See *Errand to the World: American Protestant Thought and Foreign Missions* (Chicago and London: University of Chicago Press, 1987) esp. 77-90. The same point can be made about the foreign mission movement in Europe, which began at the University of Halle, in the context of a movement of university reform, and whose most vibrant center was the Basle Mission School. See Glaue, "Heidenmission: III Geschichtlich," *Die Religion in Geschichte und Gegenwart,* various editors, 5 vols. (Tübingen: J. C. B. Mohr, 1910) 2:1979A-98B. Hereafter, R.G.G.

The most substantial Protestant response to nineteenth-century feminism was the establishment of women's colleges. See Leonard Sweet, "The Female Seminary Movement and Women's Mission in Ante-Bellum America," *Church History* 54 (March 1985): 41-55.

had long been burdened by guilt. Sometime between 1512 and 1515, primarily because of his humanistic and theological studies, he became convinced that God—solely because of the work of Christ—had forgiven him. His new faith was "a religion of conscience" that issued from:

> a particular kind of conscientious experience—namely, his unique experience of the conflict between a keen sense of divine will—and rest[ed] on the conviction that in the sense of obligation (*sollen*), which impresses its demands so irresistibly upon the human will, divinity reveals itself most clearly.[9]

Luther's experience compelled him to follow two contradictory courses of action. Since Luther's faith was profoundly personal, he had to interpret all events in terms of their effects on his own soul. Every happening was thus intensely private. But that same faith required obedience to the unconditional commands of God. Whatever pricked Luther's conscience required public action.

Luther drew the social and political implications of his religious program in his early treatise *To the Christian Nobility of the German Nation* (1520).[10] While the work advocated many changes in German life—including the establishment of more schools—its most important assertion was that the German princes were to exercise their rightful responsibility for (and authority over) the nation's religious and cultural life. The radicalism of Luther's call is easy for later observers to overlook. While church leaders had often summoned the secular rulers to attain religious purposes, Luther demanded that the government be authentically secular—to act in the world for the world's sake.

Europe's leading educators, the humanists, were baffled by Luther's secularity. The goal of the humanists had been to recover the beauty and simplicity of the classical literary works of antiquity, and by Luther's time, they had almost achieved it. Humane studies had become the center of the arts program in many universities. In addition, the printing press had made their Latin, Greek, and Hebrew grammars and critical editions of ancient authors available to the educated. The humanists feared that Luther's involvement of the princes in education would end their own program of reform:

---

[9]Karl Holl, *What Did Luther Understand by Religion?* ed. James Luther Adams and Walter F. Bense, trans. Fred W. Meuser and Walter R. Wietzke (Philadelphia: Fortress, 1977) 48.

[10]The *Address* remains a curious book. Although Luther is clearly arguing for a regeneration of faith and a rejection of the papacy as then constituted, he takes the occasion to discuss such varied topics as the need for a law against extravagance, the regulation of the spice trade, the *zynskauf*, the Fuggers, excessive eating and drinking, the toleration of brothels, and undisciplined children. See *The Address to the German Nobility*, in Martin Luther, *Three Treatises* (Philadelphia: Fortress, 1960) 100-12.

Because most schools had been religious schools in the middle ages, many common people, who were only recently converted to evangelical or Protestant ideas, associated education with Catholicism. . . . Many humanists were apprehensive about the new theology for this reason. Thus Eobanus Hesse had written to the Wittenberg theologians in 1523 to express his view that the new theology was destructive of scholarship.[11]

The humanist distaste for Luther ripened into intellectual warfare.

While Desiderius Erasmus (1469-1536), the leading sixteenth-century humanist scholar, agreed with Hesse and others that "wherever Lutheranism prevails, learning and liberal culture go to ground,"[12] his most trenchant criticism of the Lutherans had to do with their failure to transform human behavior:

Just look at the evangelical people, have they become any better? Do they yield less to luxury, lust and greed? Show me a man whom that Gospel has changed from a toper to a temperate man, from a brute to a gentle creature, from a miser to a liberal person, from a shameless to a chaste being. I will show many who have become even worse than they were.[13]

Erasmus recognized that the dispute involved two different understandings of the will. For Luther and his followers, the will was bound to either God or Satan; for Erasmus, the will, like the mind, was free to seek and do the good. To win their dispute, Protestant theologians had to show that their schools could promote good literature and good morals.

Luther alongside Philipp Melanchthon (1497-1560), professor of Greek at Wittenberg, and Johann Bugenhagen (1485-1558), appointed pastor of the Wittenberg church in 1522, began a program of school reform and construction. The crusade expanded into other areas. By 1526, the Landgraf Philip of Hesse had adopted a new educational program, designed by Melanchthon and admittedly more designed for the urban and town areas of his realm. He was followed in time by the other evangelical princes.

---

[11]W. Wright, "The Impact of the Reformation," *Church History* 44 (1985): 185. Luther himself commented on the attitude of ordinary people to the effects of his movement on education:

And because selfish parents see that they can no longer place their children upon the bounty of monasteries and cathedrals, they refuse to educate them. "Why should we educate our children," they say, "if they are not to become priests, monks, and nuns, and thus earn a support."

Letter to the Mayors and Aldermen of Germany (1524) cited in Frederick Eby, *Early Protestant Educators: The Educational Writings of Martin Luther, John Calvin, and Other Leaders of Protestant Thought* (New York and London: McGraw-Hill, 1931) 45.

[12]Ibid., 13.

[13]Ibid., 177.

Although each principality adopted its own *Schulordnungen*[14] (literally, school order or educational laws) reflecting local conditions (especially the financial resources available), their outline was similar. Often mandating textbooks prepared by the reformers (especially Melanchthon who wrote Greek, Latin, logic, and rhetoric textbooks), students began with the rudiments of German, advanced to the study of Latin and, if successful, Greek. The best then went to the university. This literary understanding of education was accepted by later Protestants.[15] When Calvin began his work in 1536, this pattern of education was part of what it meant for a nation to accept the new religion.[16]

Higher education was also restructured. Melanchthon strove for the reorganization of the universities and, in some cases (including Wittenberg and Tübingen) composed new regulations for them. Other schools also followed his lead. Since Melanchthon was convinced that theology without philosophy was blind, he identified The Philosopher's works, especially his studies of logic and of rhetoric, as a necessary point of European intellectual reference, especially in such areas as physics.

Melanchthon's neo-Aristotelianism was not a resurrection of the older university course. Not only was Scripture the judge of philosophy, but the philosophy was to be derived from the exegetical and philological study of Aristotle's own works. "Back to the sources," the great cry of humanism, was the motto for philosophy as well as theology. Serious studies of Latin, Greek, and Hebrew authors, including the new historical and philological study of antiquity, were the center

---

[14]The classical collection of these "ordinances" is Reinhold Vormbawm, *Evangelische Schulordnungen,* 3 vols. (Gütersloh, 1854–1864).

[15]Clyde Manschreck, *Melanchthon: The Quiet Reformer* (New York and Nashville: Abingdon, 1958) 142. For Scotland see Rab Houston, "The Literacy Myth? Illiteracy in Scotland 1630–1760," *Past and Present* 96 (1982): 83-99. Because of the secularization of the various chantry lands, some of which were devoted to the support of teachers, some have seen the Reformation as not supporting schools in England. However, as A. G. Dickens has noted:

> In England the advance of the Reformation cannot be truly portrayed as a period of educational decline, because it coincided with a time of marked enthusiasm for humanist schooling, and there were strong historical links between the two. It can be demonstrated that the foundation of new schools continued throughout the Elizabethan and Stuart periods; the gain from the new immensely exceeded any conceivable loss of the old.

A. G. Dickens and John M. Tonkin, *The Reformation in Historical Thought* (Cambridge MA: Harvard University Press, 1985) 346.

[16]The word *order* has been used because the more common English word *system* implies a bureaucratic hierarchy as well as a coherent understanding of education that made its various elements interchangeable. A German student could (and many did) attend a common school in Wittenberg, a gymnasium in Mannheim, and a university in Prussia without a significant change in standards.

of the curriculum.[17] The same spirit of reform influenced the other faculties, especially law, where the study of the great Roman legal texts of antiquity became standard. In England the reforms were carried even further. The traditional professional faculties were all but abolished, and university education became essentially a course in classical literature.

What did the reformers hope to accomplish by their educational crusade? The knowledge of languages was, to be sure, part of the deposit of Reformation faith. As Luther said, "Be sure of this: we will not long preserve the Gospel without the languages."[18] But the training of theologians was not the primary motive for the Protestant interest in schools. James Bowen, a noted historian of schooling, interpreted Protestant education as predominately ideological:

> In the sixteenth century, it [education] came to be appreciated as a highly important social process, especially after the stimulus given by Erasmus and Luther who argued very persuasively that the propagation and maintenance of religious beliefs—and hence political loyalty—could be controlled to an appreciable extent through the school and the procedures of education.[19]

The common goal of early Protestant educators was their desire to instruct the elite: "those qualified to teach in church and govern in the world."[20] Bugenhagen's "School Ordinance" for Brunswick used this language: " . . . that in time there may come good schoolmasters, good preachers, good jurists, good physicians, God-fearing, decent, honorable, well-grounded, obedient, sociable, scholarly, peaceable, sober but happy citizens."[21] John Knox bluntly argued for schools because "God had determined that his churche heir on earth shall be ruled not by angelles, but by men."[22] During the great expansion of English education in the period from 1600 to 1640, similar language was in the charters of new Latin

---

[17]Pielt, "Universitaeten," *R.G.G.* 5:1488-89; Manschreck, *Melanchthon,* 144-57; R. L. Harrison, "Melanchthon's Role in the Reformation of the University of Tübingen," *Church History* 47 (1978): 270-78.

[18]Cited in Bernhard Lohse, *Martin Luther: An Introduction to His Life and Work* (Philadelphia: Fortress, 1986) 132.

[19]James Bowen, *A History of Western Education,* 3 vols. (New York: St. Martin's Press, 1981) 3:4.

[20]Melanchthon, *The Articles of the Saxon Visitation* (1528), cited in Richard Gawthrop and Gerald Strauss, "Protestantism and Literacy in Modern Germany," *Past and Present* 104 (1984): 31-35.

[21]Cited in Eby, *Early Protestant,* 193.

[22]John Knox, "The Buke of Discipline," *Works,* vol. 7, ed. David Laing (Edinburgh: J. Thin, 1894–1895) 208. The spelling is Knox's.

schools, new colleges in the ancient universities, and charters of Harvard, Yale, and William and Mary in North America.[23]

While the languages were the nationalization papers required by the republic of letters, educators also valued them because linguistic studies trained students in self-discipline. The curriculum was designed to instill in the student, not so much religious faith or theological acuity, as the habits of mind needed for leadership.[24]

What is remarkable about Protestant endeavors in education was the comparative lack of religious focus. While religion, especially the catechism, was included, as were devotional exercises, the bulk of the students' time and the teachers' effort were devoted to secular subjects. In the early "grades," the primary classroom exercise was grammar, which was usually taught by the repetition of paradigms. As the student advanced, Latin translation and composition, along with drill in Greek grammar, came to the fore. Although Protestant educators preferred to use the more moralistic passages in the works of the ancients, the criteria of excellence was resolutely secular: Whether Christian or pagan, the writer had to write clearly and with literary grace.

The Protestant concern for leadership in church and state was an integral part of the Reformation vision. From its beginnings, Protestantism was dependent on the state, whether prince or city council, for the implementation of the new faith. In effect, the government replaced the hierarchical church as the source of ecclesiastical and theological legitimacy, and the various princes and city councils often legally commandeered the traditional prerogatives of the bishops. In most Protestant lands, including Calvinist Scotland, the crown was the head of the church on earth, the protector of true religion, the "nursing father of the church." In turn, the churches made the cause of the government their own.[25] The various princes and city councils were the objects of established liturgical prayers, the various wars of the Protestant states were seen as holy wars (often with apocalyptic significance), and the judgments of the civil courts, the voice of God on earth.[26] Prot-

---

[23]Bowen, *A History*, 3:131; Ian Green, "Career Prospects and Clerical Conformity in the Early Stuart Church," *Past and Present* 90 (1981): 72; Lawrence Stone, "The Educational Revolution in England, 1560–1640," *Past and Present* 28 (1974): 69.

[24]This style of education began to change in the late eighteenth and nineteenth century when educators came to see education more in terms of the mastery of a subject than the mastery of the self. But, by this point, Protestant influence was weakening.

[25]There is, of course, little that is unique about the so-called American civil religion. Protestants have always seen government as sacred and made semireligious heroes (secular saints) of political leaders. The one unique of American civil piety was that it was comprehensive enough to include (at least over time) Catholics and Jews.

[26]The Protestant ideal of law was perhaps best expressed by Sir Edward Coke, (1552–1634), whose *Reports* and *Institutes* continually referred to the Bible as the foundation of common law.

estantism, wherever it was found, aspired to be, in Benjamin Franklin's insightful phrase, "a public religion," with demonstrated "usefulness."[27]

Once the trauma of the great religious wars of the sixteenth and seventeenth centuries had ended, Protestant theologians began to envision the completion of the work of the reformers.[28] Naturally, the "new reformation" had to include changes in education as well. The "pietists" (a name invented by their enemies) were particularly interested in popular education.[29] The most active pietist reformer of schooling was August Hermann Francke (1663-1727), appointed by the king of Prussia to transform the small "knight's academy" at Halle into a new university. He summoned a distinguished faculty, including the jurist Thomasius, and began a reform of university studies that included the radical innovations of lectures in German and a program in chemistry.

Francke was determined to expand education to include the average person. Karl von Canstein, one of Francke's relatives, established the first Protestant Bible Society (the *Canstein Bibelhaus*). The new society (which published more than two million Bibles and one million New Testaments in its first hundred years)[30] used a steam press to make the Bible one of the least expensive books in Germany. But it was not enough to make the Bible available; everyone had to be able to read it, including women who had been slighted by earlier Protestant educators. Moreover, the pietists were determined advocates of universal literacy in Germany. Francke's privileged position with the Prussian nobility and king[31] made his demands "instrumental in creating the institutions through which German society achieved a high rate of literacy in the course of the eighteenth century."[32]

---

[27]Benjamin Franklin, cited in John F. Wilson, *Public Religion in American Culture* (Philadelphia: Temple University Press, 1979) 7. Significantly, the phrase was used in the context of a proposal to create an academy in Philadelphia.

[28]Philip Jacob Spener (1635–1705) put this simply: "I have never been of the opinion, and am not now, that the Reformation of Luther was brought to completion as one might hope." Cited in Eamon Duffy, "The Society of [*sic*] Promoting Christian Knowledge and Europe: The Background to the Founding of the *Christentums Gesellschaft,*" *Pietismus und Neuzeit* 7 (1981): 33.

[29]Martin Schmidt, "Epochen der Pietismusforschung," in *Der Pietismus als theologische Erscheinung: Gesammelte Studien zur Geschichte des Pietismus* (Göttingen: Vandenhoeck & Ruprecht, 1984) 82, see also 60. Horst Stephan, *Der Pietismus als Träger des Fortschritts in Kirche, Theologie, und allgemeiner Geistesbildung* (Tübingen, 1908) began the reevaluation of pietism as a cultural force.

[30]Dale Brown, *Understanding Pietism* (Grand Rapids MI: Eerdmans 1978) 65. See also Beate Koester, "Die ernste Bibelausgabe des Halleschen Pietismus: Eine Untersuchen zur Vor- und Fruehgeschichte des Cansteinschen Bibelanstalt," *Pietismus und Neuzeit* 5 (1979).

[31]See Klaus Deppermann, *Der hallesche Pietismus und der preussische Staat unter Friedrich III* (Göttingen, 1961).

[32]Gawthrop and Strauss, "Protestantism and Literacy," 54.

Although Francke characteristically attempted to effect his reforms by voluntary action, he followed Reformation precedent in asking the state to implement his educational program. From 1725 to 1775, laws requiring universal common school education were enacted in the new school ordinances of Baden, Braunschweig-Lueneberg, Hanover, Heilbron, Hesse-Kassel, Hesse-Darmstaat, Hildesheim, Holstein, Meckenberg, Prussia, Saxony, Waldeck, Weimar, Wurttemberg, and the German cities of Transylvania.[33]

In England, evangelical leaders worked toward similar goals. The Society for Promoting Christian Knowledge (S.P.C.K.), founded by Thomas Bray (1656–1730) and four laymen in 1698, set as its goal:

> to promote and encourage the erection of charity schools in all parts of England and Wales; to disperse, both at home and abroad, Bibles and tracts of religion; and in general to advance the honour of God and the good of mankind by promoting Christian knowledge both at home and abroad.[34]

The effects of the Society's resolve were felt throughout the British dominions. Griffith Jones (1693–1761), rector at Landdowror, Wales, used the resources of the S.P.C.K. to establish "circulating" or travelling schools, that used the Bible to spread basic literacy.[35] In the American colonies, the S.P.C.K. provided each rector who requested it a sufficient library—including the standard Latin and Greek authors, mathematical texts, and some studies of natural philosophy—to establish a parish school. Many Virginia gentlemen prepared for William and Mary in these "schools," which usually met in the rector's study.[36]

John Wesley (1703–1791) was a major influence on Protestant education. Like Francke, Wesley was concerned with popular biblical study, and one of the features of the various societies that he founded for his converts was the study of the Bible. Equally important, Wesley published vast quantities of literature, includ-

---

[33]Ibid, 54ff. When the pietist revision of education was complete, more than two-thirds of Protestant Germany had adopted some version of complusory education.

[34]Cited in Tim Dowley, ed., *The Eerdman's Handbook to the History of Christianity* (Grand Rapids MI: Eerdmans, 1977) 473.

[35]Griffith Jones's work, perhaps because of his connections with the Wesleys, is the best known, but the S.P.C.K.'s work was far larger, especially in the area of charity schools. See Mary Clement, *The S.P.C.K. in Wales, 1699–1740* (London: S.P.C.K., 1954). One of the factors that weakened S.P.C.K. work in Great Britain was that the Society was not able to enlist the government, as Francke did so well in Germany, largely because of the competition between churchmen and dissenters.

[36]Jefferson was painfully aware of the need to continue this educational endeavor, and his famous Bill for Establishing Religious Liberty had a companion bill that would have required Virginia to establish a system of schools. Ironically, the first bill passed, while the second was defeated. The same Virginians who refused to be taxed to support a Protestant minister refused to be taxed to support the school. The two, as always, went together.

ing sermons, abridgments of Christian classics, biblical studies, and popular medical advice, which he sold at the Methodist chapels. His message was clear: to be a good Methodist was to become a reader. The early Sunday schools, whatever their defects, had a similar purpose.

Unlike German pietists, English evangelicals never succeeded in harnessing the power of the state to their educational cause. The English elite was too wed to its system of private education for the elite to consider the expansion of education to the nation as a whole until the late nineteenth century. Ironically, the pluralism of English Protestantism may have been the primary impasse. Churchmen feared the increase of the power of Nonconformity were education to be even partly under their control, while the Nonconformists, in turn, feared the churchmen.

The Holy Cause in the New World

Oscar Handlin in his classic study *The Uprooted* reminded historians that American culture issued from the exertions of generations of immigrants who faced, albeit at different times, the problem of continuing the traditions and customs of their homelands while making a place for themselves in their new land.[37] This observation is especially true for American Protestants.[38] They continued—with very few modifications—the educational emphases that they shared with other Europeans of like faith. Thus American Protestants began with a deep concern for the education of their elites, passed through an evangelical revival that hoped to make the Bible available to all, and appealed to the state to aid their crusade.

The major difference between American and European Protestants may have been more one of degree than substance. Protestant leaders were convinced that the vastness of the continent, the freedom from customary moral restraints, and the lack of tradition put Americans only one generation from savagery. Cotton Mather, describing the founding of Harvard College, expressed the colonists' renewed sense of the importance of schooling:

> The nations of mankind, that have shaken off *barbarity*, have not *differed* in the *languages*, than they have *agreed* in this one principle, that *schools* for the instruction of young men, in all other liberal *sciences* as

---

[37]Oscar Handlin, *The Uprooted* (Boston: Little, Brown, 1951).

[38]Interpreters of American religion have often neglected the most important signal observation about American Protestantism, i.e., that "American" is the adjective, not the noun. At no point in their history have American Protestants been alienated from their European counterparts or failed to study and harken to European theology. Even denominations that were "American" in origin, such as the Disciples, have mounted European missions and been concerned with the course of European Christianity. One must be very careful about what is and what is not "American."

well as that of *languages,* are necessary to procure, and preserve, that *learning* amongst them.[39]

More than one hundred years later, Lyman Beecher in his noted *Plea for the West* argued for western schools to offset the dangers of frontier barbarism. For American Protestants, schools were the visible signs, almost the sacraments, of civilization itself.

Since schools were the thin line protecting the colonists from the loss of their culture, colonial educators devoted much effort to their charters. The legal documents creating Harvard (1636) and William and Mary (1693), America's first institutions of higher learning, outlined carefully the schools' standards and practices. The founders of these colleges were resolved to follow the best precedents available and to avoid innovations that might compromise their integrity. Both charters bristled with the language of European Protestant humanism. Harvard was devoted to "the advancement of all good literature and sciences" and William and Mary to education in "good Letters and Manners."[40] Until the Civil War, the founders of American classical and collegiate institutions followed a similar traditionalism in their schools.

The goal of the schools was to produce "learned gentlemen"[41] to serve the commonwealth as political or professional leaders. The two matrices for this preparation were a curriculum focusing on the commonplaces of Western culture (the classical languages, some philosophy, mathematics, and, especially after 1800, some science) and a period of residence in which the student learned the art of social relationships and manners. The teachers transmitted learning; the ethos created the gentleman. The basic educational program was comparatively inexpensive. The founders of a liberal arts college needed little capital, and the school's expenses might be as little as a thousand dollars per year. Any group that wanted a college could afford one.

The charters of Harvard and William and Mary did more than state Protestant educational goals. They also pointed to a major issue in Protestant education in

---

[39]Cotton Mather, *Magnalia Christi Americana,* cited in Richard Hofstadter and Wilson Smith, *American Higher Education* (Chicago: Uiversity of Chicago, 1961) 13.

[40]Hofstadter and Smith, *American Higher Education,* 12.

[41]Of course, experience did subtly change the meaning of the key term *gentleman.* Initially, colleges saw the gentleman in terms of the traditional English social structure, i.e., a gentleman was one who did not have to work with his hands but could live either from his lands, a church living, or by his own investments. In a sense, the gentleman was the truly free man because he was economically liberated from dependence on another. In the nineteenth century, the sharp class distinctions implied by the word *gentleman* were softened somewhat. The gentleman came to be seen as a person with manners and a spirit of concern for others, but its original meaning never completely disappeared. Americans, of course, were somewhat ambiguous about social class. They frequently wanted it, at least for themselves, without wanting a society dominated by class distinctions.

America: control. Both Harvard and William and Mary were placed explicitly under governing boards that were in effect boards of trust, bodies that held property and legal rights analogous to other corporations. These boards were to be controlled by noneducators. Hofstadter and Smith in their *American Higher Education: A Documentary History* wrote:

> The academic institution in America ceased practically from the beginning to be a body of self-governing scholars and fell under the control of non-resident laymen. The European universities had been founded by groups of mature scholars; the American colleges were founded by their communities.[42]

The governance of schools reflected a larger American religious pattern. Old World ecclesiastical polities, despite the desire of some groups, including the Dutch Reformed, to maintain them, did not export well. The most striking mark of American church government was lay control. In New England the predominant Puritan churches combined their inherited theology of covenant, the localism of their new settlements, and their faith in conversion to produce a unique New England congregationalism. In Virginia and later Maryland, although the governor was technically head of the church (analogous to the crown), a de facto Anglican congregationalism was established in which the vestries held effective control. Southern Anglican congregationalism proved not amenable to supervision by the various commissaries (a position roughly equal to an English rural dean) or, after independence was secured, to American bishops. In the middle colonies, where no single denomination was established,[43] each denomination developed a polity combining its old world traditions with legal requirements for holding property as a charitable trust.[44] Thus, Lutherans,[45] Presbyterians, Baptists, and Cath-

---

[42]Hofstadter and Smith, *American Higher Education,* 3.

[43]New York is one possible exception although Anglicans claimed an establishment in New Jersey, but even there the ecclesiastical laws were vague. In effect, New York's establishment law amounted to allowing the Church of England and the Dutch Reformed Churches to become legal corporations.

[44]See Timothy Smith, "Congregation, State and Denomination: The Forming of the American Religious Structure," *William and Mary Quarterly,* 3rd ser., 2 (1968): 155-76.

[45]Henry M. Muhlenberg, the great eighteenth-century Lutheran "missionary," considered the adoption of the church constitution at St. Michael's, obviously understood as a model for other congregations as something he would "sacrifice . . . [his] last hours for." The constitution

> declared that the congregation had the permanent right and freedom to elect its officers and ministers by majority vote. In addition to trustees, required by civil law to hold and transfer property, there was a provision for a church council of six elders and six deacons. The duties of the former were defined at first as primarily spiritual and of the latter as primarily temporal, but this distinction soon fell away.

E. Clifford Nelson et al., eds., *The Lutherans in North America* (Philadelphia: Fortress, 1975), Mulhenberg quote on 75; summary of constitution on 76.

olics,[46] established congregations that separated sacerdotal functions from governance. The actual management of the churches was by trustees, legally empowered to conduct business, elected at congregational meetings.

The charitable trust created an American free market in education. A college or academy was almost as easy to establish as a congregation. The colonies and later the states made educational charters easy to obtain. Consequently, whenever an American religious denomination, or a small proportion of its membership, believed that they were excluded from existing institutions or sensed an educational need that they felt was not met, they might form a corporation, raise a small endowment, seek a charter, elect trustees, and begin their institution.

The pattern was established early. The very conservative ministers of Connecticut, together with some of like persuasion from Massachusetts, wanted a college to preserve their understanding of Congregationalism.[47] Despite the very valid argument that New England did not need two colleges, they managed to secure the needed charter from the colony and to establish Yale College. Later, a body of Yale men, stung by their alma mater's treatment of David Brainerd (1718–1747), joined with revivalistic Presbyterians in New Jersey to charter Princeton College in 1746. The pattern was not, of course, confined to the scions of the Puritans. Anglicanism, whose ranks swelled in the eighteenth century through immigration and the missionary labors of the Society for the Propagation of the Gospel (S.P.G.), wanted a symbol of their strength in the middle colonies. Their leaders struggled to establish King's College (Columbia, 1753) against determined Presbyterian opposition. A decade later, Baptists (a relatively small sect in England that became an important American denomination during the First Great Awakening) campaigned for the establishment of the College of Rhode Island (present day Brown, 1763). In those cases, however, public controversy forced the sponsors to share control of the board with other groups.

Motives of place, prestige, and competition dominated the founding of western "denominational" colleges. The West was settled by successive waves of immigrants. Frederick Jackson Turner described the pattern of settlement:

. . . the Indian was sought by the fur-trader; the fur-trader was followed by the frontiersman, whose live stock exploited the natural grasses and

---

[46]Trusteeship became a major issue in the early nineteenth-century Catholic Church as the local boards often wished to appoint their own priests. Archbishop Carroll acknowledged that the American situation required modifications of established Catholic procedures:

Whenever parishes are established no doubt, a proper regard and such as is suitable to our governments, will be had to the rights of the Congregation in the mode of election & presentation of pastors: and even now *I shall ever pay to their wishes every deference consistent with the general welfare of Religion.*

Cited in James Hennesey, *American Catholics: A History of the Roman Catholic Community in the United States* (New York and Oxford: Oxford University Press, 1981) 77.

[47]Brooks Mather Kelley, *Yale: A History* (New Haven: Yale University Press, 1976) 4.

the acorns of the forests; next came the wave of primitive agriculture, followed by more extensive farming and city life.[48]

Had Turner continued his morphology, he might have noticed that this last period was also the period of dreamers and boosters. The new westerners hoped that their villages and towns might become the new metropolitan centers of an American empire.

Religious institutions followed a similar progression. Once the stage of the frontiersman was reached, circuit riders and Baptist exhorters appeared; when primitive agriculture arrived, Presbyterians and Episcopalians appeared as did primitive church buildings; and finally, as extensive farming and city life emerged, full ecclesiastical organizations—such as presbyteries, bishoprics, and associations—were established. Toward the end of this latter period, Protestant clergymen joined the dreamers and began to envision the area as a potential center of civilization. The final step, naturally, was to build academies, colleges, and seminaries.

The vast Protestant educational mission to the West was an exercise in trusteeship and control. Baptists, Methodists, and Presbyterians established strings of schools, almost "systems" of education, which were distinguished, not by their curriculum or their affluence, but by who held the legal right to control the board of trustees and to name the president.[49] Each denomination wanted to put its imprimatur on its own institutions.

Since the right to name the officers of the school implied some financial responsibility for the school, the denominations appointed agents to raise funds or, especially in the case of the Methodists, urged each minister and bishop to set aside a Sunday for the purpose.[50] As a result, American believers were continually barraged by arguments for learning. While some ministers, especially Presbyterians and Congregationalists, mentioned the training of ministers as one reason for schools, this was a comparatively minor topic. Despite resistance to the formal education of their ministry, Disciples and Methodists, for example, supported colleges as avidly as Presbyterians. In general, the agents of all churches sounded a common theme: The school was needed to promote the "religious and intellectual improvement of the whole community."[51] These passionate solicitations eventually helped convince Americans to support universal public education.

---

[48]Frederick Jackson Turner, *The Rise of the New West* (Gloucester MA: Peter Smith, 1961; reprint, New York: Harper & Row, 1906) 89-90.

[49]For a favorable account of this work in the Middle West, see Timothy Smith, *Uncommon Schools: Christian Colleges and Social Idealism in Midwestern America, 1829–1850* (Indianapolis: Bobbs-Merrill, 1978).

[50]See James Findlay, "Agency, Denominations, and the Western Colleges, 1830–1860," *Church History* 50 (1981): 64-80.

[51]Ibid., 69. The phrase is from the charter of Indiana Asbury.

The denominational imprimatur and financing rarely influenced more than the first page of the catalog. Control did not produce character. Although Christianity was an assumed part of college life, colleges were by and large free of denominational bias. As early as the presidency of John Witherspoon of Princeton (1768–1794), American educators proclaimed their schools' independence:

> The college of New Jersey is altogether independent. It hath received no favour from Government but the charter, by the particular friendship of a person now deceased. It owes nothing but to the benefactions of a public so diffuse that it cannot produce particular dependance, or operate by partial influence.[52]

The "old doctor's" insight was acute. No American school could limit its financial appeal to any one source, whether church or government, and the need for contributions from people of diverse faiths limited the power of any particular group of supporters.[53] The independence of the schools made all the more ironic the battles between denominational leaders and the various state universities, especially in the Midwest, over the appointment of presidents and professors. George Duffield, a Presbyterian clergyman and college enthusiast, spoke not only for the University of Michigan but for all educators when he wrote: "The establishment of a collegiate institute in a free state, and the conducting of its interests, should ever be upon liberal principles, and irrespective of all sectarian predilections and prejudices."[54]

Further, few colleges had enrollments in excess of one hundred. Students were in short supply, and colleges accepted students from all denominations as well as students who professed no formal system of beliefs. At best, one half of the antebellum students in America were professing Christians, and the schools needed the ritual of repeated revival to secure this percentage.

If control did not make the colleges explicitly Christian, neither did their program of studies. By the mid-eighteenth century, moral philosophy, often based on Scottish Common Sense philosophy, had displaced theology throughout the colonies. Nor were the remaining courses particularly religious. The classics were, of course, written by pagans, and no amount of bowdlerizing could make Ovid a spokesman for Victorian morality or faith. From 1790 to 1810 colleges were out of fashion with the children of the Revolutionary generation, and colleges responded, as they would to a later crisis of confidence, by adding more science to

---

[52]Hofstadter and Smith, *American Higher Education,* 143.

[53]In the twentieth century, many colleges and universities discovered that their official denominational connections embarrassed some potential supporters or limited their financial appeals in other ways. This led to the school officially withdrawing from the denomination. American schools have been denominational only when it was financially advantageous.

[54]Hofstadter and Smith, *American Higher Education,* 437.

their program.[55] Although some clerical teachers may have tried to transform science into doxology, most resisted that temptation. No sacred chemistry, physics, or geology was taught.

No formal system of accreditation existed, but college standards were remarkably uniform. Almost all colleges followed the Yale curriculum with occasional modifications to include more science. A student attending Methodist Indiana Asbury would receive the same basic education as a student graduating from Western Reserve in Ohio. The new state universities such as the universities of Georgia, North Carolina, South Carolina, and Virginia followed a similar pattern. The University of Virginia illustrates the power of this tradition. Despite founder Thomas Jefferson's brilliant outline of an elective program combining classics with the study of the useful sciences and modern languages, most pre-Civil War students elected to follow the traditional preprofessional program for learned gentlemen.

If the curriculum of the schools was more or less standard and primarily secular, were pre-Civil War American colleges nonetheless dominated by religion and religious concerns? Religious life, with the exemption of participation in certain activities, is almost impossible to quantify, but the evidence suggests that religion did not dominate. The accounts of life in these church-related schools describe a fairly vibrant youth culture, complete with pranks and resistance to authority, that reflects the nineteenth century's "discovery" of youth and adolescence. Further, apart from the revivals, especially those in the 1810s and 1820s, students do not seem to have responded favorably to the official piety of the institutions. Chapel, especially, seems to have been regarded as a bore.[56] Perhaps the most vibrant examples of piety on the campuses were the various student voluntary organizations, especially those devoted to foreign missions. Such organizations reached their zenith after the Civil War when the Young Men's Christian Association (YMCA), originally formed to help young men cope with the city, organized chapters on most campuses.

Few schools broke with this largely secular pattern before the Civil War. Oberlin College in Ohio maintained a different pattern for a few years. Led by such enthusiastic sons of the revival as Asa Mahan (1800–1889) and Charles Finney (1792–1875), Oberlin was a utopian Christian community, proud to be called "God's College," devoted to every type of reform, including a modified feminism, antislavery, homeopathic medicine, and dietary reform. The program of studies, although basically conservative, did attempt to replace the Greek poets

---

[55]See Steven J. Novak, *The Rights of Youth: American Colleges and Student Revolt* (Cambridge MA: Harvard University Press, 1977).

[56]See William C, Ringenberg, *The Christian College: A History of Protestant Higher Education in America* (Grand Rapids MI: Eerdmans and Christian University Press) 63. In general, Ringenberg argues for a position opposed to mine and sees the colleges as more genuinely religious than I do.

with the New Testament and to introduce Hebrew as well as to remove those classics, such as Ovid, that offended Victorian sensibility. However, the profession-
alism of the faculty as well as the students' desire for a standard education led to
the gradual curtailment of the innovations.[57]

Yet Oberlin was prophetic in its expansion of its clientele. American educators had a hope that education might be as extensive as the republic. Schools,
whether elementary, academy, or college, were believed to combine the wisdom
of the past with the discipline needed in the present. Thus they were crucial to the
survival of the Republic. William Holmes McGuffey (1800–1873), indefatigable
author of textbooks and school reformer in Ohio, put the theory of republic
schooling in a pungent sentence: "Let adequate knowledge be as extensive or rather
as universal as the right of our citizens to aspire to the performance of public service."[58] Elementary and academy level schools often sought to be comprehensive
by serving all people in their communities. On the collegiate level, the churches
sought to extend educational opportunity by creating new institutions for women,
often called "female seminaries," and later separate schools for Afro-Americans.

The task of educating America was finally too great for the churches. Despite
their financial and ideological resources (though neither was as extensive as later
Americans have imagined), the churches did not have the money or the teachers
to fulfill their hopes for a truly republican education. Protestant educators faced a
choice. They could continue to struggle against impossible odds to control American education or like countless generations of Protestants before them in Europe,
they could trust the state to assume the burden. American Protestants had little
difficulty selecting the latter course. In 1852 Massachusetts adopted its compul-
sory school law, and, after little more than a decade, the federal government,
through the Morrill Act (1862), committed itself to fund schools of agriculture and
engineering through grants of public lands.

Once the Civil War had ended, American education reorganized itself. The
university, only a dream for such Republic educators as Timothy Dwight, became
the standard setter for American higher education. Although some universities had
loose ties with the churches, these schools now required money for laboratories,
elective programs, and graduate studies in amounts never before imagined. The
problems of fund-raising had given the earlier colleges much freedom; the task of
supporting universities made that liberty absolute. The successful schools, including Yale, Princeton, Harvard, and Chicago, one of the last universities to be
founded by a religious body, developed elaborate networks to raise those moneys,

---

[57]For a sympathetic account by a later Oberlin president, see James H. Fairchild,
Oberlin: The Colony and the College, 1833–1883 (New York and London: Galland Publishers, 1984).

[58]Cited in John Westerhoff III, *McGuffey and His Readers: Piety, Morality, and Education in Nineteenth-Century America* (Nashville: Abingdon, 1978) 165.

and church contributions became just a penny in the pot. Although a few institutions remained "private," the majority of universities were sustained only by increasing state aid. The colleges underwent similar transformations. Government-funded schools, of course, rapidly replaced church schools on the lower levels.

Before 1960, the secularization of elementary and higher education had little effect on the nation's Protestants. They were avid supporters of public education, and their representatives resisted any attempt to secure government funds for religious schools, especially those controlled by the Roman Catholic Church. In response to cries that the schools were too pronouncedly Protestant, they gladly (almost enthusiastically) removed the offending practices from their institutions. Perhaps the most visible sign of the school's relationship to the older Protestant crusade was the persistence of the reading of a few verses from the Old Testament and the saying of the Anglican version of the Lord's Prayer. Finally, even these were removed by a Protestant-dominated Supreme Court.

Victory

When John Westerhoff III observed that twentieth-century secular school systems may well have had their roots in our nineteenth-century public schools,[59] his observation was only partially correct. The word "secularize" was early used to describe the Reformation princes who "secularized" or seized church property and used it (or its revenues) for their own ends. Whether in Europe or America, the Protestant educational crusade was part of the general tendency of Western Europeans to strengthen the government. As a general rule, Protestants did not support church control of education, and, even in America where the laws of trust allowed individual denominations considerable freedom to establish schools, those schools were consistently seen as servants of the public good. Further, the right to convey degrees was always granted by the state.

Protestant educational ideals were decidedly secular as well. Whether one samples the work of the Great Reformers or the American educational pioneers, education was valued for its own sake. Thus Protestant educators were able to adopt the humanistic republic of letters as their own and educated their young according to its standards. As science progressively replaced classical humanism as the lingua franca of the learned world, Protestants engrafted it into their educational tradition. As early as the seventeenth century, support of science was one mark of a consistent Protestant. The nineteenth-century American college used Scottish Common Sense realism, a philosophy of science, as its intellectual foundation, and American colleges, as soon as they were financially able, added or strength-

---

[59]Westerhoff, *McGuffey*, 24.

ened science departments.[60] Interestingly, President Timothy Dwight established
a department of chemistry with Yale's meager resources rather than investing the
money in a divinity school. After 1859 Protestant colleges had few problems accepting Darwin's new interpretation of organic evolution. After a very short debate, Protestant educators accepted it as a necessary component of education.
Though Charles Hodge (1797–1878), the conservative voice of Princeton Seminary, denounced Darwinism as the latest form of infidelity, President James
McCosh (1811–1894) of Princeton College accepted it with fervor. In the twenties, Protestant college presidents were in the front lines against all attempts to
restrict scientific teaching. In simple terms, Protestant educators consistently stood
for the best available scholarship.

The nature of Protestant commitments made it comparatively easy for American Protestants to surrender control of their institutions. Perhaps because Protestantism had always entrusted leadership to lay people, no established caste ever
relinquished power as readily as the American Protestant clergy surrendered their
privileged position in education. Elementary and academy education were often
taught by nonclergy from the beginning. The colleges moved more slowly. First,
the professors in the school came to be professional teachers, then the presidents
of the schools came to be elected from the ranks of the professionals, and finally
the boards became more representative of those who paid the bills.

To be sure, the surrender of Protestant control frightened some Americans.
Martin E. Marty noticed the emergence of a party in the late nineteenth century
that he calls the antimodernists.[61] The antimodernists have followed certain consistent lines: faith in biblical inerrancy, denial of the theoretical implications (but
not the practical benefits) of science, and a faith—often more touching than informed—in the past glories of evangelical America. In education, antimodernists,
fighting what Mark Noll has called a "rear guard action,"[62] created a new educational form, the "self-consciously Christian college,"[63] which, whatever the
quality of its instruction, was devoted to providing an alternative to secular educational institutions. Although this willingness to be different might be expressed
in varying ways (an emphasis on chapel, campus revivals, prayer meetings), the
Christian college's raison d'être was the "promotion of a Christian view of the
world."[64] In practical terms, the mandate was to teach in such a way as to make

---

[60]Theodore Dwight Bozeman, *Protestants in an Age of Science: The Baconian Ideal
and American Religious Thought* (Chapel Hill: University of North Carolina Press, 1977).

[61]Martin E. Marty, *The Irony of It All: 1893–1919* (Chicago: University of Chicago
Press, 1986), discusses the interplay between the various approaches to the modern world.

[62]Mark Noll, "Introduction," in Ringenberg, *The Christian College,* 33.

[63]Ringenberg provides a partial list of these institutions, *The Christian College,* 203-207.

[64]Noll, "Introduction," 34. The idea of a "Christian worldview" is, of course, a highly
abstract philosophical concept.

supernaturalism (especially the biblical miracles) the touchstone of their educational endeavors.

These schools may face a secularization similar to that of other Protestant institutions. The Christian colleges were extraordinarily prosperous in the 1970s and 1980s, and their new wealth (as well as a glut of available Ph.D.'s) enabled them to hire an increasingly professional faculty and administrative staff. Naturally, these well-trained teachers brought secular standards with them. Whether announced or not, such concepts as a "Christian" history or a "Christian" scientific interpretation of the physical world have been progressively downplayed. In time the "Christian" may be abandoned altogether. Further, antimodernist schools face, as do all private institutions, a chronic financial crisis. Bills must be paid. If past experience is a guide, the only way that the financial problem can be solved is through an increasingly broad base of support.

Parallel with the prosperity of antimodernist colleges has come the construction of a significant number of "Christian" elementary and secondary schools, devoted to the protection of the young from the "godless" public schools. But these schools, likewise, will have serious difficulty in maintaining their identity. The states are increasingly demanding that students achieve on the same or a higher level than their public school counterparts, and the standards for such achievement are emphatically secular. Further, the parents expect the same, and often see the schools as offering the advantages of a "private" school (more personal attention, a disciplined approach to study, and the like). Finances will also have a secularizing influence.

What happened to the educational crusade among mainstream Protestants? The religious leaders of the Protestant center have been strangely silent about educational matters in recent years. This may be traceable, in part, to an unheralded Protestant victory. The passion for education has become part of American idealism, and the schools are in a real sense America's secular church. The sons and daughters of mainstream American Protestants often attend colleges and graduate schools, and each generation has seen progressively larger numbers of Protestant young people seeking more education than their parents. Significant numbers of Protestants continue to teach in and to administer America's educational establishment.

Further, the Protestant confidence in secular education has increasingly gained ground. For instance, Catholics have increasingly abandoned their belief that classroom and church ought to be coordinated, and Catholic colleges are progressively becoming less controlled by the hierarchy or by religious orders. In education, as elsewhere, "the characteristic contribution of American religion to American civic understanding . . . has been not perspective, wisdom or depth of insight, but the rousing of . . . sentiments and energies."[65]

---

[65]William Lee Miller, *The First Liberty: Religion and the American Republic* (New York: Knopf, 1986) 266.

We began this essay by discussing Jaeger's masterful work, *Paideia,* and wondering if it provided any clues for the understanding of American Protestantism. In Jaeger's portrait, Greek society made education a settled and steady habit, part of the very fabric of civilized life, and one of the assumptions of serious thought itself. Greek *paideia* was a magnificent achievement. The Protestant crusade in education had a similar, if less magnificent, outcome. In the United States, one of the by-products of Protestantism was a belief in education that has become part of the bedrock of the American character. In this sense, Protestant education was transformed from a crusade to a true *paideia* in its own right.

Yet another significant parallel should be drawn. Ancient Greek *paideia* was, to a greater degree than many imagine, one by-product of the work of philosophers who lived in the "twilight of the gods" and were willing to secularize many ancient cultural values to secure the foundations of the civil life of the polis. Greek religious institutions were forced to the margin, and the best insights of Greek religion lived by becoming habits of the heart. Much the same can be said about Protestants and education in America. Events, especially the high cost of post-Civil War education, forced American Protestantism slowly to relinquish its control of educational institutions and to accept a place on the margins of the larger enterprise. But, as with the Greeks, that very secularization enabled the basic educational values of the churches to become part of the habits of the American heart.

The Future

Present-day Americans are deeply concerned with education. Whatever else may be true about education, people seem to feel uneasy about its present outcomes. Recently, Allan Bloom's book *The Closing of the American Mind*[66] climbed to the top of the best-seller charts and sparked a lively debate, despite weaknesses in argument, documentation, and conception. How should Protestants participate in this debate? Does their history as educational crusaders offer any guideposts for the present? One must be very careful here. Despite assertions that history repeats itself, the world never completely returns to its past situation, and each age or epoch is irreducibly unique. Within these cautions, allow me to offer some suggestions.

Protestants must learn to live with the consequences of their victory. From Luther to Francke to Finney, Protestants crusaded for a society in which education was a primary social norm. In America they succeeded beyond their earlier dreams. The nation has built one of the most comprehensive school systems in the world, and each generation uses the resources to a larger extent than its parents. The price of this success was the same price that Luther had to pay for his more modest educational success: control by the state and the loss of room for voluntary action.

---

[66]Allan Bloom, *The Closing of the American Mind* (New York: Simon and Schuster, 1987).

Further, the dream has necessarily involved the loss of some substance. If everyone is to be educated, then schools must include people of varying abilities, social classes, and interests. Comprehensiveness must be protected at all cost, including the cost of the loss of distinctive Protestant cultural elements. If mainstream Protestants retreat here, they will imperil their earlier victory.

The ancient Protestant goal of comprehension may also enable us to be true pioneers of new educational ventures. And such pioneering is occurring. In recent times, for example, the churches have responded to the expanded employment of women by developing (often on a parish level) church day care centers. Although these were originally little more than baby sitting services, they have gradually evolved in the direction of true schools. Many states have adopted standards for day care centers, universities have placed a renewed emphasis on early childhood education, and many centers have begun to hire professional staff.

If such pioneering efforts are to remain true to Protestant tradition, sooner or later the churches will have to retreat from leadership and encourage the state to bring its far greater resources to bear on the problem. One model for Protestant educational pioneering may be the nineteenth-century church-related college or the heavily Protestant "public" schools system of that era. Once Protestants have successfully established the social goal, they need to know when to call for state help to complete their revolution.

To participate in the current discussion, Protestants must remember that their earlier victory was made possible by the state. Despite their deep concern with education, Protestants have rarely believed that the church should be the primary educator of the nation. Even in America, despite a brief period in which their churches served as sponsors for colleges and academies, the sons and daughters of the Reformation quickly returned to their traditional advocacy of governmental action and control. For good or ill, Protestant *paideia* is linked to the state and its agencies.

These observations suggest that one of the current problems in Protestant thinking about education is the lack of a contemporary theology of the state. Present-day Protestants have no equivalent of the reformers' trust in the "godly" prince, the nineteenth-century American evangelicals' confidence in the Christian Republic, or the progressives' belief in bureaucratic management by good people. In fact, opposition to any positive understanding of the role of government often seems to be almost a given. To the neoconservative, the only purpose of the state is to secure a place for true religion; for the neoliberal, government is often too easily related to oppression.[67] But, if Protestants want to participate in the larger discussion over education (and many do not wish to do so), they must renounce

---

[67]Are there bases for such a positive view of government? I believe that there are even in such unlikely dialogue partners as Barthianism and, particularly, process theology.

their antiestablishmentarianism and embrace, as they historically have, the state as the primary educator.

Further, Protestantism must recognize that the modern secular order is their own creation. Luther removed the schools from church control, and each Protestant generation has embraced the belief that education was essentially secular. The classics were the basis of early Protestant education, and no one ever dreamed of a "Christian" Ovid, a "Christian" Tacitus, or a "Christian" mathematics. The same is true of the new "arts and sciences" that gradually replaced the older curriculum. Protestant thinking about education has to begin at this point. Protestants should not ask how they can somehow make a religious contribution to education, but how they can help to keep education secular in its aims and purposes.[68]

The most difficult part of such thinking will be to allow the "trappings" of traditional religious intervention in education to pass from the scene and to recognize their essential hollowness. Just as nineteenth-century American Protestants learned that it contributed little to education to require the president of a college to be a church member, so twentieth-century Protestants must learn that religious clubs and chaplains do little to promote either piety or learning. Protestants must recognize that the ministry of Word and Sacrament for students, as for nonstudents, is best conducted within the churches. Most important, Protestant leaders must learn to trust their laity. A Protestant presence in education will not be secured by the presence of clergy on the staff or courses in "Christianity." The real influence will be exerted by the faithful men and women who do their job as educators as well as it can be done. In the last analysis, serious Protestant thinking about education must begin with the people who do the job in the world.

---

[68]This may also involve a recognition that theological education itself ought to be done in secular institutions conducted according to secular standards. What is the difference, for example, between a historical critical study of the New Testament in a university and the same study in a seminary?

11

Revolutions, Quiet and Otherwise: Protestants and Higher Education during the 1960s

Dorothy C. Bass

A quarter of a century after Selma, the presidential assassination, and the Gulf of Tonkin resolution, Americans are still struggling to absorb the reality and interpret the meaning of one of the most turbulent decades in our history. It is too soon to view the 1960s with dispassion; most of us over the once-suspect age of thirty carry memories of naive optimism and paralyzing rage, some of them vaguely embarrassing after all these years. Nostalgia and bitterness mark not only the outer limits of public discourse but also the inner dynamics of individual reflection on this troubled and troubling time. Particularly for liberals, whose visions arced and whose plans unraveled amidst the tumult,[1] getting straight about the sixties is and will continue to be a touchy, but crucial task.

Though near in this sense, however, the sixties are already distant enough that the self-consciously modern language printed in numerous paperbacks and pamphlets now sounds strangely antique. The era, which claimed to be ''unprecedented,'' ''radical,'' ''revolutionary,'' ''secular,'' ''cybernetic,'' and ''futuristic'' (these terms appear again and again in the pronouncements of the established as well as those of the rebellious), is receding into the past in spite of itself, and the task of historical interpretation is beginning. The rapid social and cultural change

---

[1]See Allen J. Matusow, *The Unraveling of America: A History of Liberalism in the 1960s* (New York: Harper & Row, 1984).

of the period left a deep impression on the major institutions of American life, and
the time has come to discern more precisely what that impression is.

The aim of this essay is to examine the impression of the 1960s on a relationship much older than American culture itself: the relationship between religion and higher education. As heirs of a long tradition of stewardship for higher
education, the older Protestant churches—those associated with America's religious "mainline"—encountered in the powerful and tumultuous universities of
the 1960s a set of challenges they had no desire to ignore. Amid the storms of the
sixties, however, activity in this arena, which many viewed as the most advanced
outpost of the unprecedented-secular-technological future, exposed the theological and institutional resources of such Protestants to furious winds indeed. In the
encounter of religion and higher education during the sixties, many of the characteristic features of liberal religion became evident, and some aspects of the sixties were disclosed.

In common memory, the apparent calm of the 1950s has stood all along as a
contrast to the turmoil of the '60s. The growth, prosperity, and prestige of mainstream Protestantism in the earlier decade make it seem in retrospect, to some, the
halcyon time before the storm.[2] Together with other institutions of the white middle class, the churches were benefiting from a postwar revival of faith. Whether
the faith was in the United States of America or in God is difficult to determine,
but in any case indicators of earthly success were high. At universities across the
land, the Protestant denominations funded the work of hundreds of campus pastors. In 1959 the growth of a strong student Christian movement of considerable
theological sophistication and ecclesiastical self-consciousness was capped by the
creation of the interdenominational National Student Christian Federation. A national Faculty Christian Fellowship, briefly associated with the National Council
of Churches earlier in the decade, called attention to a lively conversation about
Christian faith and higher learning, and the powerful Danforth Foundation poured
millions of dollars into both campus ministry and the education of spiritually and
ethically committed academics.[3] And an impressive generation of theologians, led
by Reinhold Niebuhr and Paul Tillich, won for Protestant theology substantial respect throughout the intellectual world.

Yet the theological and social transformations that would soon overtake the
relatively comfortable denominations of mainstream Protestantism were already
underway as the sixties began. Within months, for example, a sit-in in Greens-

---

[2]William R. Hutchison disputes the accuracy of this common view in "Past Imperfect:
History and the Prospect for Liberalism," in Robert S. Michaelsen and Wade Clark Roof,
eds., *Liberal Protestantism* (New York: Pilgrim Press, 1986).

[3]On the National Faculty Fellowship, see Franklin Jung Woo, "From USCC to UCM:
An Historical Inquiry with Emphasis on the Last Ten Years of the Student Christian Move-
ments in the U.S.A. and Their Struggle for Self-Understanding and Growing Involvement in
Social and Political Issues" (Ed.D. diss., Teachers College, Columbia University, 1971) 171ff.

boro, North Carolina, provided the rising generation with a model of protest, and on Easter weekend of 1960 the Student Non-Violent Coordinating Committee was born. Members of mainline Protestant student organizations, which had never abandoned the social concern that had attended the birth of the student Christian movement in the late nineteenth century, were among the first white students to follow the lead of blacks into the civil rights movement, with southern Methodists and those influenced by the human relations work of the student YMCAs and YWCAs in the forefront.[4]

Theological change was also on the horizon. After a 1960 World Student Christian Federation meeting in Europe, an American delegate reported that if she had heard one message there, it was this: "Only when we who are the Church are willing to lose our institutional life in love for and service to the world, will we discover the nature of our true life, our mission, and our Lord.'"[5] Neoorthodoxy's theme of letting the church be the church lost appeal as Bonhoeffer's advocacy of "world" Christianity became known to a generation eager to be part of historic struggles taking place in the secular arena. And so, at some point early in the decade, the persuasive resolution of the relationship between modern thought and classic themes from the Christian tradition that had dominated the postwar theological scene collapsed. By mid-decade a "radical" theology of doubt and secularity had claimed center stage, and theology as a whole had entered a transitional and uncertain period in which no single position could obtain consensus.

A "hushed-up revolution" was taking place in the churches, reported Martin Marty in an article written in the middle of 1964. And there were already two "sides": the "foot-draggers," who were comfortable with familiar middle-class ways, and the activists, who were "united in their vision that our way of life is called in question by the world's technological and political great awakening and by secularization in our culture." Students and campus ministers, he observed, were almost all on the activist side. If Marty's basic sympathy for the activists was a commonplace of mainline commentary, his concern that "the quiet revolution . . . is becoming more cut off and has not faced the future seriously"[6] was much more remarkable.

Central to the Protestant witness to the secular university of the 1960s was a deep discomfort with the institutional church. "Solemn assemblies"—typical American Protestant congregations—made "noise" as a comfortable religious

---

[4]Sara Evans, *Personal Politics: The Roots of Women's Liberation in the Civil Rights Movement and the New Left* (New York: Vintage, 1979) 30-37. "In the late fifties, throughout the south the MSM [Methodist Student Movement] harbored the most radical groups in most campuses," 30. See also Julian Bond, "Impetus and Impact: Students and the Civil Rights Movement," *motive* 26/1 (October 1965): 41-45. I am grateful to Ian Oliver for his assistance in researching *motive* and other sources of the student Christian movement.

[5]Student (unnamed) quoted in Woo, "USCC to UCM," 102.

[6]Martin E. Marty, "The Hushed-Up Revolution," *motive* 25/7 (April 1965): 5-7.

establishment, trapped by social and economic forces in a conservative position irrelevant to the massive global changes of the day. So argued Peter Berger in his 1961 book, a work commissioned by the National Student Christian Federation as a study document and, by 1963, read by more campus ministers than any other recent volume.[7] "Let there be no uncertainty as to what we are saying," Berger wrote; "we are suggesting that Christians may freely choose *not* to become members of local congregations, *not* to identify themselves with a denomination, *not* to join in the weekly traffic jam of the religious rush hour on Sunday morning." Moreover, he concluded, such decisions might be directly grounded in commitment to the Christian faith, as an expression of a legitimate Christian vocation appropriate to the times.[8]

For Protestant leaders concerned about higher education, the perception that religious institutions were not necessarily the privileged location of God's activity meant reconsidering both their social analysis and their theological assessment of the church's relationship to the university. "A society which once hinged around the church is now more and more pivoting around the university, and the church is marginal to that university," declared Robert W. Lynn in a 1966 address. Far from considering such a shift disastrous, however, this Presbyterian educator welcomed the churches' release from the tasks of building and sustaining institutions. This change, he argued, constituted "a new call of the people of God to be a critic on the margin of American society." Displaying the mood of the era while turning the necessities of Protestantism's disestablishment into virtue, he rejoiced that "we can forgo cultural imperialism and begin to take and select that which most needs to be done at this moment . . . free from excess dependence on the patterns of the past."[9] Lynn's theological openness to the new situation and the social analysis upon which it relied were widely held by other Protestant educational strategists as well.

Three major developments comprise the story of mainstream Protestantism's relationship with higher education during the 1960s. In two of them—campus ministry and the student Christian movement—the denominations' official representatives in the universities embraced with gusto the role of marginal critic. In the process, the internal resources of this stream in American religious life were severely tested, not only in the encounter with the university itself but also in the maelstrom of political conflict. The third development was of another sort, com-

[7]Peter L. Berger, *The Noise of Solemn Assemblies: Christian Commitment and the Religious Establishment in America* (Garden City NY: Doubleday, 1961). On campus ministers' reading, Phillip E. Hammond, *The Campus Clergyman* (New York: Basic Books, 1966) 58.

[8]Berger, *Noise of Solemn Assemblies*, 177.

[9]Robert W. Lynn, "A Ministry on the Margin," in Kenneth Underwood, *The Church, the University, and Social Policy: The Danforth Study of Campus Ministries*, 2 vols. (Middletown CT: Wesleyan University Press, 1969) 2:20.

ing from different origins than the first two but confirming, like them, the continuing shift of cultural power from the churches to the university. Especially during the second half of the 1960s, scholarship that was independent of ecclesiastical institutions and defined by the norms of the secular university carved out a new place for religion in higher education, as the academic study of religion grew at a spectacular rate.

Denominational Ministers in Changing Universities

Campus ministers stood at the forefront of the mainstream Protestant churches' encounter with the university in the 1960s. Campus ministry as an enterprise, however, occupied an exceptionally difficult position, simultaneously squeezed between two mighty cultural forces and kept at arm's distance from each. Thus commentary on campus ministry in the 1960s displays some of the ambiguities that the ministers themselves experienced. Typical campus ministers were too churchy, the secular theologian Harvey Cox charged; they were too caught up in the busy-ness of developing programs to encourage denominational loyalty, coordinating activities with ecumenical peers, and sustaining a religious realm that was divisive to the life of the university as a whole. Sociologists Phillip Hammond and Jeffrey Hadden analyzed the situation differently, observing that campus ministers were often isolated from the churches.[10] Both points of view, however, identified the enduring quandary of campus ministry: how to forge a relationship between dissimilar institutions with different aims. Moreover, two factors made this quandary, always a pressing one, exceptionally strong during the 1960s. One was discomfort with the institutional church. The other was the massive self-confidence of the modern university.

The decade was one of startling expansion for higher education. The number of students more than doubled, and the percentage of college-age youth who were currently enrolled substantially increased (from 22 percent to 32 percent).[11] Located almost entirely in the government-sponsored sector, this acceleration of postwar growth was accompanied by heightened awareness of higher education's role in a complex modern society. "We are just now perceiving that the university's invisible product, knowledge, may be the most powerful single element in our culture," affirmed California Chancellor Clark Kerr in his noted 1963 address

[10]Harvey Cox, *The Secular City* (New York: Macmillan, 1965) 197; Hammond, *The Campus Clergyman*, 98-106; Jeffrey K. Hadden, *The Gathering Storm in the Churches* (Garden City NY: Doubleday, 1969) 194-97. Like Berger's *Noise of Solemn Assemblies*, *The Secular City* was written as a study document for the National Student Christian Federation.

[11]*Campus Ministry in the United Church of Christ* (New York: United Church Board for Homeland Ministries, 1981) 32; Seymour E. Harris, *A Statistical Portrait of Higher Education* (New York: McGraw-Hill, 1972) 269.

on *The Uses of the University*. In phrases that recall the tone of the Kennedy administration's best and brightest strategists, Kerr declared that the university was being called upon to "produce knowledge" for a wider range of purposes than ever before—"for civic purposes and regional purposes, for national purposes, and even for no purpose at all beyond the realization that most knowledge eventually comes to serve mankind"—and to transmit knowledge "to an unprecedented proportion of the population." In the process, the university was acquiring a web of complicated relations with government, foundations, and industry that would further transform it.[12]

Kerr's image of the large, impersonal, fragmented, cosmopolitan "multiversity" hardly described the majority of colleges and universities in the United States. Yet the multiversities—schools like Berkeley, Wisconsin, Columbia, Michigan—were the decade's pace-setters. In one sense, Protestant ministries in such settings were in place from the outset: Interested observers had already noticed that there were, for example, four times more Methodists in Iowa's state universities than in its Methodist colleges, and denominational programs at the University of Iowa and similar campuses all over the country had been created.[13] The organized student Christian movement was also strong. In another sense, however, the continuing secularization and fragmentation of knowledge and the institutions where it was "produced" (as Kerr put it) placed ever greater distance between the dominant forces in higher education and the inherited educational style of American Protestantism. Church-related colleges, which had given American higher education its distinctive form until around 1900, had long since lost their normative status. During the sixties, these colleges received relatively little denominational attention, and reports early in the next decade discovered widespread lack of clarity about their mission. More importantly, the ever-increasing dominance and confidence of the cultural forces represented by the multiversity seemed further to weaken religion's claim to be a center of value.[14]

---

[12]Clark Kerr, *The Uses of the University* (New York: Harper & Row, 1963, 1972) vi-vii, 122.

[13]Robert Michaelsen, "Religious Education in Public Higher Education Institutions," in Marvin J. Taylor, ed., *Religious Education: A Comprehensive Survey* (New York: Abingdon, 1960) 306.

[14]Robert Wuthnow, *The Restructuring of American Religion* (Princeton NJ: Princeton University Press, 1988) 158ff.; Manning M. Pattillo, Jr., and Donald M. MacKenzie, *Church Sponsored Higher Education in the United States: Report of the Danforth Commission* (Washington DC: American Council on Education, 1966); and C. Robert Pace, *Education and Evangelism* (New York: McGraw-Hill, 1975; Carnegie Commission on Higher Education). Dorothy C. Bass, "A Ministry on the Margin: The Protestant Establishment and Education in the Age of the University," forthcoming in William R. Hutchison, ed., *The Protestant Establishment in the Earlier Twentieth Century*, treats the diminished influence of mainstream Protestant churches in higher education after 1900.

Although varied forms of campus ministry took place at large and small schools of many sorts throughout the decade, both contemporaneous and retrospective reflection on campus ministry demonstrates the hold of the multiversity on the imagining of the sixties. To some of the unconventional ministers who chose this field and their advocates, the multiversity represented a religious new frontier. There the diversity, secularity, and social engagement lacking in ordinary congregations were present, in all their "revolutionary" potentiality. "The vast intellectual, political, and social changes sweeping the world confront the leadership of the churches in the theories and data of the strategic centers of higher education," wrote Kenneth Underwood, appropriating Clark Kerr's case for use by liberal Protestants. Campus ministers were pioneers on the challenging trails the whole church would need to travel in the not-too-distant future.[15]

This vision was stirring, but it was not the reason for which the denominations had thus far supported campus ministry. Founded as state schools overtook church-related colleges in the early twentieth century, campus ministry was first of all the church's effort to "follow its students," as guiding spirit Clarence P. Shedd of Yale had put it in 1938. Even during the 1950s, providing distant collegians with a church home-away-from-home was the predominant motive for generous financial support from the denominations. The ideal campus minister was a master programmer, an ivied version of H. Richard Niebuhr's 1950s clergy prototype, the pastoral director.[16] During the sixties, however, this model came in for serious criticism. Propelled by genuine attraction to the vibrant political and intellectual life of the multiversity as well as by frustration at the difficulty of building a traditional program in its midst, many campus ministers were seeking "wider-ranging and less institutionally inhibited roles." In the view of campus ministers at the University of Wisconsin, a mid-decade sociological survey concluded, "the traditional notion of a student religious group is as archaic as it is ineffectual."[17]

The historical development of higher education had produced change in the style of campus ministry, and the result, not surprisingly, was considerable confusion about the role. A 1963 survey of personnel in ten denominations showed that they were disproportionately young, of short tenure, and uncommitted to long-term service in the field. They believed that the churches wanted them to produce quantitative suc-

---

[15]Underwood, *The Church, the University, and Social Policy,* 1:xvi, 3, 8.

[16]Clarence Prouty Shedd, *The Church Follows Its Students* (New Haven CT: Yale University Press, 1938). On campus ministry in the 1950s, see Barbara Hargrove, "Church Student Ministries and the New Consciousness," in Charles Glock and Robert Bellah, eds., *The New Religious Consciousness* (Berkeley and Los Angeles: University of California Press, 1976) 208. On the pastoral director, H. Richard Niebuhr, *The Purpose of the Church and Its Ministry* (New York: Harper & Row, 1956) 79ff.

[17]N. J. Demerath III and Kenneth J. Lutterman, "The Student Parishioner: Radical Rhetoric and Traditional Reality," in Underwood, *The Church, the University, and Social Policy,* 2:139.

cesses, but they were unsure of how and even why to do so. They received little ac-knowledgment from either church or university. And, paradoxically, it seemed that they were caught in a spiral that must only make their isolation more severe. The more cosmopolitan (that is, the less religious) their university, the more innovative their style became; and the more innovative their style became, the less acknowledgment they were likely to receive from the church.[18]

Faced with this conundrum, most chose innovation. In part their reasons were theological. "The clearest thing of all is that the future shape of the church in the university will occur only when Christians live with responsibility within it and for it, and not in and for the denominational churches that have only succeeded in weakening and fragmenting the university's life," wrote Harvey Cox in his pop-ular book, *The Secular City*, showing the influence of Dietrich Bonhoeffer.[19] Considerably more liberal than other ministers, theologically and politically,[20] these ministers were open to new ways. (For a time, coffeehouses were models of inno-vation, though one wonders whether even secular theologians would have accepted a Yale undergraduate's proud claim that coffeehouses represented the church " 'giv-ing up' her sacred heritage and position and becoming, once again the servant of the world."[21] Campus ministers may also have been emboldened to stretch their ties to the churches as far as possible by the financial generosity of denominational sponsors in a prosperous age. The earliest signs of diminishing resources appeared at a United Ministries in Higher Education meeting in February 1966, but the sharp decline in support that the next decade would bring was not foreseen.[22]

Innovation in the 1960s was not only the style of campus ministers but also the leading theme of a culture. So the choice of Protestantism's official represen-tatives in higher education to stretch their ties to the churches and to Christian tra-dition itself is understandable. Yet the troubling likelihood exists that the ties were stretched so far that many campus ministers lost touch with the distinctive word that they might have spoken in a realm hungry for meaning. When this happened, innovation amounted to accommodation. For some, this entailed accommodation to the university. In his massive Danforth-supported study of campus ministry, for instance, Kenneth Underwood seemed dazzled by the modern university. Advo-

---

[18]Hammond, *The Campus Clergyman*, 13, 70-71, 80, 101, 115.

[19]Cox, *The Secular City*, 207.

[20]Hammond, *The Campus Clergyman*, 42-44; and Hadden, *The Gathering Storm*, 195-96.

[21]John D. Perry, Jr., "Coffee Houses: Evangelism or Evasion?" *motive* 25/6 (March 1965): 11.

[22]Daniel E. Statello and William M. Shinto, *Planning for Ministry in Higher Educa-tion* (New York: United Ministries in Higher Education, n.d. [1970s]) 25. E.g., in the Bay Area UMHE there were seven ministers with a $176,365 budget in 1966 and five ministers with an $87,776 budget in 1972. The national staff contributed to UMHE by ten denomi-nations fell from 31 to 14.5 between 1970 and 1981; *Campus Ministry in the UCC*, 83.

cating campus ministers' involvement in the university's tasks of "social policy research," Underwood assumed the superiority of the university and sought ways for campus ministers to fit in. For others, this entailed immersion in the political movements that played so large a part in campus life as the decade proceeded.

The Student Christian Movement and *the* Movement

Students, the supposed recipients of Protestant efforts in higher education under the traditional model, were throughout much of the 1960s a powerful force pushing it into new forms. "We settle not for the pious cliche or hollow admonitions of sterile conformity," declared a 1965 editorial in *motive*, the publication of the Methodist Student Movement. "Wrong, impractical, immature, improvident, idealistic, we may be. But anesthetized . . . never!" Many campus ministers, though scapegoats for the churches' anger at student rebellion during the late sixties, were nonetheless drawn to and encouraging of student passion. It matched their own on the pressing political issues of the day, particularly civil rights and Vietnam.[23] Student rebellion also, however, included features that threatened mainline Protestantism's longer commitment to stewardship in the realm of higher education. Its development would both lead to a startling institutional disruption and disclose a range of problems that were not limited to students but were rather characteristic of liberal Protestantism as a whole.

The message American students heard from world Christianity in 1960—"only when we who are the Church are willing to lose our institutional life in love for and service to the world, will we discover the nature of our true life, our mission, and our Lord"[24]—could hardly have come at a more timely moment. The civil rights movement in the South was calling for student volunteers, and in tones that evoked deep religious response. And so organized Christian students joined the larger movement of students to promote equality, peace, and freedom. From the 1960 sit-ins and freedom rides through the voter registration projects in the summers of 1964 and 1965, thousands of students were directly involved, while millions more watched intently. As initial idealisms were confronted by encounters with real danger and frustrating systemic opposition, the political education of a generation began. Then in the fall of 1964 Berkeley's Free Speech Movement brought the new confrontational politics and the rhetoric of freedom and justice to a northern campus. It was the beginning of an accelerating train of campus-based protest. Opposition to United States' involvement in Vietnam, sharpened for young people by the draft, fueled further political activity and analysis. The most visible

---

[23]B. J. Stiles editorial in *motive* 25/8 (May 1965): 5; Statello and Shinto, *Planning for Ministry in Higher Education*, 23.

[24]Student (unnamed) quoted in Woo, "USCC to UCM," 102.

and thoughtful students, deeply shaken, feared that the American Dream had become the American Nightmare. And the majority of all students by 1970 participated in at least one demonstration.[25]

Between 1960 and 1970, the student Christian movement did indeed lose its institutional life in love for and service to the world. At many points along the way, the loss was gain; care for organizational stability flagged, to be sure, but spirited involvement in issues of genuine importance was high. Even so, the story of institutional loss is an important story, for it tells not only about students but also about some of the tendencies of the 1960s, or at least of liberal and radical religionists of the '60s.

The decade opened auspiciously. The organization of the National Student Christian Federation in 1959 reflected the ecumenical spirit of the day, bringing the student movements of the various denominations into closer association with one another and with the National Council of Churches. In addition, in 1960 Presbyterians, Disciples, Brethren, and the United Church of Christ formed an organic union of their student movements and campus ministries in the United Campus Christian Fellowship. These successes of denominational ecumenism marked, in a sense, the final passing of an era: The older nondenominational organizations that had initiated and shaped student work were passing from the scene, as the Student Volunteer Movement, the Inter-Seminary Missionary Alliance, and the student Ys took subordinate places within NSCF. In another sense, however, the tide was already beginning to turn against denominationalism itself, even in its interdenominational forms. The YMCA and YWCA tradition of student work—evident in support for radical causes since the 1930s, in the human relations workshops that spurred students' civil rights involvement, and in a style of openness to the whole life of a campus—would later be recognized as an important precedent for the radical style soon to appear.[26]

A turn to politics early in the decade set the apparently strong student Christian movement on its decisive course. A major study on the Life and Mission of the Church, undertaken with enthusiasm in 1958, was barely mentioned after its completion in 1962. A major study on faith and learning, introduced in 1960 to summarize fourteen years of lively discussion on the topic, met with little audience. The chief periodical of the student Christian movement, the Methodist mag-

---

[25]On student protest, see Evans, *Personal Politics,* and Julian Bond, n. 4 above; Matusow, *The Unraveling of America.* Robert McAfee Brown employs the image of nightmare in "No Promise without Agony," in G. Kerry Smith, ed., *Agony and Promise: Current Issues in Higher Education, 1969* (San Francisco: Jossey-Bass, 1969) 266. On student participation in demonstrations, Helen Lefkowitz Horowitz, "The 1960s and the Transformation of Campus Cultures," *History of Education Quarterly* 26 (1981): 12.

[26]On the contributions of the student Ys, see Cox, *The Secular City,* 196-97; Woo, "From USCC to UCM," 49; Horowitz, "The 1960s," 15; "Mary King," Chicago *Tribune* (23 August 1987) 6:3.

azine *motive*, carried an increasing number of articles on politics.[27] And little wonder. The issues were pressing, the momentum of the larger student community was compelling, and the theological justifications for political involvement and against religious self-absorption were in place.

The NSCF was concerned about southern Africa early in the 1960s and about Vietnam soon thereafter; in 1974, in an unprecedented move, it endorsed the Johnson/Humphrey ticket. Civil rights and urban policy were prominent NSCF concerns as well. Even so, before 1966 the organization did not officially cosponsor antiwar demonstrations, and its interdenominational structure, affiliated as it was with a host of "adult" institutions, stayed in place.[28] Then, in 1966, the "second sixties" began, and student activism pitched leftward. Myron B. Bloy, an Episcopal campus minister, described how the shift affected universities: "Tenured department heads and SDS leaders used to share an assumption that, however great their ostensible differences, if they dug deep enough they would eventually come to the common ground on which they could join to build the new academic Jerusalem," he reported from a vantage point in 1970. "Those halcyon days of easy hope are over now."[29] Liberal institutions and their customary structures, far from being the force for peace and justice activists in the "first sixties" had expected, had become part of the problem, according to a radicalized generation of students, black leaders, and opponents of American imperialism. And among such institutions, student Christians determined, was the church.

In 1966 the National Student Christian Federation was reorganized and renamed the University Christian Movement. The Articles of Operation urged that institutional structures "be kept as minimal and as flexible as possible in order that it may be free to serve as an enabling instrument of creative responsible 'movement.' " Denominational student Christian movements, heretofore loosely joined in a federation, suspended their independent existence so that grassroots groups of student Christians would constitute the new organization. The ecumenical spirit extended far beyond the bounds of conciliar Protestantism: Roman Catholic and Orthodox student groups joined up, and soon UCM leaders also began to speak of an "issue-oriented ecumenicity" linking them to SDS and other

---

[27]Woo, "From USCC to UCM," 6-7, 171ff., on discussions of faith and learning; *motive* was published by the Methodist Board of Higher Education, Nashville TN, from 1941 until 1971.

[28]Woo, "From USCC to UCM," 150-70.

[29]Myron B. Bloy, "Counterculture and Academic Reform," in Martin E. Marty and Dean G. Peerman, eds., *New Theology No. 8* (New York: Macmillan, 1971) 230-31. On the "first" and "second" sixties, see Leonard I. Sweet, "The 1960s: The Crises of Liberal Christianity and the Public Emergence of Evangelicalism," in George Marsden, ed., *Evangelicalism and Modern America* (Grand Rapids MI: Eerdmans, 1984) 30; and Martin E. Marty, "Religion in America Since Mid-century," in Mary Douglas and Steven M. Tipton, eds., *Religion and America* (Boston: Beacon, 1983).

student movement organizations. Any group that claimed to agree to the Articles could belong to and vote in UCM. Governance—which treated equally college freshmen and denominational officials, campus ministers and dropouts—was turned over to a large General Committee.[30]

As the founders had hoped, this structure was responsive. In fact, it was so responsive that UCM priorities shifted annually, a common pattern in left-of-center organizations during the startling, fast-paced years of the late '60s. Year by year, UCM's objectives expanded beyond the realm of the university. In September 1966, UCM president Charlotte Bunch Weeks expressed the organization's initial goal in a "fraternal" letter to SDS: "We share with you the desire to build a movement on the campuses of this nation responsive to the moral imperatives for equality and justice now confronting us." In 1967, UCM redefined its task as "to bring about social change through the reformulation of the university." And by 1968 the stated goal was "to work for the termination of American economic and cultural exploitation at home and abroad."[31] With this, all the world became UCM's parish.

In an expansive development similar to that which carried the movement's goals beyond the university, UCM's Christian identity was also growing tenuous. Early on, egalitarianism crippled the organization's theological capacity. The Theological Reflection Committee, formed in 1966, soon disbanded on the grounds that theology should be the task of all members as they reflected on their active social involvement, not the specialty of a designated group.[32] (Whether or not all members reflected theologically within their practical situations cannot be determined. If they did, no records of it remain.) An SDS leader joked that UCM had not come into being in order to use religious influence in building an economically democratic America, as it claimed, but rather out of fear of "losing its flock on leftward moving campuses."[33] *Motive,* which the Methodists agreed in 1966 to publish on behalf of UCM, increased further its political emphasis. And in December 1967, with the aid of $50,000 from the Danforth Foundation, UCM culminated a year-long grassroots study project on social issues with a 2,500-person convention in Cleveland. The open-minded campus ministry veterans who evaluated the week-long event for Danforth reported that it was dominated by "peace symbols, calls for political action of the liberal and radical varieties, political graffiti, a profusion of McCarthy and Kennedy buttons, and strobe lights at the conference-sponsored rock dances." Its access to Christian resources appeared to be slight, however: The convention was held together by "moral conscience, but a

---

[30]Woo, "From USCC to UCM," is a very valuable study that includes the details of these structural changes. Robert Lynn directed this dissertation.

[31]Ibid., 193, 60, 68.

[32]Ibid., 11-12.

[33]Ibid., source unnamed, 59.

morality with few roots into spiritual disciplines and into continuing communities of faith."[34]

It is likely that some of the young men who burned their draft cards at a worship service that week experienced more spirit, discipline, and faith than this judgment implies. Yet it is also true that discourse on politics and ideology almost completely replaced explicitly religious discourse in the University Christian Movement. As the larger student movement became more alienated from liberal politics and dominant cultural institutions in the wake of confrontations on the campus of Columbia and the streets of Chicago, UCM shared the leftward move. Moreover, the critique of injustice in America would not find a stopping place; it continued to expand, often in ways that divided even radicals from one another. In 1968 a women's caucus was born in UCM, and by early 1969 several other caucuses—black, "radical," international—further segmented the organization. The problem of clarifying UCM's political position was both increasingly complex and, in the view of many, increasingly pressing. And so a Task Force on Ideology was appointed.

The Task Force delivered its report to the General Committee in Washington, D.C., at the end of February 1969. The report urged UCM to identify itself as "a community of organizers committed to a sense of total alienation from the present society," viewing social change "only in terms of total dismantlement of that society" while operating in thoroughly collective style. The debate became convoluted and heated— frustrating to most participants, no doubt. At the moment of frustration, a member of the black caucus rose to declare UCM's entire debate and strategy totally irrelevant to the needs of the black community. Therefore, he demanded, UCM should turn over $50,000—the major portion of its budget—to black caucus control.

The black caucus demand hit the white UCM majority at its most vulnerable spot, both politically and religiously. For all their radicalism and theoretical sophistication, these were young people who had only lately responded to the religious appeal of the civil rights movement. And they can hardly have been expected to find what had eluded their elders: a way to reconcile black with white—or, as difficult, a way to reconcile their own guilt with their own confusing reluctance to relinquish all race privilege. Paralyzed, the University Christian Movement adjourned for the night. The next morning, those present declared it dead. The session concluded with "a sharing of bread and wine."[35]

Looking back a decade later, Robert Ranking of Danforth ruefully reflected that the foundation had, at his urging, "furnished the UCM with sufficient funds

---

[34]Evaluation report by Jackson W. Carroll and David S. Wiley, quoted in Robert Rankin, ed., *The Recovery of Spirit in Higher Education* (New York: Seabury, 1980) 13-14; see also Woo, "From USCC to UCM," 199-206.

[35]Woo, "From USCC to UCM," 71-75.

to purchase a fifty-thousand dollar gun with which they committed suicide." As he was quick to add, however, UCM's action was in a sense a representative one "during a time when people, young and old, seemed to enjoy destroying things—an unlovely product of the Vietnam War."[36] Looking back, indeed, it is evident that the mood of UCM was like that of people, young and old—and liberal Protestants in particular—in other ways as well. Charlotte Bunch Weeks's anger that the churches had to spend so much energy on institutional maintenance when the world had pressing needs echoed at many a denominational strategy meeting. Another UCM staffer's chagrin at being stuck in the Interchurch Center in New York, isolated from her real constituency, pointed to a weakness shared by the denominations and UCM alike. And Steve Schomberg's lament that the emergence of caucuses had cost the movement its unity and vitality was fast becoming familiar throughout liberal circles.[37]

Many of those who closed down UCM anticipated a greater life of service in the broader movement, where they could work unhindered by institutional confines. This view was not simply the romantic dream of expressive individualists; it was also the tragic conclusion of deeply committed, thoroughly discouraged advocates for justice and peace. The institutional church, from whose shadow UCM could not escape alive, was itself involved in the denial of equality, negligent of moral contradictions, and as caught as other prominent American institutions in the guilt and grief of Vietnam. Worse yet, these advocates recognized, so were they. Amid the political realities of 1969, theological "silence" and institutional suicide—"forgo[ing] familiar but inadequate structures even when successors to them are undefined"—seemed the only course.[38]

The death of the American student Christian movement—so quickly, and after such a long period of growth—was a severe loss. With the exception of the Lutherans, denominational student organizations were not reconstituted. UCM continued to operate in New England under the leadership of Lynn Rhodes, a Methodist, but it had lost its wider base. Efforts to include American students in the World Student Christian Federation, whose members in other countries stuttered in disbelief at UCM's self-destruction, were made only sporadically in the coming years. In a related loss, the Methodist church and *motive*, a creative and important voice for nearly three decades, found it impossible any longer to live together, especially as editorial radicalism expanded to include issues of gender and sexuality. At first eager for independence, once they had it the editors were

[36]Rankin, *Recovery of Spirit*, 13.

[37]Weeks's and Schomberg's statements on the demise of the UCM appear in *motive* 30/1 (October 1969): 50-59; the other statement is from an unnamed staffer quoted in Woo, "From USCC to UCM," 267.

[38]UCM leadership statement on the need for "silence" in the current situation is quoted in Statello and Shinto, *Planning for Ministry*, 23; Charlotte Bunch Weeks on "forgoing . . . inadequate structures," *motive* 30/1 (October 1969): 53.

unable to sustain the publication. It died in 1972. And campus ministry entered a new phase, reduced by financial constraints, deprived of a natural constituency in the student movement, and shaken by the shifting mood. By 1970 the organizational initiative on college campuses was passing into new hands, as Campus Crusade, Inter-Varsity Christian Fellowship, and other groups began a period of impressive growth.[39]

The Academic Study of Religion

The difficulties of campus ministry and the demise of the student Christian movement seriously weakened the mainline Protestant presence in American higher education, particularly in the large secular universities that dominated the system. Religion more broadly considered, however, did not lose ground in the universities during the 1960s. Rather, as a subject for study in accordance with the academic norms of those universities, religion attained much greater attention than previously. Reversing the trajectory of official Protestant presence, the upward movement of the field of religious studies won from the modern pluralistic university at least a grudging respect for the importance of religion in human affairs.

Mainstream Protestants, whose liberal theological perspective was not at odds with the historical and scientific study of human religious activity, were generally supportive of the trend. However, in institutional terms the advance of the academic study of religion was neither their initiative nor their victory. The social and intellectual location of the study of religion, once the territory of theological faculties and church-related colleges, had been changing throughout the century, and especially so since World War II. As higher education grew in size, self-confidence, and secularity, scholars in the field of religion addressed—successfully, on the whole—concerns about their academic legitimacy. Pursuing the 1935 Princeton University plan of drawing a clear distinction between "the study of religion and the practice of it," the field had entered a formative period that brought it by 1968, in the judgment of John F. Wilson, to substantial self-understanding and clarity. James M. Gustafson agreed: The field had made great strides in the academy, and differentiation among the several types of concern for religion—in arts and sciences, in preparation of professional leadership, in religious care of students—had made a crucial difference.[40]

Working from a "posture of analytical rigor, of disinterested objectivity, and sometimes of disinterested irreverence," the field of religious studies was show-

---

[39]Ronald B. Flowers, *Religion in Strange Times: The 1960s and 1970s* (Macon GA: Mercer University Press, 1984), reports on the rise of the evangelical campus movements.
[40]Paul Ramsey and John F. Wilson, eds., *The Study of Religion in Colleges and Universities* (Princeton NJ: Princeton University Press, 1970) 14, 332.

ing great scholarly productivity and attaining substantial institutional success. Might this success have been related to the corresponding decline in the churches' influence? The differentiation of religion's various tasks in higher education, with one clearly at the center and others on the margins, would suggest that this was the case. In addition, John Wilson believed, theology's intellectual hold on thinking about religion had weakened. This was due in part to the current confused state of theology, he reported; no theological option "so articulated and expounded as to transform (or be intended to transform) cultural attitudes and social institutions" was on the intellectual scene. Moreover, theological schools played an ever smaller role in the social structure of the field, taking a decreasing place in the preparation of religious studies faculty members after 1950.[41]

If this analysis is correct, growth in the academic study of religion was partly the result, by a curious twist, of the expansion of secular ways of thinking in the American academy. Even more clear is its link to another important event in the secularization of American education. Concern about the entanglement of church and state, which had long deterred many state universities from offering religious studies curricula, was quieted by the U.S. Supreme Court's 1963 ruling in *Abingdon School District v. Schempp*. "It might well be said that one's education is not complete without a study of comparative religion or the history of religion and its relationship to the advancement of civilization," wrote Associate Justice Tom Clark in his majority opinion prohibiting the devotional reading of the Bible in the public schools, which also addressed the issue of the nondevotional teaching of religion. "Nothing we have said here indicates that such study of the Bible or of religion, when presented objectively as part of a secular program of education, may not be effected consistent with the First Amendment."[42]

Programs in religious studies, which had grown steadily but unimpressively early in the decade, multiplied rapidly after 1964. Nationally, undergraduate enrollments increased by 150 percent between 1964 and 1969, while total enrollments rose by only 55 percent. In public institutions, the rate of growth was even greater. By 1970, nearly all accredited four-year institutions offered courses in religion, and two-thirds of them had a program or department. Moreover, the scholarly approach adopted in state universities was having an impact in departments of "theology" or "Bible" in nonsectarian and liberal Protestant colleges as well. A "quiet revolution" had occurred, Claude Welch concluded in his definitive 1971 survey for the Council on the Study of Religion.[43]

---

[41]The "posture" phrase is Gustafson's, in ibid., 335; Wilson, ibid., 15-19.

[42]*The Study of Religion in College and University* (New York: Department of Higher Education, National Council of Churches, 1967) 7; Claude Welch, *Graduate Education in Religion: A Critical Appraisal* (Missoula: University of Montana Press, 1971) vii.

[43]Welch, *Graduate Study in Religion,* 167-75, 193.

The Churches, the University, and the Sixties Generation

Those who argued during the 1960s that the complex modern university embodied the advanced development of modern society were in many ways correct. There diverse cultural and religious groups met, under the protective canopy of secularism. There the knowledge upon which technological advance and social policy would be constructed was discovered, though how to combine knowledge with faith or ethics was not a privileged question. When political turmoil erupted, it soon involved the universities and those who taught, studied, or ministered there; universities and their denizens could not escape the issues of the time, but neither did they hold in common a way of resolving them. Thus the resolute modernity and ethical complexity of the universities of the sixties brought to a new intensity the tension between religion and higher education in America, which had begun to come to light with the emergence of the modern university nearly a century earlier.[44]

Advocates of the academic study of religion fared well in the changing university environment, accepting as they did its genuine diversity and adopting a scholarly posture that could receive respect from other disciplines as well as within their own. While many of them were, no doubt, from mainstream Protestant backgrounds, the "quiet revolution" they led was in principle pluralistic and detached from the churches. It matched the self-understanding of the university and contributed in helpful ways to its offerings.

Mainstream Protestantism's official representatives in the university moved less effectively upon the changing scene. Like their predecessors in the liberal religious tradition, campus ministers and their denominational backers were at home with modern thought and affirmed its implications for the university: religious inclusivity, opposition to sectarianism, the separation of the practice of religion from its study, and the extension of scholarly investigation to all realms of human activity. Indeed, on the basis of liberal religious confidence some, such as Kenneth Underwood, celebrated the university's importance in leading humanity into the future. Yet neither he nor others persuaded a large constituency that the church had a significant role to play as even one of the university's several partners on the journey.

As the sixties came to a close, concern for that partnership took second place to involvement in national and international politics, at least among the leaders of the student Christian movement and many of the campus ministers who worked with them. The urgency of events, they believed, required that institutions and their sustenance take low priority. The hasty dissolution of the University Christian Movement was the most vivid and probably the most unfortunate instance of urgency's triumph over institutional sustenance; it brought to an end nearly a cen-

---

[44]Bass, "A Ministry on the Margin," treats this tension in the years after 1900.

tury of student organization, and it has not yet been replaced. Yet the dissolution was not an odd event but rather a characteristic one.

An air of freedom from constraining religious institutions had characterized this stream of Christianity at least since the era of the Social Gospel: An immanent God could and did work outside of the church, and Christians could and indeed must join in God's historic, manifestly secular work.[45] During the 1960s, not only student radicals but also campus ministers, denominational strategists, and rising theological professors exhibited both the power and the problems of this stance. A tradition of prophetic criticism of the church was renewed; insightful and usually well-founded, these criticisms both cleared the way for fresh faithfulness and tempted critics to a religious elitism that threatened to cut them off from crucial resources, spiritual as well as institutional. Forming alliances with others of similar vision was also an already-accepted approach, standing behind 1960s alliances with university social policy makers, civil rights activists, or socialist students. In each of these very different alliances, however, Protestant clarity about what their distinctive contribution could be was lacking, and their appropriation of their allies' views was often insufficiently discriminating. And the mandate to action even to the point of spending the life of the church in service to the world, though it received fresh impetus from the worldly theology and heightened political conflicts of the time, had a longer history than sixties innovators often stopped to ponder. It would remain as a spur against political complacency and a temptation to unspiritual impatience for the middle-class, university-educated leaders of mainstream Protestantism.

Together, the self-destruction of the student Christian movement and the ecclesiastical isolation of the campus ministry exemplified these larger tendencies in mainstream Protestantism. Although the tendencies could be ignored most of the time in some congregational settings, they could not be ignored in ministries located on the margins of the university. There liberal Protestants were continually challenged to acknowledge their own modernity. This, for the most part, they readily did.

For Protestants such as these, the sixties were a classic and poignant moment of encounter with a tension that stood (and still stands) at the center of their religious identity. In some renderings, this is the tension between tradition and modernity; in others, the tension between accommodation to culture and sectarianism. Where the educational task of the church is at stake, it is the tension between response to the present moment and responsibility for the faith of generations already gone or yet unborn. Vital involvement in the aspirations and struggles of

---

[45]William R. Hutchison, ed., *American Protestant Thought: The Liberal Era* (New York: Harper & Row, 1968) 13, interprets the 1960s theology as a reassertion of some classic themes of liberal theology.

the present day is the particular genius of this stream of Christianity. Forgetfulness of the fragility of Christians' presence in history is its weakness.

Amidst the urgency of events and the demands of change, which extended well beyond the campuses as many aspects of American culture were restructured during the 1960s,[46] the genius of liberal Protestantism shone brightly. These Protestants responded to God's activity in the world with a love of justice and a freedom from ecclesiastical self-absorption that brought the Christian faith into lively, contemporary expression. Yet in their haste, they also stumbled into the shadows that characteristically accompany liberal Protestantism's light. In their disdain for real churches, their abandonment of Christian organizations, and their neglect of historic expressions of faith, they both deprived themselves of resources that could have deepened their responses to the present age and did less than they should have done for the Christian education of the next generation.

In 1965, a *motive* editorial identified the tension and hinted at the rising generation's stake in exploring it.

> If we [the youth] err in contemporaneity, then we invite the church to surround us with authentic historicity and viable tradition. If we wallow in jargon or soar in false erudition, then we ask the church to expose our failures by showing us the magnitude of the church's prophetic witness. Our invitation: God, Make us honest.[47]

B. J. Stiles, the young leftist who issued this invitation, surely did not intend to abandon contemporaneity. Rather, he was hinting at an insight that represents the most truthful and faithful manifestations of liberal Protestantism. Honest Christian witness takes place when a hearty, unapologetic contemporaneity is nourished and corrected by the authentic, vital traditions of the church.

Every variety of Christian faith must work out a way of understanding the relationship between its own historical context and the traditions it has received. At its moments of greatest truthfulness, liberal Protestantism has represented an understanding of this relationship that is vibrant with possibilities for service and witness in the modern world. If its vibrancy is to be true and enduring, however, the churches and their educators at every level must be prepared to respond to Stiles's invitation.

Today, as the students of the sixties prepare to send their own children off to college, many of those Protestants for whom friendliness to modernity has become a tradition are troubled about the future of the denominations to which they belong and, more importantly, of the irenic and engaged faith to which they have adhered. The denominations of mainstream Protestantism have, by and large, not reached the student generation of the sixties and are thus suffering membership

---

[46]See Wuthnow, *The Restructuring of American Religion*.
[47]B. J. Stiles, editorial, *motive* 25/8 (May 1965): 5.

losses.[48] In addition, the longstanding divisions and injustices that these denominations recognized during the sixties are proving so difficult to resolve that hope and strength sometimes wear thin. Indeed, the end of "liberal," "Mainstream" Protestantism is being widely announced, and it is at the very least clear that emerging awareness of global realities are rendering such naive and nationally framed labels useless.

As this particular branch of the Christian family enters a new period of history, it must change—and it will by its nature welcome change. Many of its features will surely be transformed. Yet it is likely that its characteristic genius, entailing openness to and engagement with the present age, will continue to be manifest, *if* those charged with the educational mission of the churches help them to avoid its characteristic weakness.

---

[48]Wade Clark Roof and William J. McKinney, *American Mainline Religion* (New Brunswick NJ: Rutgers University Press, 1987) 60-63.

12

Public Happiness and Higher Education

William F. May

In a haunting novel, *The Temple of the Gold Pavilion,* Mishima describes a Buddhist acolyte's obsession with the temple he serves. The beautiful building stands for the entire realm of outer forms—those made by human hands and by the gods—seemingly obdurate and indifferent to the pitiful impotence of the acolyte himself.

Mishima uses a fine image to convey the split the acolyte feels between his own inner life and the outer world. He is a stutterer. Other men pass easily through the doorway between the inner and the outer, but every time the hero of the story attempts to pass through the door, he turns the key only to discover rust in the lock. The young acolyte both loves and hates the beautiful temple. He resents it and yet feels drawn to its cold beauty. Eventually, he sets fire to the sanctuary, in an ecstasy of destruction.

Once again, Mishima uses a fine image to describe the deed. He tells us that the young incendiary does not think of himself as starting a fire; rather he releases those fires already *latent* in the universe.

The Loss of Public Happiness

The first part of this essay concentrates on the first of Mishima's themes. Toward the whole world of outer forms, institutions, and ceremonies today, we sometimes feel like Mishima's stutterer. We have difficulty connecting our own interior life to those external forms that dominate the public scene. Our private happiness seems to have little to do with the public realm. This divorce between the public and the private is what the Germans sometimes call an *Ur-problem* that underlies others, such as the specific problems of poverty, unemployment, environmental issues, racial injustice, and deficit spending. Entire institutions—schools, churches, synagogues, corporations, governments—seem to interlock, reinforce one another, and persist without touching and nourishing inner lives.

At first glance, this divorce between the inner and the outer seems to have begun with the middle 1960s. The radicals had a word for the repudiated public realm: the "establishment" or the "system." In the late 60s, young radicals protested against a system resented because they believed it mutilated lives. The most savage statement of this protest came not from an American under 30 but from the then 40-year-old Scottish psychoanalyst R. D. Laing, who, in *The Politics of Experience,* complained of the brutalities of our modern educational system. Parents, maneuvering their children to succeed in a harsh world, pressured them to become efficient overachievers, shrewd little connivers, clever in cadging the grades that would open the doors to the best schools, clear the way to the best jobs, turn the keys into the best houses, and open the gates to the best cemeteries. Parents pressed for all this achievement in the name of a tough-minded realism about the outer world. Laing compared their frantic realism to the London beggar who used to maim and mutilate his children in order to equip them to overachieve in the family trade.

Gothic exaggeration to be sure—to compare a high-powered educational system to the low cunning of a Fagin. But some of us over 40 were too much acquainted with some of the psychic mutilations of an educational system and lifestyle that meant too much insomnia and hypochondria, too many tranquilizers and too much alcohol, too many broken homes and burnt out cases to deny altogether the charge against our generation.

The militant protest against the system in the 1960s gave way in the early 70s to withdrawal. It is a complicated subject, but an illustration from the field of religious studies may suffice. The 1970s saw a striking interest in nonwestern religions—and much of this interest was positive. I will not try to enter into all the good reasons for this interest. However, the restlessness of the interest from year to year was baffling. One year students enthused about Zen Buddhism; another year, Krishna Consciousness; still another, Transcendental Meditation; the religion of the South Dakota Sioux, Sufism, and, then, Kundalini Yoga. In fact, a single, questing spirit provoked this restlessness in religious studies and practice across a decade. These traditions possessed one important feature in common; namely, they were *somebody else's* religion, *not* one's own and *not* the religion of one's parents. Enthusiasms shifted but the driving force remained the same: the cult of romantic love, a fascination with the faraway princess. Students responded to the lure of traditions under whose social and political precipitate they had not had to live. They knew rather too well the warts and goiters and hair curlers and pot belly of Christianity and yearned for faraway possibilities. They wanted to have little to do with what T. S. Eliot once called the hippopotamus church.

For similar reasons, students of that decade withdrew from politics in general and political parties in particular. The purity of their ideals forbade them to deal with anything so ponderous and imperfect as a political party, appropriately symbolized by the most prosaic of farm animals—the donkey—and a pachyderm.

Clearly the responses of protest and withdrawal in the middle 60s through the early 70s attested to a profound dissatisfaction with the public realm. But the radicals of the counterculture mistakenly supposed that they had invented the split between inner meaning and outer form. Two decades earlier people had already sensed this split and summed it up with the word *conformity*. Metaphors from the 1950s—the "windmill," the "grind," and the "rat race"—betrayed the fact that people expected to find little happiness in the public realm. In the face of an outer world that they found unfulfilling, people in the 1950s responded through passive conformity to the world's demands while pursuing their careers. Meanwhile they reserved to themselves—behind a shelter of thoughtful sermons on conformity— or jokes in the *New Yorker*—a sanctuary of private life that was their own.

Thus only the solutions have changed. Successive generations tried conformity in the 50s, rebellion in the 60s, withdrawal in the early 70s, and have returned to a somewhat individualistic careerism in the 80s; but all alike betray considerable despair over the arena of public life and affairs. Whatever happiness people are likely to pursue and attain they associate with their private lives.

We have lost a sense of connection between inner life and outer forms and institutions that led the thinkers of the American Revolution to declare this country a republic (*res publica*, a public entity). The most important political principle for John Adams at the time of the American Revolution was the concept of *public* happiness. Adams backed the principle "no taxation without representation" *not* because taxes would reduce his purse and thereby subtract from his *private* happiness. (The taxes against which Adams and others protested were minuscule.) Adams objected rather to being "without representation." That state of affairs deprived him of his *public* happiness; that is, his right to be seen and heard, and to make himself felt in public forum and in political commerce with his fellows. Without such public space in which to live and act in concert with others, the merely private life—as variants of the word itself suggest—becomes the diminished life: "privative," "deprived," impoverished.

Hannah Arendt, the political philosopher, has argued that it was an unfortunate day when the great phrase, "life, liberty, and the pursuit of happiness," gradually came to mean exclusively, "private happiness." From that day forward we began to treat the public realm as though it were a necessary evil, as though it merely served private flourishing. We did not experience or savor happiness in the public domain.

Liberals, radicals, and conservatives—all for their different reasons in the past century—have inveighed against imperialistic and oppressive institutions. But they have not recognized that beneath the growth of imperialistic institutions often lies an equally imperial concept of the self. Following the literary critic, Quentin Anderson, we may define the imperial self as the self that accepts no limitations upon itself at the hands of others.[1] Half indifferent and resentful of the public domain, the imperial self fails to invest itself in the growth of strong, nurturant, and self-restraining institutions. One needs for the latter task, the cultivation of the civic self.

The civic self, as opposed to the imperial self, understands and accepts itself as limited by others. At the same time, it recognizes that it experiences an expansion of its life in and through its participation in community. Thereby it participates in public happiness. The civic self includes both a subjective and an objective element. Subjectively, the civic self must cultivate the capacity to work in concert with others. This skill of cooperativeness refers to the goods of process in a democracy. But these goods of process must not be shorn of their object—the common good. Otherwise, the art of acting in concert with others may terminate merely in those larger aggregates of self-interest known as interest groups or factions. Thus, objectively, the art of acting in concert with others must orient—at least in part— to the goal of the common good. (Men and women, to be sure, must orient partly to their own private good. We are not a species of angels. Self-interest and the interest of groups have their place. But a society, wholly driven by self-interest would tear itself to pieces, no matter how ingenious its constitutional mechanisms.) Therefore, the leaders of the revolutionary and constitutional periods in American life recognized the importance of "public virtue" in a citizenry. "No phrase except 'liberty' was invoked more often by the revolutionaries than the 'public good.'"[2] Public virtue consisted in some measure of readiness to sacrifice one's own self-interest to the common good.

John Adams recognized that the constitutional republic that he and his colleagues had devised would not long survive the corrosive power of self-interest without the active engagement of two institutions in the formation of the American character: religious institutions and educational institutions. Rightly conceived, both types of institutions contribute to public happiness. Other essays in this volume deal with the importance of religious institutions in the formation of the citizen. This essay will restrict itself to educational institutions, and most particularly to our institutions of higher learning, in exploring their responsibility for contributing to public happiness by cultivating the civic self.

Higher Education

If our educational institutions are to help us to recover a sense of public duty and happiness, we will need to acknowledge the ways in which they have both helped to form the citizen and partly contributed to the current decline in civic

---

[1]Quentin Anderson, *The Imperial Self: An Essay in American Literary and Cultural History* (New York: Knopf, 1971).

[2]Mortimer J. Adler and William Gorman, *The American Testament* (New York: Praeger Publishers, 1975) 87.

consciousness. This essay will compare three different visions of higher education and their continuing power to determine, for good or for ill, the civic consciousness of graduates: the liberal arts college, the modern positivist university, and the counterculture reaction to that university. No effort will be made to write a history of the complicated relationships of these differing educational visions to the formation of the citizen. But neither can we retreat to a purely typological analysis that ignores historical change. The liberal arts college in this country largely developed in the nineteenth century and in the setting of small town Protestant culture. The British "colleges" in the setting of Oxford or Cambridge provided the basic template for a liberal arts education. In the American transplant, each college sat on its own bottom as an institution and supplied its students with their terminal degrees. The liberal arts college persists in the twentieth century partly on its own terms but more often as vestibule to advanced technical degree programs in the context of the twentieth-century positivist university.

The United States in the twentieth century followed the continental rather than the British pattern of education. The German and the French universities provided the basic model for the university oriented to the advanced degree. For several reasons this choice of models prevailed. First, America, as an industrial democracy in the twentieth century, needed to supply corporations with large numbers of skilled persons. The Ph.D. system and its ideal of specialized research fit into that social need. Further, America, as a continent rather than an island, opted for an educational system better suited to a continental scale. America is largely a society of strangers rather than a community of friends. Understandably it opted for an educational system based on impersonal credentials rather than on the informal networking of friends in an insular setting.

The counterculture movement has not produced an institution comparable to the liberal arts college or the positivist university, but in many ways it helps throw in relief the commitments of these more enduring institutions. It also reflects in its own right and turn persistent themes in American culture that affect civic consciousness. This essay will compare the three differing visions of higher education on a grid that covers the following issues: (1) the educational ideal to which the institution aspires; (2) the view of intelligence that it presupposes and the kind of teacher that it prizes; (3) the social setting of the institution and the social destiny it assumes for its students; (4) the social virtues that it tends to foster and the understanding of vocation that it espouses.

The Liberal Arts College. The nineteenth- and twentieth-century liberal arts college has tended to define its ideal as the cultivation of the well-rounded person. To that end, it imposes upon its students a highly structured education. While it offers students the possibility of majoring in one of the several branches of knowledge, the chief emphasis falls on a common educational experience achieved either through distribution requirements or core courses that it expects all students to take. It offers students the more immediate goal of self-realization, but we misinterpret this goal if we think of it as wholly narcissistic. In the setting of idealist philosophy, educators believed that students could realize themselves only by connecting themselves effectively and fruitfully with the goals and purposes of the society at large.

The Intelligence and Its Teacher. By and large the liberal arts college has held (and still holds) to an aesthetic interpretation of the intelligence. It acknowledges (and seeks to develop) the human capacity to appreciate a wider range of goods and values than is available to instinctually driven animals. The study of art, music, math, history, and other conventional subjects in the curriculum broadens horizons. Clearly this emphasis on aesthetic intelligence in the nineteenth century did not escape criticism. In Europe the existentialist Soren Kierkegaard challenged the Hegelian philosophy that sponsored it. Kierkegaard doubted whether intelligence so conceived served much more than human enjoyment. The broadening of horizons hardly served (and often deferred) moral decision-making. A "de-cision," Kierkegaard believed, etymologically indicated and morally required the cutting out of possibilities. Too much of life, he felt, merely floundered in the possible. In America, early inventors and industrialists also dismissed the importance of aesthetic intelligence. They valued pragmatic rather than aesthetic intelligence. *Homo faber* did not need a college education and its broadening of horizons in order to be successful. Just what social purposes of leadership aesthetic intelligence might serve eluded the practically oriented on the American frontier. Nevertheless the liberal arts college aimed at that broadening of intelligence which the well-rounded person required.

The liberal arts college prized the teacher for wisdom and insight more than specialized expertise. He or she was, for want of a better term, an intelligent amateur. Often teachers did not earn their living from their vocation. Independent incomes allowed them to teach for love rather than for money. Moreover, they did not need a Ph.D. in order to secure appointments in some of the most prestigious of institutions. The tradition of independence from formal credentials remained alive in the Eastern women's colleges as late as the 1950s. Students scrupulously called their teachers Mr., Miss, or Mrs., rather than Doctor or Professor, as a way of indicating that formal credentials and hierarchical rank did not of themselves generate that respect which a teacher might hope for.

The British Isles, which provided the template for the prestigious American liberal arts college, only recently and defensively began to grant the Ph.D. degree. Private tutorials and conversation at the faculty table and tearoom provided better evidence than formal credentials as to talent, culture, and breeding. Those who held to this ideal of the intelligent amateur into the 1950s viewed with some alarm the descent of the barbarians into modern academia: careerists, freshly equipped with their Ph.D.'s, whose ambition permitted them little sense of loyalty to the local institution that temporarily employed them. Needless to say, the ideal of the intelligent amateur did not escape those considerable professional deficiencies associated with the injustices and mediocrities of the old boys' network.

Social Setting and Destiny. The nineteenth-century liberal arts college was small, highly structured, collegially oriented, and personal. More recently, counterculturalists have valued smaller scale institutions on the grounds that they permit an unstructured and informal educational experience. But the nineteenth-century liberal arts college did not associate smallness with informality. Both the education and student social life were highly structured; nevertheless, they allowed for personal contact. The college consisted of a small community of names functioning largely in the environment of a small town. Both faculty members and students oriented to the college as a significant social unit commanding their loyalties. Many of these institutions, of course, emerged under the sponsorship of the Protestant religious traditions whose chief strength in America lay in small town America. Higher education in America until recently has largely been a rural enterprise. Colleges afforded students the chance to get away from the small towns that their own parents led but in a setting that institutionally resembled the towns of their origin.

By and large, the liberal arts college prepared students for eventual leadership in small town America. What better place to provide for that task than in a small college and in a small town that greatly resembled the experience of their parents? Meanwhile, however, the education helped broaden horizons and thereby provided graduates with a partial antidote to the narrowing and restrictive tendencies of life in a small town. The enlargement of sensibilities helped prepare students for a more spacious leadership role in the towns to which they would return.

One should not, however, so emphasize this social destiny of students as to overlook the importance of the liberal arts college in producing graduates who eventually helped lead America in its transition to a modern industrial state. A young student at Oberlin College developed in his chemistry class there the electrolytic process indispensable to the production of aluminum. He eventually helped establish this important sector of American industrial life and thereby symbolized the social importance of the liberal arts college in shaping the country's next stage of development.

Social Virtues and Vocation. The college largely relied on a value consensus that shaped its life. This value consensus oriented to ends and goals; to substance rather than merely to process. Reflecting this consensus, the president of the college offered a course in ethics for all graduating seniors. This arrangement may have meant that the course was badly taught but the symbolism was inescapable. The subject of ethics was not reduced to a merely technical subspecialty in the field of religion and philosophy; it served rather as the very crown of the educational experience.

Various factors contributed to the possibility of this value consensus in the liberal arts college. First, the college often owed its existence and support to a particular religious tradition. Second, both its faculty and its student body often reflected this homogeneity in background. Third, even as the college distanced itself from its specific religious origins, its faculty members had not so far disappeared into various areas of specialization as to lose their sense of themselves as a *collegium*. Faculty members focused on the college rather than treating the college as a temporary local identity utterly subordinate to their enduring identity with a technical discipline. Fourth, although explicitly religious values faded as the unifier of the college, faculty members informally subscribed to a generally agreed upon list of the "greats," the *auctores*, an acquaintance with which defined the truly educated person. These authors constituted a quasi-religious, sacred canopy under whose sheltering presence Western civilization would presumably continue and flourish.

On the whole the value consensus that the liberal arts college presupposed fostered a sense of vocation which William Perkins, the early seventeenth-century English Puritan, defined as "that whereunto God hath appointed us to serve the common good." The term *vocation* has a public ring to it that our more modern terms *career* and *job* do not. The ultimate end and purpose of a vocation is the common good. Public happiness does not wholly reduce to private good and private happiness. Further, the "that" to which Perkins referred includes not only one's work life but also one's further duties as a husband, wife, parent, citizen, church member, and participant in voluntary communities. The ideal of well-roundedness correlates subjectively with a vocation that includes more comprehensive responsibilities than to one's work life alone. Thus the liberally educated draw upon and transmit a *pleroma* of shared values that let them play out a variety of social roles within the setting of the common good. So goes the ideal.

The Twentieth Century Positivist University. The fate of the college president's course in ethics symbolizes the shift from the nineteenth-century liberal arts college to the twentieth-century positivist university. No longer the crown of the enterprise, ethics was rapidly reduced to a subspecialty in the field of philosophy and even there, strictly speaking, ethicists could not properly deal with normative questions. At best they could report on the history of ethics or focus analytically on the nature of moral discourse. They could not offer serious recommendations as to how one ought to act and decide since the positivist university disclaimed moral reflection and nurture as part of its mission. Normative questions had no place in the classroom inasmuch as professors could teach facts but not values. The positivist university generated disciplines that deemed it their special vocation and glory to remain aloof from questions of value and utility in the disinterested pursuit of the truth. Values reflected only subjective, emotive preferences. They did not adhere to things; we read them into things. They were too spongy and slippery to deserve a place in the classroom. The faculty member could not make value judgments without descending into subjective propaganda and advocacy. In his justly famous essay, "Science as a Vocation," sociologist Max Weber both described and recommended this restriction of the university to purely factual, objective inquiry. Weber put the question rhetorically: Do you want to be a leader or a teacher? A demagogue or a pedagogue? If you want to be a teacher or a pedagogue, then you must hang up your values on a peg outside the classroom in the cloakroom along with your hat and coat.

This ascetic restriction of the university to purely factual, objective inquiry especially dominated American universities during their manic phase of expansion after World War II through the mid-1960s. While this ideal of the university did not altogether eclipse the function and task of the traditionally conceived liberal arts college, it did increasingly dominate ideologically the various disciplines within the liberal arts college and shape the self-understanding of the professional schools. The universities of the twentieth century increasingly came to shape the professions and their ethics at approximately the same time that many faculty members began to exclude value questions from the university's domain.

The interior commitment of the university faculty to the ideal of objectivity justified itself socially on the grounds that the acquisition of objective knowledge eventually produced a skilled person. These skills, in turn, had a marketplace value that enabled the graduate to pay for those goods that aesthetic intelligence enjoys. Ultimately, the objectivism of the university produced opportunism and careerism in its student body. Since the university did not offer an arena in which reasoned discourse, debate, and discriminate judgments about values could occur without deteriorating into propaganda or advocacy, the information that it offered went up for grabs to the highest bidder. Who was to say otherwise? Ends were only a matter of subjective preference. Since ends had no objective public status, who could deny the claim that knowledge itself was a personal possession, not a public trust, to be manipulated for private advantage alone in the sale of marketable skills?

Intelligence and the Teacher. The modern university concentrated on the cultivation of technical intelligence. While aesthetic intelligence enlarged the student's capacity to enjoy a wider range of goods, technical intelligence enhanced those skills important in producing goods—largely economic goods. Max Weber observed that an education cannot offer one much help in making judgments about which goods one ought to choose and serve, but it can offer objective information important in the choice of means useful (or inconvenient) in reaching various ends. The university can enhance the development of technical reason— reason in the service of preferences. But the university cannot help sort out among those preferences, the noble and the ignoble, the worthy and the spurious. Technical reason illuminates the paths that we travel but not the ends to which we travel. It leaves the choice of ends, goals, or values to bare feeling or preference.

The standard of the formally credentialed professional replaced the liberal arts ideal of the intelligent amateur. The transition in the United States occurred massively during the 1950s. Middle-aged teachers at such institutions as Smith College, who often had independent incomes to supplement the modest salaries that the institution paid, viewed with alarm the arrival of young married careerists during that period. Some distinguished literary people there still taught without their Ph.D.'s, but young ambitious people recognized that rapid promotion required the leverage of offers from outside institutions. The young teacher without a Ph.D. made himself or herself wholly hostage to favor within the local institution. Increasingly, loyalty shifted from the college where professionals worked to the discipline to which they belonged. Disciplinary leaders at the graduate schools determined job offers, and therefore even job promotions in the institution from which one drew one's salary. While academics read David Reisman's *The Lonely Crowd* and viewed with alarm the dominance of the other-directed person in American society, academic institutions themselves became increasingly other-directed. Their own sense of self-esteem depended upon the approval of gatekeepers elsewhere in the several disciplines. Decisions for promotion traditionally depended upon the criteria of research, teaching, and service, but, inevitably, the emphasis on distant, disciplinary peer review meant that the primary *desideratum* for the appointment, retention, and promotion of the academic depended upon excellence in research.

The meaning of research itself substantially changed. An industrial model obtained. Researchers engage in manufacturing and wholesaling; mere teachers serve as retailers. The teacher packages and retails what others have distantly produced. Within the restrictions of this model, one lost the sense of discovery that occurs in teaching at its best. Further, publishing scholars lost a sense that they in fact taught a wider audience through their writing. Within the reward system of the modern positivist university, one wrote *up* to impress the gatekeepers in one's field rather than outward to an intelligent audience of inquirers. Thus writing became increasingly filial rather than collegial.

It must be conceded that the specialization of knowledge within a discipline that the university fostered led to extraordinary progress in some fields. Clearly in the sciences, but, even in the humanities, thoughtful reflection on detail sometimes allowed a new theory to heave into view. But, on the whole, specialization in the humanities only too often led to the miniaturization of knowledge. To demand that graduate students mimic their colleagues in the laboratories and write a thesis on a new subject only too often forced them out into the desert of the trivial. Further, the ambitious young academic, pressured to make tenure within a five- to six-year period, could not afford to live with a great idea that might not reach its maturity within that time. He had to choose carefully a manageable thesis topic in order to convert it into a book and if not into a book, a series of brief, publishable articles. Apologists justified this period of indentured servitude on the grounds that after five or six years, the security of tenure would now position the academic to pursue a major project across a lifetime. But meanwhile the socialization of the academic has made it more and more difficult to undertake a more ambitious topic.

Too much crawling to achieve tenure has made it difficult to walk and run once it has been won.

Social Setting and Destiny. The large scale of the modern university has accommodated to the extraordinary variety of disciplinary subspecialties that have developed both in its professional schools and in its own version of the liberal arts college. Within that setting, the institution offers a highly structured education, though, apart from basic distribution requirements, departments largely control that structure. While professionals think of themselves as colleagues, the organization, as a whole, arranges itself hierarchically. The hierarchical strains against the collegial. Hierarchical distinctions obtain not only between different ranks of faculty members, but, just as important, between the basic cadre of faculty members and students. The university assumes a greater gulf between faculty members and students than traditionally obtains in liberal arts colleges where the two groups usually come from similar social and cultural backgrounds.

The university has increasingly restricted the scope of its responsibility to the university's educational mission alone. It has largely shed responsibility for the student's personal and social life, renouncing the role of *in loco parentis*. This renunciation fits into its general orientation to the future rather than the past. It orients itself less than the college to the community of birth and more to the economic and organizational identities that students will assume on graduation. In the language of the German sociologists, the university is *gesellschaftlich* rather than *gemeinschaftlich*. It is oriented not toward origins but toward destination, not toward past tradition but toward future possibility. It is less a community than an organization. Since, moreover, the institution specializes and fragments, it often provides no more than a site, a campus, on which many kinds of educational and research enterprises happen to intersect. Thus it often relies on nonsubstantive activities to provide a kind of surrogate for that unity which it intellectually lacks. A new class of specialists, athletes, help provide the university with liturgical forms that gather the community together and thereby atone for its lack of unity at more substantive spiritual levels.

The university helps provide students with their own complicated social transition from *Gemeinschaft* to *Gesellschaft*, from status in a community to some kind of future identity in an organization. The latter identity depends partly on the acquisition of formal credentials but also upon the acquisition of a social style that helps one cope with the rigors of anonymity and at least temporary marginality. The social style that the nineteenth-century, largely rural, liberal arts college encouraged relied heavily on the rhetoric and speech of understatement. In small towns, self-advertisement tends only to isolate the advertiser and proves that he does not belong, that she possesses no status. A more anonymous twentieth-century university (and society at large) relies more heavily on verbal hustling. It emphasizes and develops skills in self-display, as one attempts to silhouette oneself against a dark horizon. The demands of application forms, sorority and fraternity selections, job interviews, and the verbal free-for-all of the beer blast and the cocktail party varyingly require the cultivation of these skills.

Social Virtues and Vocation. The university does not claim that it possesses an extensive set of shared values. Indeed, one could argue that the university fits into an America that increasingly depends upon four mechanisms, rather than a specific set of shared values, to allow the country to function without requiring too much virtue of its citizens. Those mechanisms include the U.S. Constitution that allows people of varying interests to pursue their diverse goals within a legal framework of checks and balances that keeps various factions within the society from tearing themselves to pieces. Second, the mechanism of the marketplace allows people to pursue exclusively their own self-interests, and yet, through marketplace exchanges, to contribute indirectly to the well-being of all. Third, the mechanism of the large-scale organization, the corporation, mobilizes purely technical skills and provides economies of scale that increasingly crowd out the ma and pa stores and dominate the marketplace. Finally, the country relies on the university as a mechanism through which young, unformed people can develop those skills saleable to large-scale organizations that increasingly dominate the marketplace within a constitutional framework. Together, these mechanisms allow a highly pluralistic and interest-group oriented society to work together despite substantive differences among its citizens.

This emphasis on process and mechanisms in American social life has led Americans to value what might be called the secondary rather than the primary or substantive virtues. One needs less those virtues that flow from shared goals than those that contribute to the process of reaching whatever goals people choose. Thus the university tends to encourage and inculcate those virtues required for the attainment of skills: sufficient stamina to stick to a program of long, arduous, and sometimes boring professional training; sufficient discipline to defer personal gratifications for its sake; and the cooperativeness upon which the successful operation of the large-scale organization depends. Second, while the university, through its regularized grading standards, does not encourage in its students (any more than in its faculty members) unusual, heroic, or extraordinary achievement, it does emphasize reliable performance, precisely that kind of achievement so convenient in large-scale organizations whose specialization of function demands that one expect from one's fellow workers predictable work rather than maverick performance.

In this setting the traditional doctrine of a vocation converts increasingly into a career. One focuses less on the common good than on one's own private good, achieved and monetarily sustained through a career. A career is a self-driven vehicle through life whereby one enters into the public thoroughfares but moves toward one's own private destination. Students' orientation to their own careers, however, does not mean that their lives altogether lack public significance. A kind of fit exists between the skills that the young may attain for their own private rea-

sons but that an industrial and postindustrial society nevertheless needs in the fulfillment of its public purposes. Further, since a market economy establishes an
ontological break in identity and dignity between the employed and the unem-
ployed, the acquisition of marketable skills gives to the careerist some sense of
belonging. It bestows a limited public significance upon his or her life. Membership is the first of social goods, not only because it supplies the member with the
ticket to other goods, but because it is a good in itself. As indicated earlier, students in the universities tend to detach from origins. In this respect, they resemble
the immigrants to this country in the late nineteenth century who boarded the great
mother ships, leaving Europe for this country, to escape the limitations and misery
of their origins. Now students flock to the universities as the new mother ship that
will carry them out of the city ghettos and working class neighborhoods. They acquire at the university a degree that will license them to move, with some kind of
recognizable public identity, from city to city and from the city to the suburbs of
America. Still, the fulfillment of public purposes and goals in a careerist society
depends excessively upon the degree to which they dovetail with private agendas.
The virtues of cooperativeness suffice as long as no fundamental disputes erupt
over the ends toward which collaborators move.

Universities could neglect the issues of public life and goals in the late 1940s
and 50s in the afterglow of shared national purpose during the war years but no
longer as two issues divided the nation in varying ways: civil rights and the Vietnam War.

The Counterculture Protest. The third moment in higher education on this grid
did not reflect or determine an established institution but pitted itself against the
prevailing institutions of its time. Briefly characterized, the counterculture movement sought immediacy in relationship to people, power, truth, and morals and
rejected any and all mediated relations in these spheres. Its quest for immediacy
in relationship to people made it suspicious of all large-scale organizations and
their hierarchies. It rejected the constraints upon people that traditional roles im-
posed. Its quest for immediacy in relationship to power led to its affirmation of
participatory, as opposed to representative, democracy. Communes preferred doing
business as a committee of the whole rather than trusting to the several mediations
of delegated authorities, working subcommittees, or deputized representatives.
Such traditional representative devices, the movement believed, distanced any
given gathering of people from the expression of its power. The quest for an immediate relation to truth led to a profound suspicion of the liberal arts college and
the positivist university. The college depended upon the mediations of truth through
a tradition; the university, upon the mediations of truth through the expert. Finally, the counterculture's conviction that we can have an immediate relationship
to morals led to its emphasis upon the virtue of moral indignation and energized
both its militant engagement in politics and its disapproving withdrawal from the

political arena. These counterculture commitments display themselves across our grid for higher education.

The Ideal. The protest movement rejected the received ideals of the well-rounded self and the skilled self. Instead, the movement in its political form aimed at raising consciousness; and, in its religious form, at altering consciousness. Religion ultimately tinged both aims. In effect, the movement associated authentic education with alchemy. The traditional liberal arts college did not expect to achieve a radical transformation of the self. It simply aimed at fulfilling the self's already established capacities. The positivist university expected to develop individual skills that would considerably transform the external circumstances of life but not the self's interior life. The goals, however, of raising consciousness and altering consciousness aimed much higher spiritually. In its political version, the movement held that authentic education must lift students above the false consciousness that oppressive institutions impose. In its religious version, the movement resorted to meditative techniques, which help devotees transcend the common sense polarities of subject and object, self and world, human and natural, cosmic and divine. The alteration of consciousness entailed moving beyond the surface polarities that engage the superficial self to the deep self, where the self dissolves and unites with the world and the divine. The specific religious inspiration for this ideal came from the East rather than the West as one rejected that Western distinction from which so many other basic distinctions and polarities derive: the distinction between the Creator and the creature.

Intelligence and the Teacher. Critics of the political counterculture objected to its hostility to the intellect. But its anti-intellectualism, such as it was, reacted less to the classical confidence in substantive reason than to the positivist reduction of reason to purely technical reason. From the perspective of student radicals, purely technical intelligence served patently false goals to which the society subscribed and for which the university so assiduously prepared its graduates. Further, the evils of the Vietnam War and racial oppression were self-evidently wrong. The immediacy and self-evidence of moral truth made the radicals disdainful of the convoluted training of technical intelligence. Young teachers emphasized the cognitive significance of feelings and criticized the distancing tendencies of technical reason that but emulated academically the bombing at a distance that occurred in the war. The religious version of the counterculture movement more ambitiously protested against not simply the myopia of technical intelligence but the inherent boundedness of discursive reason. The propensity of reason to analyze, define, and circumscribe removed it from that union with all things to which the religious person aspired.

The counterculture both dethroned and elevated the teacher. On the one hand, it criticized the positivist ideal of the teacher as specialist. Placards in the French student protest of 1968 put it simply: Eliminate the expert. A few teachers complied by handing over the substantive choices in course syllabi to students. On the

other hand, the ideals of a raised consciousness or an altered consciousness elevated a few teachers to the role of guru. This role bestowed upon the teacher a
more redemptive significance and power than either the intelligent amateur or the
specialized professional possessed.

Social Setting and Destiny. Counterculture students objected to the huge size
of the positivist university and celebrated the small as beautiful. They pressed either
for a relatively private, tutorial, custom-made education within the confines of the
larger institution or created a contrapuntal free university—small, unstructured,
and relieved of the demeaning burden of a grading system and other of the controls
upon which a meritocratic society insists. This preference for a small-scale setting
differed from the liberal arts college ideal in that it also opted for the unstructured.
One needs to distinguish, however, between the first and second stages of any reaction against structure. As the free churches long ago discovered in their protest
against highly ritualized liturgical and institutional forms, the original charismatic
impulses quickly settle into their own new routines. Further, the protest of young
faculty members against a highly bureaucratized university had its own ironical
outcome. Young Turks, suspicious of the academic bureaucrats, proceeded to establish more and more procedures, the immediate purpose of which was to hem
in administrators. But these new procedures cumulatively further elaborated bureaucracy. Thus, bureaucracy happily metastasized through the contributions of
those who were its sworn enemies.

One also needs to distinguish between the first and second stages in the conception of the student's destiny. In its first stage the student radicals repudiated
the very notion of social destiny. The movie *The Graduate* symbolized that repudiation. Education, if successful, should not lead to that plastic promised land
that its middle-class sponsors offered. Haight-Ashbury and other gathering places
of the flower children symbolized this repudiation and disturbed the parents of the
young as leading to a personal cul-de-sac. The rejection of a military-industrial
civilization led to romance with the rural, a preference for the organic rather than
the plastic, the self-sufficient rather than the specialized. But the parents' nightmare persisted: The flower children would become the cut-flower children.

In its second stage, of course, the apparently permanent, irrevocable, irre-
versible repudiation weakened. Rejection, for many, turned into a merely temporary moratorium. Many radicals eventually finished off professional degree
programs and joined the upwardly mobile in a society over which Ronald Reagan
could not have presided so readily unless substantial numbers of their generation
had not returned to conventional careers. The astute social critic Richard Sennet
anticipated this development in his early essay *The Uses of Disorder*. There he
observed that the apparent turbulence and anomie of the young covers, at deeper
levels, the fixing of forms. More than one powerful antiauthoritarian of the sixties
has turned out not to be globally opposed to authority as such but rather simply
impatient for the exercise of his own.

Social Virtues and Vocation. The social virtues that the counterculture fostered resembled those that flourished in the left wing of the Reformation in the sixteenth century. The virtue of moral indignation energized the political militants. The Vietnam War was self-evidently wrong. Therefore, one had very little grounds for either patience or tolerance toward those who supported the war. The quest for a communal purity motivated the more religious version of the cultural protest. In a sense, the assumption of innocence and purity underlies the responses of both militance and withdrawal.

Attention to the virtues alone, however, would miss another important way in which the protest movement rejected the ethos of the liberal arts college and the positivist university. A deep change occurred at the level of manners. Edmund Burke once observed that the French Revolution's breach with decorum, its challenge to manners, offended the Western world more than its moral and political ideas. The same might be said of the sixties. Manners serve the very useful social function of veiling ourselves in the course of revealing ourselves to others. Social style functions as a sort of fig leaf that spares us the anguish of total exposure. It is hardly an accident that the new culture movement began with the free speech challenge at Berkeley. Students assaulted the nervous system of their elders less by their ideas than by their hair length, their ragtag clothing, unwashed bodies, their littered pads, their noisy music, and their ready resort to the rich loam of Anglo-Saxon four-letter words. Shared manners as much as shared virtues give coherence to a civilization, but the manners of the bourgeois West seemed no longer to be decent clothing but indecent hypocrisy.

A sense of vocation often works itself out in a specific kind of orientation to time. The liberal arts college oriented generally to the past, to the transmission of a valued tradition. The positivist university oriented generally to the future, to those transformations of the world and one's own life that the controlling power of technical intelligence made possible. The counterculture movement oriented emphatically to the present, earning its epithet as the "Now" generation. It clearly rejected the past, certainly the past as the positivist university largely mediated it. It also rejected emphatically the future that political leadership offered the nation—winning the war—and the personal fulfillment that the successful career would place within reach.

We need not rehearse here the rejection of the rejection in which so many students of the current generation and their elders have enthusiastically participated, as they have returned to a mix of the aesthetic and the technical ideals.

Reconnecting Higher Education and Public Happiness

My title for the concluding part of this essay misleads. I do not want to argue that higher education is wholly disconnected from questions of public happiness. The nineteenth-century liberal arts ideal of the well-rounded person had a civic as well as a personal justification. Educators expected their students emerging from college to provide leadership in small-town America. Appropriately, therefore, education took place in a setting not too dissimilar from the environment to which they would eventually return. The liberal arts college both broadened students and provided them with a foretaste and trial of life to come.

But in the course of time the ideal lost its tie with the social order. Graduates moved out of the small town into a large, anonymous, mass society. Thus the merely well-rounded person sank into obscurity unless he or she acquired technical skills useful to a rapidly developing industrial and urban society. The ideal of the broadly educated person lost its tie to civic life. It described merely the individual who was intellectually and culturally well-larded, who knew something about a lot of things that contributed to his or her quality of life. It signified a capacity for savoring but it required now marketable skills to finance a privately defined happiness.

The twentieth-century positivist university also connected, in a sense, with public happiness even though students pursued there the means to their private happiness. It turned out people with the skills that allowed them to function in the huge bureaucracies of the Ford Motor Company, the Pentagon, IBM, the hospitals, and law firms of the country, whose scale and structure the university increasingly resembled. Further, the university dramatically broadened and diversified the population that received a university education and to that degree allowed a much wider range of Americans to acquire a stronger public identity.

Neither of these goals of education—the well-rounded and the skilled person—should be disdained. But the quality-of-life and the careerist arguments, taken together, are today too narcissistic, too self-preoccupied, to be the sufficient aim of education. The counterculture produced a kind of institutional spasm that reflexively acknowledged that fact. Yet its reaction against a too-narrow understanding of the intelligence too often led to anti-intellectualism instead of the recovery of substantive reason. And its reaction against a politics gone awry in its commitments and goals too often led to the protests and withdrawals of the imperial self instead of the recovery of the civic self.

Higher education can fully contribute to public life and happiness only if our institutions of higher learning recover three ancient purposes of a liberal education. This recovery can occur because all three purposes have had their continuing, though muted, influence in the university, even during its burgeoning positivist years.

Critical Intelligence. The university needs first to recover its sense of vocation in the cultivation of critical intelligence. The word *critical* has its roots in the Greek verb meaning to judge or decide. Accordingly, the task of criticism in the intellectual life includes making judgments as to worth and value in the spheres of politics, art, economics, religion, philosophy, and morals. Operational intelligence tells one how to get from here to there; critical intelligence raises questions as to whether the there is worth getting to. It asks what recently and incessantly has been called the question of values. The work of the intellect includes the task of normative as well as descriptive inquiry. This is precisely the activity of the intellect called for in professional life but deemed by many professionals in the academy to be merely subjective and emotive and, therefore, an inappropriate intrusion in the classroom.

The professional schools especially need the work of critical intelligence, that is, reflection on ends, goals, and values. Behind many of the quandaries in medicine—whether to pull the plug or not, whether to tell the truth or not—loom critical questions about the basic goal of medicine. What defines the end of medicine? an unconditional fight against death? the relief of suffering? or the pursuit of health? What basic goals should shape the legal system? Does the law find its ultimate justification in the values of truth and justice or in the sometimes opposing value of order? On these questions turn the justification and the potential reform of the adversary system. What defines the goal of the corporation? Milton Friedman's maximizing profit? Or a somewhat more socially complicated notion of economic performance at a profit?

To the degree that the university ignores these questions, it threatens the professions with their moral impoverishment, as they turn out technicians incapable of, or hostile to, critical thinking. It also diminishes the university itself in its intellectual life. The university is precisely the site where critical inquiry ought to occur, posing alternative goals for the society at large and the professions in particular. We concede too little to the range of the human mind and grant too little to the capacity of the university to organize itself for civil and fruitful discourse if we assume that the only alternative to objective inquiry is subjective advocacy. Critical inquiry is not only licit but required in the institution devoted to the cultivation of the whole of the human mind.

The Civic Self. Second, the university has an ancient, related, and continuing responsibility for the cultivation of the civic self. The university must recover its own early heritage, dating back to the Greeks, that accepted as part of its most comprehensive purpose the cultivation of the civic self—the art of acting in concert with others for the common good.

In the United States we have democratized education, but, at the same time, to our own disadvantage as a people, we have also privatized it and justified it for what it can do in enlarging merely private opportunities. All of this is salutary in its own way but extraordinarily fragile. Private opportunity, in the long run, flourishes only in the context of healthy institutions, and healthy institutions depend upon selves with some sense of public identity and responsibility. When the social covenant is weak and the professional thinks of himself as an opportunist alone, uninvested with a public trust, then our institutions suffer, and people get hurt when their institutions are hurting. Both by its ancient traditions and by the terms of its modern social support, the university can ill afford to deny its public function and the civic destiny of its trained professionals.

This point would be trivialized if it were reduced to the strategy of tacking onto the university curriculum courses in ethics and civics or courses that strained for relevance: for example, *Macbeth* and Watergate, *Romeo and Juliet* and juvenile delinquency. Cultivation of the citizen requires a more fundamental change in the university that connects its life throughout to critical inquiry. Ultimately, the nurturing of the civic self and the encouragement of critical inquiry overlap and reinforce one another as ideals if value questions are not merely matters of private, subjective preference. To engage in critical inquiry is itself a social act that teases the mind out of the bottle of private preference and opens it out toward a community of inquirers. It makes a person publicly accountable and responsible for her judgments and decisions and assumes these judgments to be interpretable in civil discourse. The classroom is a public place; the library, a commonwealth of learning; critical inquiry among peers, a kind of parliament of the human mind. Such inquiry is indispensable to a professional life that has more than technical services to offer for personal gain.

Good Teaching. Finally, the university must turn out professionals who are good teachers. This point needs to be made at a time when the teaching vocation itself seems to be drying up. The Business School of Indiana University recently enrolled within two percent as many degree candidates as the entire student body of the College of Arts and Sciences. Students (and the best students) have flocked to the so-called nonacademic professions. These professions have increasingly defined themselves as dispensers of technical services, in which case, it would appear that the academy needs to concern itself less and less with the teaching prowess of its graduates. (Professors have reacted to this development with self-pity. They no longer get to produce teachers for the public schools, colleges, and universities. They bemoan their lot. Turning out Ph.D.'s had been the functional equivalent of immortality in academic life. But teachers today have fallen into the position of mules and Shakers who, for differing reasons, cannot reproduce their own kind.)

The task of the liberal arts college looks somewhat different, however, if modern professionals and business managers must be good teachers in order to perform their tasks well. At first glance, this line of argument does not appear to be too promising. Professionals, generally, have a low estimate of the ability or interest of their patients or clients in learning. Corporation executives prefer to run the enterprise by command and obedience rather than persuasion. The quarrel on this issue in medicine is very old. The "rough empirics" in classical Greece (who were familiar with treatments but not with the scientific reasons for their success) used to ridicule the more scientifically oriented physicians who sought to teach their patients. The empirics argued: Patients do not want to become doctors, they want to be cured! The scientific physicians replied, if one fails to teach one's patient, one is merely engaging in a veterinary practice on men and women. Since then the increasing complexity of medical knowledge has only increased professional skepticism about the therapeutic value of teaching patients.

Yet the physician must teach if she would enlist her patients more actively in their own health maintenance. To the degree that the physician accepts her patient as partner or collaborator in the pursuit of health, she must perceive shared truth as an important ingredient in that partnership. Preventive medicine, rehabilitative medicine, and chronic care medicine all require effective patient education. Words are to a prescription what a preamble is to a constitution, argued P. Laine Entralgo, the distinguished Spanish historian of medicine. They help to interpret what is going on in the whole process. Teaching helps to heal the patient, to "make whole" the distracted and distressed subject.

Other professionals must also teach. The nurse and the social worker must engage in teaching their patients and clients if they would do their work well. The lawyer, to be sure, offers technical services in drawing up contracts and appearing before the bar. These tasks resemble acute care in medicine. But the really good lawyer knows how best to keep his client out of the courtroom in the first place. He must effectively teach his clients. Counseling is the functional equivalent of preventive medicine in the practice of law. The very title *rabbi* means teacher. Some Protestant denominations define the minister as the teaching elder. Politicians, public administrators, and corporate executives must also teach if they would lead their subordinates at least partly by persuasion. It was a tragedy of his tenure in office that President Jimmy Carter was not an effective teacher to the nation. He knew little about the presidency as a bully blackboard to the nation.

One does not want to exaggerate here. Leadership depends partly on command, not entirely upon persuasion. But our leaders of huge hierarchical organizations will function better if they learn something about the art of persuasion, if they follow the political development of Athens and not simply the military development of Sparta. Military Sparta was essentially a taciturn society. It relied on the bark of command and the grunt of obedience. Athens, on the contrary, depended primarily on the word, *logos rhetor,* the art of persuasion. The *word* helps create the polis, the public domain—not only in politics but in the work place and in the professional exchange. (A liberal education is hardly the sine qua non of the art of persuasion. The prophets of Israel make it amply clear that one does not need a higher education to be skilled in the *word.* But a modern society does not live by inspiration alone. Education can help.)

If professionals and leaders must be good teachers to wield their powers effectively and responsibly, then one needs to rethink the liberal arts component in both undergraduate and professional education so as to cultivate the fundamental qualities of the teacher—a capacity for critical inquiry, a direct grasp of one's subject, a desire to share it, verbal facility, and sensitivity to one's audience. Theoretically, at least, requiring a liberal arts background for professionals and locating professional education in the university should produce professionals today who are more pedagogically skilled than the "rough empirics" of whom Plato complained. Unfortunately, however, academicians have assumed that only some of their graduates become teachers; the rest do not. Therefore, they have treated teaching as a segregated profession. Teaching constitutes, of course, a special profession, but at the same time it ought to be the aim and purpose of a liberal arts education to turn out good teachers whether students go into the teaching profession or not. Nonacademic professionals and leaders must teach, even as they dispense esoteric services. How else will they be fit practitioners of their art and contributors to our public life and happiness?

Rightly understood, the three aims of education interconnect. The young person who makes his or her first stammering moves out of the sphere of private likes and dislikes into the arena of critical discourse and judgment has begun to develop a civic self. She or he enters into that public domain— however tentatively and modestly—that eluded Mishima's stutterer. At the same time, the professional who learns how to teach what she knows and the leader who persuades and does not simply command help to enlarge and empower and sustain that public domain. In the course of relieving even private distress, they contribute to public happiness.

Four

Paideia
and Profession

13

The Education
of Robert Lynn

Elizabeth Lynn

> Any present is linked to the past by obvious or hidden continuities, any future will be affected by the way those continuities are understood and transmitted.
>
> —*Robert Wood Lynn*[1]

My father has never much liked to talk about himself, and so his personal history has been something of a mystery even to his children—a vague image of wide skies over struggling farms, a father with a gift for enduring hard times, a mother with a battleship bosom and an endless supply of potato recipes. And yet, somehow, from this thin soil and diet grew four ambitious and creative children: Greg, who became a general; John, an engineer; Margaret, a designer—and Robert, a Protestant educator.

William McGregor Lynn, Sr., the father of these four, came from a Scotch-Irish Presbyterian family in which the double values of religion and education were well rooted. The son of Missouri pioneers, Will attended a small Presbyterian college in Tarkio, Missouri, where he seems to have divided his attention equally among academic studies, football games, dates, and a passion for oratory. As a senior in 1906, Will represented Tarkio College in a statewide oratory contest. His speech on "The Race Problem" brought third prize. "His self-possession was superb," noted a local reviewer, "and his manner though reserved showed deep conviction." The speech contains many conventional moments: an opening image, heavy with descriptive adjectives, of a slave ship unloading its human cargo on American shores; a topic—"the Negro Question"—popular for the period in which the failures of Reconstruction had become fully apparent. And yet the solution posed by "the Tarkio orator" stood out as one of personal conviction. "Ed-

---

[1]Robert Wood Lynn and Elliot Wright, *The Big Little School* (New York: Harper & Row, 1971) xi.

ucation and Christianity,'' he argued, ''are the two great powers that have raised races and individuals; but they must go hand in hand. Intelligence without Christianity makes men dangerous. Christianity without intelligence makes men bigoted, superstitious, or fanatical.''

Will's belief in the mutual necessities of ''Intelligence and Christianity''— or, in the lexicon of the next generation, education and religion—carried him eastward after graduation to Princeton University, where he sampled the wares of theological education offered at its seminary and, on the basis of that sampling, made plans to enroll the following year. At the same time, however, a different frontier had opened up—and Will had been energetically sampling its wares as well. At Tarkio College the thoughts of most young men had not focused on religion and education. ''The prominent and prevailing thought and ambition of everyone,'' as Will later reflected, ''seemed to be to acquire land, buy every acre you could, borrow every dollar you could, buy more land—it was the source of all wealth.'' In the summer of 1905 midway through his Tarkio years, Will had traveled to Wyoming, and he had seen some of that land: a territory around the brand new town of Torrington that had just been opened to homesteaders. At that time, Torrington consisted of two grocery stores, a bank, a hotel, three saloons, a company of cowboys and gamblers, and land—land unfenced and unending. The promise of this land enticed the young man into filing for a homestead; and so, since 1905 William Lynn had been a part-time settler on the Wyoming frontier. When, in the spring of 1907, he decided to enroll at Princeton, Will returned to Wyoming to ''produce the wheat crop and prove up on the homestead.'' The homestead, however, needed more proving up than Will had anticipated: He never returned east but settled into Torrington to become a full-time homesteader.

Thus began Will Lynn's life as a farmer. Although he abandoned the possible careers of minister and educator offered by Princeton, he spent his life working as a layman for the cultivation of ''Intelligence and Christianity'' in the newly developing world of Wyoming. Commitment to a religious community was one of his first acts of settling in that new world: Within months of having moved to Torrington, he ''brought his letter'' to its United Presbyterian Church and for the next half-century served his denomination variously as elder, trustee, clerk, and moderator. Church participation led to participation in community education as well; for the activities of church and school were not clearly separated in Will's mind or in his Wyoming world. In 1920 conversation at a Lynn family gathering drifted around to the question of Presbyterian representation on the local school board. Having decided that someone should represent the ''U.P.'s'' in school affairs, the Lynns drew lots for the privilege—and Will soon found himself a member of the local school board. He served for fifteen years on that board and for five years on the board of trustees for the University of Wyoming.

Thus church membership led to community leadership—and in time Will's ''community'' expanded outward to include all of Wyoming. Local school boards were then, and perhaps still are, every town's best lesson in politics. Will learned the lesson, liked it well, and in 1934 ran successfully for the Wyoming state legislature. From then on he pursued politics and farming, in combination and alternation; when one failed (as it invariably did, given the vicissitudes of agricultural markets and of political parties), he would turn to the other.

Jane Reid had been one of the reasons Will Lynn did not return to Princeton. Born in Iowa, raised in Colorado, she, too, came from a Scotch-Irish Presbyterian family in whom the double values of religion and education were deeply rooted and as deeply intertwined. Her father J. F. Reid, had, as his obituary reported, "received his education at Amity College, College Springs, Iowa, there becoming equipped for wielding the large influence which he exerted in every community where he lived." In that same early period of his life, he had also "united with the Presbyterian Church . . . and through his long life lived an earnest Christian life in that communion." His six children—male and female alike—duly received the double blessings of Presbyterianism and a college education. Jane Reid, the youngest, was a college student in Greeley, Colorado, when she and Will Lynn met in the summer of 1905; in fact, her father had been one of the men accompanying Will on his first trip to the newly opened territory of Torrington. Together, the Reids and the Lynns became settlers on that territory, and Jane and Will were married in 1912.

After her marriage, Jane Reid Lynn's sphere of activity rounded about the farm, the family, and the church. She did not challenge that circumference outwardly; instead, she inhabited her assigned roles energetically, idealizing the creative powers of Mother, Wife, Homemaker, and Church Member. She kept a perfect house, filled with collections of colored glass, little altars of clarity and light amidst the Wyoming dust; she made potatoes taste interesting night after night; she fought beside her husband in his struggles with farming and politics; she raised her four children; she participated actively in the local Presbyterian church.

And yet, as I have discovered over the years, Jane Reid Lynn had a restless heart behind that battleship bosom and a voracious appetite not only for new potato recipes but for new ideas. She seems to have satisfied her restlessness and hunger in two principal ways: by reading and by living imaginatively. Her adult education had begun, but did not end, in college; she remained throughout her life a constant and curious reader, with a particular love of Shakespeare and Emerson but a willingness to explore any other books that came along. She also continued her education vicariously through her children: When Robert went East for college, for instance, she asked him to send home his book lists, and she read those she could find in order to discuss them with him on his visits home.

She also wrote. The circle of a farm woman's life could not be escaped, but it could be expanded imaginatively. She did not travel—but she read about the rest of the world, and when done with the books, she wrote long pieces about lands she had never seen, in which she extended a sympathetic imagination to the ways of others, including the ostensible enemy of the age, Russia. But mainly Jane wrote about what she knew from new and highly experimental perspectives. She converted all things encountered in her little round of experience into imaginative symbols, turning them now one way, now another, mining them for their larger meanings. In her poetic projects I see the inspiration of Emerson, who called all persons to be poets, and all objects to be explored imaginatively—whose mission, as Irving Howe has so accurately said, was a "democratization of the sublime." All things, even the most common and low, wrote Emerson, could be perceived as invested with sublime meaning. Jane Reid Lynn took this promise seriously— perhaps, at times, a little too literally. She served lavish meals to her husband's guests—and afterward she wrote short stories about those dinners, reliving the experience from the perspective of the dining room table. She even went so far as to write an "Ode to Teeth," which she submitted (unsuccessfully) to *Oral Hygiene* magazine.

Jane Reid Lynn also mothered her four children with the passion and intensity of an artist creating four human works. Indeed, a short piece she wrote about the children when Robert was only a toddler suggests that she contributed decisively to their future forms, not only of character but of vocation. In that piece she placed each of the four children in activities that accurately symbolized their future occupations: Greg, in the army; John, in engineering; Margaret creating houses; and Robert (then just learning to walk) she placed in the barnyard, reading Browning!

Like Will, Jane was an active member of the Presbyterian Church from the beginning of her adult life. The church provided an acceptable public arena for women, an arena that she (like many other women of her time) exploited to the full, becoming a member of many organizations and, eventually, a delegate to the Presbytery. As Will proudly wrote in his memoirs, "It was in this church, where on being given the opportunity, her ability, especially as a speaker and leader of religious life really began to emerge. . . . I have sat and listened with deep admiration and love to her speaking to an audience without a single note because the outline of her speech was so clear and there was no hesitation in the flow of her words." While she gladly utilized the speaking opportunities in the church, however, Jane was no passive receiver of its doctrine. She rejected the highly conservative teachings of the Torrington church (whose minister fed the family a steady diet from the book of Revelation) and sought her own theological nurture elsewhere— in the heretical thought of Harry Emerson Fosdick, for instance, whose writings she read secretly and then hid from her pastor, a frequent caller at the Lynn family farm.

For Jane and for Will, then, life was one of active participation in religious and community activities, nourished on the side by independent reflection and reading. A constant flow of guests through the Lynn family home reflected their "multiple worlds of allegiance" within the Wyoming community: There were informal dinners at which a governor, senator, university president, minister, and friends from neighboring farms might all be present.

It was also a life of hardship. Will's constant attempts at new agricultural markets brought just as constant debts and disappointments; his participation in public life was all too often determined by the changing political climate, the ins and outs of parties and platforms. Will and Jane Lynn weathered a continual series of failures and disappointments throughout their life—and yet they maintained a determined faith in the continuing progress of their world toward eventual perfection. Every loss could be converted into a gain if approached from the proper perspective; every apparent curse was, in one of Will's favorite phrases, "A Blessing-in-Disguise." As the chairman of the Torrington School Board, Will had put a plaque on the elementary school wall that read, "Let No Occasion Pass That Now Smiles—Milton." According to Bob's sister Margaret, this became a favorite family phrase, "quoted with some zest."

In his reminiscences, William McGregor Lynn, Sr., gives no account of the paths each of his children followed from the family farm to their distinctive (and distinctively nonagricultural) vocations. His single remark takes the form of an appreciation—an appreciation for the way in which all four saw to their own education. Their substantial worldly accomplishments are not mentioned, must less enumerated. Will's only praise is for that first step forward, for "their ambitions to get an education when there was practically no help from home in a financial way." And yet that very ambition *was* the gift of their parents. "There just was never any question that we all wanted to and would go to college," notes Margaret. "Education was an 'Absolute.' "

Robert Wood Lynn, "the baby with big ears," was born to Will and Jane Lynn on 3 April 1925. Those big ears were signs of heights to come: By adolescence Robert Wood towered above the other members of his family and had earned, by dint of his long thin frame, the local nickname of Bobby Splinter. His height was apparently not inherited. He did, however, inherit a severe case of asthma from his father's side—and from his mother's side, a dissatisfaction with farm life and a love of books. As his sister Margaret says, rather tactfully, "Bob did not really understand or like farming." Moreover, because of his asthma, Bob could not work on the farm. Instead, he had to spend his boyhood afternoons resting, and he to took to books for entertainment. He read every book he could find in the small town of Torrington, including textbooks. Of his "formal" education in Torrington at the local elementary school, I know little; he recalls his schooling as a series of teachers—as my mother says, he remembers every teacher he ever had—and a vast, somewhat indiscriminate consumption of books.

When Bob was just out of elementary school, his father ran unsuccessfully for the state Senate. Meanwhile, farming, too, had become a losing gamble: and so, when Will was offered a seat on the State Board of Equalization in 1937, he took it, and the Lynn family gave up the farm and moved into a small house in the state capital of Cheyenne. As Will would later write with characteristic cheerfulness, the loss of the Senate race was "A Blessing-in-Disguise," for it enabled their youngest child, Robert, to graduate from a Cheyenne high school. The Torrington schools, thought Will, would never have prepared his son for the education that lay ahead. In Cheyenne, Bob enrolled at the Lula B. McCormick Junior High School, and he, too, remembers that change of schools as crucial. As the family story goes, the teacher told him he was lazy, which got him mad and got him working. He graduated from a Cheyenne high school in 1942 and, as class valedictorian, gave a speech consonant with his parents' progressive faith. Life, he assured his class, could be beautiful—if you just made it that way.

That, in foreshortened form, is the "long foreground" to the emergence of Robert Wood Lynn. Following his high school graduation, he left Cheyenne for an Army training camp in California, where he discovered that life could not, after all, always be made "beautiful" at will. His allegiance to his parents' progressive faith seems to have taken a beating in this period, but nothing emerged as a clear alternative. Severe asthma made him ineligible for service in the war. Hence, in 1944 he retraced his father's path east to Princeton with vague but ambitious plans for a career in law or publishing.

In his first year at Princeton, Bob's Wyoming education served him well— so well, in fact, that he was excused after one class from a required English course. Looking for something to fill the gap, he wandered into an elective with Princeton's first professor of religion, George Thomas. The course with Thomas initiated my father into what Alfred North Whitehead called the "romance stage" of education, a period of ferment when "the subject matter has the vividness of novelty; it holds within itself unexplored possibilities half-disclosed by glimpses and half-concealed by the wealth of material."[2] In Whitehead's scheme, this "romance stage" is intended to be just the first of three steps—but it is a stage from which Robert Lynn never quite graduated. My father has managed, in the four decades since his college days, to retain that sense of romance in his professional work and in his private reading. Indeed, if asked to characterize his ideal of education, he invariably refers to it as a kind of romance with thought. (At the same time, I would say, he has moderated that romanticism with an acute sense of the historically conditioned character of educational experience. While making education an "Absolute" for his children, as his parents had made it for him, he has never attempted to turn his own experience into a timeless ideal. His keen sense of history has advised him of the historicity of his own experience.)

The subject matter in Robert Lynn's romance stage was religious thought, especially the new neoorthodox theology of Reinhold Niebuhr. The teachers through whom Bob encountered this thought—George Thomas and Paul Ramsey, in particular—were themselves the first explorers of a new frontier; for the academic

---

[2]Alfred North Whitehead, *The Aims of Education* (New York: The Free Press, 1969) 17.

discipline of religious studies, like the doctrine of neoorthodoxy, had just arrived, and doctrine and discipline combined to create an exciting new world. It was, in other words, not just a moment of romance for this one individual, Robert Lynn, but a moment of romance for the field of academic religion itself, a moment heavy with promise.

A time of "romance" is one way in which my father has characterized his educational ideal; a time for "repentance" is another. In the neoorthodox thought of Reinhold Niebuhr, Paul Tillich, and others, Bob found, at a crucial moment in his life, an alternative to the progressive optimism of his parents—a way of looking at the world which, as he himself wrote in *The Big Little School*, "refuted the liberal reliance on progress, electing instead to emphasize God's sovereignty and the decisive revelation of the Bible."[3] With its stress on the constancy of sin in human desire and action, its emphasis upon history as a necessary and yet always partial or conditioned arena for Christian activity, neoorthodoxy called its listeners to action in the world *and* to humility in that action; it called for an attempt to understand and live fully the historical moment, without deifying history or one's self in the process. In my father's confrontation with this revitalized doctrine of original sin and divine election, he found, I think, the necessary and compelling alternative to his parents' battered faith in progress. He found at once a call to repentance and a call to action.

In the following years, Bob moved ever further away from the world of his parents: He stayed East and became "a liberal intellectual." He left the family's Republican fold and became a Democrat. But the most serious conflict between the generations did not arise over life-styles or politics; it occurred when he announced to his mother that he "no longer believed in progress." As I have noted, Jane Reid Lynn was a woman of great sympathetic and imaginative powers, a woman willing to experiment with a variety of different perspectives. But she could not imagine the world seen without the animating principle of progress. It might have been easier for Jane to understand, had her youngest son said he did not believe in God. Progress, however, was not a debatable proposition; indeed, it was not a "proposition" at all but the unquestionable axis around which her other beliefs and practices revolved.

At the risk of overstatement, I would suggest that my father's encounter with neoorthodox theology was a moment of conversion. Neoorthodoxy *made sense* of his discontentment with the world into which he had been born. It gave a new and more adequate meaning to the disappointments suffered by his family, disappointments that his parents tirelessly converted into "Blessings-in-Disguise." And it acknowledged the inevitability of human failure without depriving human effort altogether of hope or possibility. That initial year at Princeton gave Bob Lynn a

---

[3]Lynn and Wright, *The Big Little School*, 91.

compelling new picture of the world, one that he has never abandoned—one that he could no more abandon than his mother could abandon "progress."

Central to that picture of the world, perhaps at its very axis, is the shared work of a community. The sinfulness of individual human desire and action cannot be countered simply by the regular recognition, confession, and repentance of one's sins; it must be more productively disciplined by a transcendence of the self in activities with others. Moreover, those activities take the distinctive form—not of worship, nor of leisure—but of reflective study. Bill May, who met Bob in his second year at Princeton, was struck right away by Bob's stress upon the communal nature of his academic life. "Young men who do what Bob did, who go from public school to the university, usually have an attendant anxiety, as they enter, about their performance," May remarks. "Yet with Bob it was never, 'How am I doing?' It was always 'How are *we* doing?'" That characteristic emphasis upon communal activity has remained with him throughout his life. As colleague Barbara Wheeler observes of his years at Union Theological Seminary and the Lilly Endowment, Bob has always found ways to work with others. In contrast to the academic norm, he has not been a solitary scholar, making his own contribution in isolation from others. Instead he has sought out, and sometimes actively created, a "public" or community for what he perceives to be the work at hand.

If work within a community is one distinctive aspect of the world picture of Bob Lynn, the nature of that "community" is another. The kind of companionship the young man sought at Princeton, and in the years after, was not all-inclusive. In keeping with the Calvinist underpinnings of neoorthodoxy, it took the form of an elite. As May reports, "There was, in Bob, even at Princeton, a strong Calvinist tendency to seek out an elite—the elders of the larger community, in the Presbyterian sense." Two qualities were required of that elite, says May: talent and commitment. At Princeton, and throughout his career, Bob has sought out the partnership of persons who are not only talented but committed as well to something beyond their own advancement. In this emphasis there are echoes of his own father's pronouncements about "Intelligence and Christianity" in 1905. Father and son may have disagreed about the prospect for human perfectibility in this life— but they seem to have agreed that intelligence alone merely "makes men dangerous," and that commitment without intelligence makes them "bigoted, superstitious, or fanatical."

In his Princeton years, Bob Lynn's own picture of the world crystallized; but a clear sense of vocation, a way of participating in that pictured world, did not immediately emerge. He has told me that he arrived at his vocation by a process of elimination, rather than in an "aha!" moment. In the wake of his encounter with neoorthodoxy, he traded in ambitions for the law and publishing for the ministry, but he approached the pulpit with a detectable lack of enthusiasm. According to Bill May, Bob liked to say, "Everyone has big ambitions, but I figure I'll just go back to Chugwater, Wyoming, and be a pastor."

The road back to Chugwater passed through Yale Divinity School, however, and there the new divinity student came under the transforming influence of H. Richard Niebuhr. In 1949, the year of Bob's arrival, Niebuhr was lecturing to students from the materials that were to become *Christ and Culture*. Those lectures, and the book itself, sparked Bob's interest in the historical relationship between Christian faith and culture, and drew his attention to education as a focal center for that relationship. Christian faith, asserted Niebuhr, is not a static set of attitudes or actions amid a shifting panorama of paganism; nor, however, can it achieve the easy harmony with the culture of its moment, the flexible self-accommodation or reflex "relevance" to society advocated by many liberal Protestants of the progressive era.

In my father's subsequent reflections upon the history of religion and education, and in his own restless movement between the institutions of religion and education, I see an effort to work out the historical and the personal implications of Niebuhr's insight. After graduation from Yale, Bob duly followed the road back West, not to Chugwater but to Denver, Colorado, where he served as assistant pastor on the staff of a large Presbyterian congregation. Church life, however, seemed to sacrifice critical reflection for the (omni)presence of a committed community. The role of pastor required too much piety and too little thought; he "fought the robes," as his sister Margaret puts it, and used the pulpit to teach rather than preach. In 1959 Bob abandoned the ministry for a teaching career and, in 1976, gave up "the robes" altogether. Only in the last decade has he found his place in the church, not in the pulpit but in the pew—and especially in the Sunday school classroom.

Upon leaving Denver in 1959, Bob returned East, to a Ph.D. program at Union Theological Seminary. There he remained for almost two decades, moving rapidly from the role of student to that of teacher and administrator. The community of theological education presented problems of its own, however. While leaving it to others to describe and analyze those years at Union, I will say that my father's most enduring critique of academic life has focused upon its "individualism"— the tendency of its members to use their intelligence for self-aggrandizement rather than in service to a public beyond themselves. "There are," as he said in 1985, "few places in American life where the problem of individualism is more rampant."[4] Lest that sound like a Jeremiad against the moral fiber of the current academic generation, I would add that he understands academic individualism as a symptom of a more serious problem: namely, the problem of the disintegrating relationship between public service, learning, and faith. The dominant intellectual pictures of the world today do not enable, indeed *disable,* a public life. There is, in his words, "no Torah now" through which to interpret the aims of education.

---

[4]Robert Wood Lynn, "The Harper Legacy: An Appreciation of Joseph M. Kitagawa," *Criterion* 24 (Autumn 1985): 6.

Will and Jane Lynn, it might be said, had such a "Torah": For them, piety, learning, and public service were relatively organic aspects of life, aspects bound together by participation in the newly developing community of Wyoming. In his Princeton years, my father made a sharp movement away from that world and way of life; his sharpest departure came in rejecting his parents' progressive faith for the more tragic tones of neoorthodoxy. Yet, in the years that followed, he did not abandon, but reformulated within a neoorthodox perspective, the importance of an integration of faith, learning, and public life.

For Bob, unlike his parents, however, a context for the integration of these activities has been much harder to find. In his work, he has moved somewhat restlessly between a variety of institutions—most obviously the church, the seminary, and the foundation. He has shifted from preaching to teaching, from the pulpit to the pew, from the administrative offices of a seminary to those of a foundation. Whatever the institution and whatever his means, however, he has consistently sought in each situation to help others cultivate or renew the bonds between faith, learning, and public service. He has done that mainly by providing opportunities for individuals and institutions to reflect upon their past; for in that past, as in his own past, the roots of religion, education, and public life may be found deeply rooted, and deeply intertwined.

The biography of Robert Lynn says something, I think, about the disintegration of piety, learning, and public life in our century: A larger context, a community that relates these allegiances and activities, has been lost. But his work also tells us where we must look in an effort to reintegrate religion, education, and public life: not to the church alone, nor to the seminary alone, nor to serving institutions alone—but to the common historical ground upon which each of these institutions now stands.

There are, as my father has so often said, continuities as well as breaks between past and present. Only by understanding how those continuities have been transmitted, can we understand the tyrannies of our present time—and the possibilities of our future.

Contributors

Dorothy C. Bass is Associate Professor of Church History at Chicago Theological Seminary, a contributor to *Between the Times: The Travail of the Protestant Establishment in America, 1900–1960* (edited by William Hutchison), a minister in the United Church of Christ, and President of the Board of the United Campus Ministry at the University of Chicago.

Edward Farley is Drucilla Moore Buffington Professor of Theology at the Vanderbilt Divinity School. He is the author of *The Fragility of Knowledge: Theological Education in the Church and the University* and a forthcoming book tentatively entitled *Human Condition: A Theo-ethical Exploration.*

James W. Fowler is Charles Howard Candler Professor of Theology and Human Development and Director of the Center for Research in Faith and Moral Development at the Candler School of Theology, Emory University. He is the author of *Faith Development and Pastoral Care, Becoming Adult, Becoming Christian,* and *Stages of Faith.*

Neil Gillman is Aaron Rabinowitz and Simon H. Rifkind Associate Professor of Jewish Philosophy at the Jewish Theological Seminary of America. He is the author of *Sacred Fragments: Recovering Theology for the Modern Jew.*

Robert T. Handy is Henry Sloane Coffin Professor Emeritus of Church History at Union Theological Seminary in New York. He is the author of *A Christian America: Protestant Hopes in Historical Realities* and *A History of Union Theological Seminary in New York,* and is currently working on a volume for the Project on Church and State at Princeton University.

Sara Little is Professor Emerita of Christian Education at Union Theological Seminary in Virginia. She is the author of *To Set One's Heart: Belief and Teaching in the Church,* and has contributed to *Education for Citizenship and Discipleship* (edited by Mary C. Boys).

Robin Lovin is Associate Professor of Ethics and Society at the Divinity School of the University of Chicago. He is the author of *Christian Faith and Public Choices,* the editor of *Religion and American Public Life,* and a United Methodist minister.

Elizabeth Lynn is a doctoral candidate in religion and literature at the University of Chicago. She is the author of *Taken from the Ground: Leeds, Maine in the Twentieth Century.*

William F. May is the Cary M. Maguire Professor of Ethics at Southern Methodist University. He is the author of *The Physician's Covenant: Images of the Healer in Medical Ethics* and *The Patient's Ordeal,* and a former President of the American Academy of Religion.

Glenn Miller is Professor of Church History at Southeastern Baptist Theological Seminary. He is the author of *Piety and Intellect,* forthcoming from Scholars Press.

Henri Nouwen is a Catholic priest from the Diocese of Utrecht in Holland and currently is a member of the L'Arche-Daybreak (a community with and for people with a mental handicap) in Toronto, Canada. Among his recent books are *The Road to Daybreak* and *Seeds of Hope.*

Parker J. Palmer is an independent writer, teacher, and activist, working in the areas of education, religion, and social change. He is the author of *The Active Life, The Company of Strangers,* and *To Know As We Are Known.*

Barbara G. Wheeler is President of Auburn Theological Seminary. She is the editor of *Congregation: Stories and Structures,* by James F. Hopewell, and coeditor, with Joseph C. Hough, Jr. of *Beyond Clericalism: The Congregation as a Focus for Theological Education.*

John F. Wilson is Collord Professor of Religion at Princeton University and Director of the Project on Church and State at Princeton. He is the editor, transcriber, and author of introduction and annotations of Jonathan Edwards's *A History of the Work of Redemption,* the editor of two volumes of *Church and State in America: A Bibliographical Guide,* and author of *Public Religion in American Culture.*